Y0-BXK-284

THE EUCHARISTIC PRAYER

265.3
Rya
c.1

The Eucharistic Prayer

A Study in Contemporary Liturgy

by
John Barry Ryan

Novitiate Library
Mont La Salle
Napa, California

PAULIST PRESS
New York / Paramus / Toronto

10293

Copyright © 1974 by
The Missionary Society
of St. Paul the Apostle
in the State of New York

All rights reserved. No part of this book may be reproduced or transmitted in
any form or by any means, electronic or mechanical, including photocopying,
recording or by any information storage and retrieval system, without permission in writing from the Publisher.

Library of Congress
Catalog Card Number: 73-94215

ISBN: 0-8091-1834-3

Published by Paulist Press
Editorial Office: 1865 Broadway, N.Y., N.Y. 10023
Business Office: 400 Sette Drive, Paramus, N. J. 07652

Printed and bound in the
United States of America

ACKNOWLEDGMENTS

The author would like to express his gratitude to the publishers indicated for
their kind permission to quote from the following works:

The Experimental Liturgy Book by Joseph Hoey. Copyright © 1969 by Herder
and Herder, Inc. Used by permission of the publisher, The Seabury Press.

Prayers, Poems & Songs by Huub Oosterhuis. Copyright © 1970 by Herder
and Herder, Inc. Used by permission of the publisher, The Seabury Press.

Open Your Hearts by Huub Oosterhuis. Copyright © 1971 by Herder and
Herder, Inc. Used by permission of the publisher, The Seabury Press.

Man Becoming: God in Secular Meaning by Gregory Baum. Copyright © 1970
by Herder and Herder, Inc. Used by permission of the publisher, The Seabury Press.

Eucharistic Theology by Joseph Powers. Copyright © 1967 by Herder and
Herder, Inc. Used by permission of the publisher, The Seabury Press.

The Church and the Catholic and the Spirit of the Liturgy by Romano
Guardini, translated by Ada Lane. Copyright © 1935 by Sheed and Ward, Inc.
Used by permission of the publisher.

Livre de la Prière by Thierry Maertens *et al.* Copyright by Fides Publishers,
Inc. and to be published in the spring of 1974 under the general title *Contemporary Prayer.* Used by permission of the publisher.

The Documents of Vatican II, edited by Walter Abbott, S.J. Copyright © 1966 by American Press, Inc. All rights reserved. Used by permission of the publisher.

The Shape of the Liturgy by Gregory Dix. Copyright © 1960 by Dacre Press: A & C Black Ltd. Used by permission of the publisher.

Eucharist by Louis Bouyer, translated by Charles Underhill Quinn. Copyright © 1968 by University of Notre Dame Press. Used by permission of the publisher.

The Mass of the Roman Rite (Missarum Sollemnia) by Joseph Jungmann, translated by Francis A. Brunner. Copyright © 1950 by Benziger Brothers. Used by permission of the publisher.

Eucharistic Faith and Practice: Evangelical and Catholic by Yngve Brilioth, translated by A. G. Herbert. Copyright © 1930 by SPCK. Used by permission of the publisher.

Liturgies of the Western Church, edited by Bard Thompson. Copyright © 1961 by Meridian Books, Inc. Used by permission of the publisher.

The Religious Man: A Psychological Study of Religious Attitudes by Antoine Vergote, translated by Marie-Bernard Said. Copyright © 1969 by Pflaum Press. Used by permission of Gill & Macmillan, Ltd.

The Holy Bible, translated by Ronald Knox. Published 1954 by Sheed and Ward. Used by permission of His Eminence the Cardinal Archbishop of Westminster.

CONTENTS

To
the Brothers
of the Christian Schools

Abbreviations

DACL	Dictionnaire d'archéologie chrétienne et de liturgie
DB Sup	Dictionnaire de la bible supplément
DS	Denzinger Schönmetzer, Enchiridion Symbolorum
Eph. Liturg.	Ephemerides liturgicae
JJS	Journal of Jewish Studies
LJ	Liturgisches Jahrbuch
LQF	Liturgiegeschichtliche Quellen und Forschungen
LTK	Lexikon für Theologie und Kirche
MGWJ	Monatsschrift für die Geschichte und Wissenschaft des Judentums
NRT	Nouvelle revue théologique
QLP	Les Questions liturgiques et paroissiales
RB	Revue Biblique

FOREWORD

After Vatican Council II, at the same time that three Eucharistic Prayers were added to the Canon used for fifteen centuries as part of the Roman Missal, numerous other Eucharistic Prayers composed by private individuals were being used and published. Of course, time must pass before the historian and the theologian can accurately evaluate the various aspects of such a phenomenon. Nevertheless a study or, more exactly, an in-depth study of each of them is possible and necessary if one is to answer several questions: What are these Eucharistic Prayers, what is their purpose, and how do they achieve it? How should they be judged in light of the Catholic faith and the traditional structure of the Eucharistic Prayer? How widespread are they and what are the causes motivating their creation and use? Does the phenomenon reveal the need for definite types of celebrations or groups that merit consideration by Church authorities? The distinction between public and private worship has been fundamental for the Catholic Liturgy (at least since the Middle Ages) as well as for the Anglican Liturgy. Is this distinction losing its viability only for certain small groups in their celebrations (which resemble what were formerly called private celebrations) or is liturgy generally speaking in the process of taking on another form?

These questions, all of which are important for the common welfare of the Catholic liturgy and its proper administration, go beyond the capacities of a single person and belong to several approaches: liturgical analysis from a literary, historical and theological point of view; pastoral sociology; ecclesiology as well as the study of ecclesial institutions. It is on the first question especially that John Barry Ryan has concentrated his efforts. With regard to the others, he adds some elements of information and criticism but refrains from giving any definite answer. It would be possible to object that in any case one cannot dissociate the study of contemporary Eucharistic Prayers from that of the literary and theological genre of the Eucharistic Prayer. The objection is exact insofar as the Church, or the liturgist for his part, by reason of the very faith commitment, needs to arrive at criteria or to verify anew the value of those held at the outset.

1

But from a methodological viewpoint the objection does not hold up, and it is possible that a certain Anglo-Saxon pragmatism aids fairness without betraying dogma: before judging one must make the effort to understand, not the reverse. When an author discusses new Eucharistic Prayers, one often knows almost *a priori* what he is going to say. Already from this point of view, we can thank John Ryan for bringing some fresh air into the debate.

His analysis covers three languages (Dutch, English, French) and three different genres: American compositions linked more or less to traditional structures; the thematic constructions of Thierry Maertens; and finally but especially the Eucharistic Prayers of Huub Oosterhuis. Is such a sampling sufficient to represent the diversity of tendencies? I think it is, although certain special questions such as the one concerning Eucharistic Prayers for children would require their own study.

The present sampling makes quite evident the literary superiority of Oosterhuis. The other Prayers may have been successful at given celebrations but alongside those of Oosterhuis they appear non-existent. On the other hand, from the theological point of view, it is the Oosterhuis Prayers that are the most problematic: starting from the traditional *eucharistia* he seems to have evolved toward a testing of the limits of the literary genre and a sort of existential cry of groping faith beautifully rendered. But it is difficult to see how the Catholic Church could acknowledge this as an adequate expression of ecclesial faith in Christ and of the celebration of his memorial.

However, the real problem goes beyond the doctrinal adequacy of any given text, and it should not be hidden behind stands for or against the authority of the Apostolic See or of the Bishops in the liturgical domain nor behind a theoretical discussion of creativity. The true problem, I think, consists in this: is it desirable that there should be alongside the present Eucharistic Prayers in the Roman Missal other Prayers equally orthodox and entering more completely into the language and culture of men of today? Even those who will not agree on every point with the judgments of John Ryan will be grateful to him for having shed light on this question by a serious and objective study.

Pierre-Marie Gy, O.P.
Director of the
Institut supérieur
de Liturgie de Paris

PREFACE

Not quite ten years, that is the time it took from the promulgation of the Constitution on the Sacred Liturgy (December, 1963) to the publication of a circular letter (April, 1973) containing strong warnings against the use of unauthorized Eucharistic Prayers in the Roman Rite. The April document showed how the three newly authorized Eucharistic Prayers (1968) could be adapted to introduce within them greater variety. While deeming it inappropriate at the present time to allow episcopal conferences to create new Eucharistic Prayers, the possible development for special cases is left open. The brief and carefully worded document, found in the appendix, is a valuable statement by the Sacred Congregation for Divine Worship on the nature of the Eucharistic Prayer.

However, behind such a document lies much that is not generally known to pastor or parishioner or, at best, poorly understood. Everyone knows, for example, that besides the three official Eucharistic Prayers added to the Roman Missal, there are other unofficial Prayers used in small group gatherings. Some of these Prayers were written before the appearance of the official ones and many more have appeared since. The simple fact is that for every official Eucharistic Prayer there are more than a hundred unofficial ones. Particularly abundant in Western Europe and America, they are found around the world.

To shed light on the dynamics of this phenomenon, we have chosen to study four groups of contemporary Eucharistic Prayers: the three new Eucharistic Prayers in the Roman Missal, selected American ones taken from the *Experimental Liturgy Book,* ten "Table Prayers" of Huub Oosterhuis, and ten *Eucharisties* of Thierry Maertens.

Steeped in tradition and the result of a great deal of reflection by some of the best liturgists of our time, the Roman Prayers are an obvious choice for they are *the* Prayers of the Roman Rite, and it is over against them that unofficial Eucharistic Prayers should be set. The American Prayers follow for it is primarily to an English-speaking audience that this study is directed. Furthermore, since these latter

Prayers are greatly influenced by the same models used for the Roman Prayers, placing them second does not disrupt the continuity as might be the case if either of the next two groups were considered there.

As might be guessed, the Dutch have played the greatest role in writing their own Eucharistic Prayers. Among the Dutch, no one person has had more influence than Huub Oosterhuis. That is why we have chosen to study a corpus of ten "Table Prayers" recently translated into English. These Prayers show considerable differences, not only from the Roman and American ones, but almost from one another. Our final choice of study was Thierry Maertens' ten *Eucharisties*. Two reasons guided our selection: first, Maertens has been widely known in many countries for his efforts toward a revitalized liturgy; second, these *Eucharisties* represent options not found in the other groups. Furthermore, Maertens' book will soon be available in English.

It is obvious that with such a large group of Prayers no exhaustive study could be made. That is why we have chosen several points of view from which to study all the Prayers, thus limiting the scope of the study but at the same time taking into account the most essential aspects. First of all, we have examined the structure of these Prayers with a view to appreciating the different options taken, thereby understanding better the form of the literary genre called "Eucharistic Prayer." Our next interest was to discover the manner in which the "voice" in these Prayers referred to God, to Jesus Christ, and to itself. In this part we did not undertake a study of what these Prayers say *about* God even though this would have been revelatory of certain theological positions. At the same time, this aspect is not totally neglected since it comes into play in other parts of the study. The next two viewpoints were of more immediate concern to us: What does the praying community have to say about Jesus Christ and what action is the praying community conscious of performing? Here we found ourselves confronted with such important matters as the expression of the divinity or Lordship of Christ and the Eucharistic celebration considered from its sacrificial aspect. Last of all, we studied the role given the Holy Spirit in these Prayers.

The study opens with a background chapter, tracing the movement from the one canon to the many Eucharistic Prayers. This information tries to place in context the whole situation that has led to the present period which began even before the creation of new Roman Eucharistic Prayers. The final chapter, besides presenting and comparing our findings, attempts to place the problem of Eucharistic Prayers in the broader context of the Reformation and present ecumenical discussion as well as the problem of religious language.

There was a certain urgency about this study, not only because the situation with regard to unofficial Eucharistic Prayers has evolved rapidly, but also because of the great confusion presently reigning with regard to the Eucharistic Prayer even among well-instructed Catholics. This confusion will not disappear by fiat, but whatever light can be brought to bear upon the problem should aid those in positions of responsibility.

In comparing "official" and "unofficial" Eucharistic Prayers, we do not intend to put them on the same footing. In the Church, the maxim, *nil sine episcopo*, is most sure when speaking of the liturgical assembly that celebrates the Eucharist. Also it must be noted that the term Eucharistic Prayer embraces both an action and a discourse. Thus, the Eucharistic Prayer used at mass accomplishes something that is not accomplished by reading it privately in one's room. We have, nevertheless, found no better term than Eucharistic Prayer to designate the discourse that begins with the Preface and ends with the Doxology. Hence, we abide by a current use of the expression even though we acknowledge that those who hold that the Eucharistic Prayer is something *done* rather than said have a correct understanding of the Eucharistic Prayer.

Finally, it is not our purpose to enter into present Christological or ecclesiological debates even though at certain points we must touch on Christology or ecclesiology. What we wish to do is let both official and unofficial Eucharistic Prayers speak for themselves. The different options taken in them shed light on the whole situation.

We would like to thank our confrères who encouraged this study, Père Gy, who shepherded it, and all those who have helped us during the time of its composition, especially Dave Delahanty of Lloyd Hall at Manhattan College and Father Bertels and his staff at the Woodstock Library.

1
FROM THE ONE CANON TO THE MANY ROMAN EUCHARISTIC PRAYERS

Fixed in print, dated and signed, an end and a beginning, the document announced the use of three new Eucharistic Prayers in the Roman Church, thus bringing to an end the 1500-year-old reign of the Roman canon as its one and only Eucharistic Prayer. Those who signed the document, Cardinal Gut and Bishop Antonelli, were not primarily responsible for the new Prayers, the date affixed was in itself unimportant, and the document's title was official and forgettable.[1] In such wise can the printed word lock up in itself and strip of all drama events of great significance.

In fact, the change announced was monumental, inevitable and, ten years earlier, would have been unbelievable, at least to the liturgical specialist. It is easy to speak of something as inevitable after it has happened, and it would be impossible to chronicle the myriad of persons and things that rendered the event inevitable. However, in the case of the Eucharistic Prayer, there are a number of elements that can be singled out that show rather clearly why a change in mentality was able to come about, for it is nothing less than a change of mentality with which we are concerned. These elements, even though they do not in themselves call for the creation of new Eucharistic Prayers, are all the more important as witnesses to another way of doing things.

Before studying the individual contemporary Eucharistic Prayers, it will be of use to review the elements that led to this change in mentality. They can be grouped under three different headings: The Liturgies of the Eastern Churches, the Jewish Roots of the Eucharistic Prayer, and Western Liturgical Tradition.

[1] Decree promulgating the Eucharistic Prayers and the New Prefaces, *Notitiae* 4 (1968), p. 156.

The Liturgies of the Eastern Churches

For centuries, in the words of Goar [2] and Renaudot [3], and more recently in the collection of Brightman [4], liturgical scholars in the Western Church had admired and studied the Oriental liturgies. The best of these liturgies were marvelously rich in theological content, dignity of style, and coherent structure. To be sure, in comparison with the Roman canon they could be judged long, but in the context of their own cultures this could not be considered a criticism.

The structure of the Roman canon—a variable Preface and a longer invariable (except on certain feast days for the *Communicantes* and, more rarely, the *Hanc Igitur*) oblation prayer—differed from the Eastern practice of several anaphoras within a given Rite. Their parts were also more clearly distinguished from one another structurally than were those of the Roman canon. In fact, one could also speak of different liturgical traditions according to the way the parts were arranged in the overall structure. There is no question here of evaluating the merits of either practice, but the sheer fact that the Oriental liturgies proposed an alternative to the Roman one was in itself of the utmost importance.

Variety alone would not give one pause for reflection if this variety were not accompanied by a content wedded to a literary style that often caused admiration in erudite Westerners assisting at an Oriental Liturgy or even simply reading the texts. In rich and expressive language, the themes of God's glory and the redemptive work of the Son play a large role in the Oriental anaphoras. In the words of one present-day admirer, the anaphora is "this contemplation in and by the Church of the mystery of God and his gracious plan of salvation." [5] In the anaphora, one speaks fittingly of God only by allowing himself to be formed by His Word until it resounds in us into praise and thanksgiving. In recalling the mighty deeds of God and all He has done to constitute and free His people, the Church can do no

[2] Jacques Goar. *Euchologion sive Rituale Graecorum,* Paris, 1647.

[3] Eusèbe Renaudot, *Liturgiarum orientalum collectio,* Paris, 1716.

[4] F. E. Brightman, *Liturgies Eastern and Western,* Vol. I, *Eastern Liturgies,* Oxford, 1896.

[5] I. H. Dalmais, "Quelques grand thèmes théologiques des anaphores orientales," *Eucharisties d'Orient et d'Occident* (Lex Orandi, 47), Paris, 1970, p. 181. It should be noted, however, that Dom Cabrol (+1937) tirelessly defended the Roman canon when compared to the Eastern anaphoras with regard to form and content. See his *Les Origines liturgiques,* Paris, 1906, pp. 89ff.

other than turn suppliant in order to request the full accomplishment of the plan of salvation: that all be gathered up into unity by the communion in the gift of the Spirit in such a way that it is clearly seen that the Church is the Body of Christ, harmoniously organized by the diversity of its functions, building itself up to full adulthood. Everything is put into action in order to render a full ecclesical consistency to an existential theology, expressing the right relationships of man and of God the savior.[6]

The diversity of the Oriental liturgies is particularly striking because, despite definite theological options in them, they generally have a certain similarity among them. This is a result of their reliance on the Bible for inspiration. They have a certain universal character in their expression, and, since they developed out of a tradition, they show a certain continuity.[7]

It is no wonder then that, in the announcement of the creation of new Roman Eucharistic Prayers, the document refers specifically to the Oriental practice when it says that no single anaphora can contain all the pastoral, spiritual, and theological richness desirable. A variety of texts has to make up for the limits of each one.[8]

Jewish Roots of the Eucharistic Prayer

In wishing to emphasize the specificity of Christianity and, perhaps, because of the whole idea of the rejection of Jesus by the Jews, Christian scholars generally neglected the deep Jewish roots of Christian Prayers. Baumstark, the famed German lay liturgist, had insisted that the comparative history of liturgies had to take into account the cult of the synagogue. However, he called for a certain prudence because of difficulties in chronology: often Jewish witnesses were posterior to corresponding Christian ones and, in addition, the Christian liturgy had undergone non-Jewish influences.[9] However, even as recently as 1966, Bouyer found it necessary to write at the beginning of his *Eucharist:*

---

[6] *Ibid.,* pp. 181-182.

[7] "Epilogue," *Eucharisties d'Orient et d'Occident, op. cit.,* p. 293ff.

[8] "Indications pour faciliter la catechèse des anaphores de la messe," *Notitiae* 4 (1968), p. 151.

[9] Anton Baumstark, *Liturgie comparée,* Chevetogne, 1939, pp. 11-12 and 52-58; in English, *Comparative Liturgy,* revised by Bernard Botte, F. L. Cross, trans., Westminster, Maryland, 1958, pp. 10-11 and 46-51.

It is true that the Christian liturgy, and the eucharist especially, is one of the most original creations of Christianity. But however original it is, it is still not a sort of *ex nihilo* creation. To think so is to condemn ourselves to a minimal understanding of it.[10]

To be sure, Bouyer sees that the Catholics were misled by Protestant scholars who were insisting that Christian originality was to be, at the very least, limited to and by a substitution of themes coming from Hellenistic thought for those from Jewish thought.[11] However, it would make as much sense to say that strong conservative impulses had to be overcome before Christians (whether Catholic or Protestant) would look beyond the Christian beginnings to arrive at Jewish origins in their most sacred of Prayers.

There were other reasons why the Christian scholarly world was kept from acknowledging the dependence on Jewish origins: one was that they simply did not yet have enough evidence to force them to it; another was that the scholars' efforts were spent on other things, for example, the relationship between the Christian liturgy and pagan rites (especially in the mystery religions) and the nature of the Last Supper meal.[12]

From the end of the 19th century on, a certain number of scholars, Christian and Jewish alike, studied the influence of Jewish prayers on Christian prayers. In particular, the Jewish scholar Kaufmann Kohler had called attention in 1893 to Christian interpolations added to Jewish prayers in the Apostolic Constitutions (Books VII and VIII).[13] Later, the Protestant scholar W. Bousset gained much wider notice when he took up the same subject.[14] In English, W. O. E. Oesterley's *The Jewish Background of the Christian Liturgy*[15] gained a wide audience, and W. Gavin, studying the research up to 1925, published his lectures in which he discussed the Beraka as a

[10] Louis Bouyer, *Eucharist,* Charles Underhill Quinn, trans., Notre Dame, Indiana, 1968, p. 15.

[11] *Ibid.,* p. 18.

[12] Joseph Coppens, "Eucharistic," *DB Sup.,* Vol. II, Paris, 1934, cols. 1146-1215.

[13] Kaufmann Kohler, "Über die Ursprunge und Grundformen der synagogalen Liturgie," *MGWJ* (1893), pp. 441-451 and 489-497.

[14] W. Bousset, "Eine jüdische Gebetssammlung im siebenten Buch der Apostolischen Konstitutionen," in *Nachrichten von der K. Gessellschaft der Wissenschaften zu Göttingen, Philologische-Historische Klasse, 1915* (1916), pp. 435-489.

[15] W. O. E. Oesterley, *The Jewish Background of the Christian Liturgy,* London, 1925.

source of the Eucharistic Prayer.[16] All of these authors, even Kohler later on although not without reservations, were indebted to the work of the renowned Jewish scholar I. Elbogen, who had studied Jewish worship.[17]

In 1949, Dom Botte, basing himself on Dugmore and Rankin as well as his own acute sense of what is a fact and what is only a hypothesis, rejected what he regarded as an unscientific attempt to see more influence than was actually warranted by the paralleling of texts. He did not, however, attack a parallel of form or genre, but he emphasized that in the composition of prayers the Old Testament was a common source for Jews and Christians.[18] Rankin played down the determining of influence based on the paralleling of texts, but he accepted the influence of forms. He acknowledged that there were a number of topics, themes, and doctrines common to Jesus and to the Jewish Christians and that it cannot be supposed that the latter, of the same race and culture, devised a linguistic technique for praying concerning the same things in ways different from their brethren.[19] Among the Jewish scholars, Spanier had popularized the *Formgeschichte* method,[20] and, later, Werner would use the method in his study *The Sacred Bridge*.[21]

Prior to Botte's article, Dom Dix [22] and Abbé Chirat [23] had pointed out the parallels existing between the Beraka and the Christian prayer forms. Chirat suggested that the consecratory prayer took the place of the solemn Beraka. Like it, it was preceded by an invitation to give thanks whose formula—supplemented by Christian additions—resembled that said by the Jews when ten or one hundred persons were present. Justin's formula and that of Hippolytus, he found, showed an analogy with the Beraka. This latter, it could be said, was revised in the light of the New Covenant; without being

---

[16] F. Gavin, *The Jewish Antecedents of the Christian Sacraments*, London, 1928, esp. pp. 59-98.

[17] I. Elbogen, *Der jüdische Gottesdienst*, Leipzig, 1913.

[18] Bernard Botte, "Liturgie chrétienne et liturgie juive," *Cahiers Sioniens* 7 (1949), p. 215ff.; C. W. Dugmore, *The Influence of the Synagogue upon the Divine Office*, London, 1944.

[19] O. S. Rankin, "The Extent and the Influence of the Synagogue Service upon Christian Worship," *JJS*, Vol. I, No. 1 (1949), p. 30.

[20] A. Spanier, "Zur Formengeschichte des altjüdischen Gebetes," *MGWJ* (1934), pp. 438-447; "Stilkritisches zum jüdischen Gebet," *MGWJ* (1936), pp. 339-350.

[21] E. Werner, *The Sacred Bridge*, London, 1959.

[22] Gregory Dix, *The Shape of the Liturgy*, Westminster, 1945.

[23] Henri Chirat, *L'Assemblée chrétienne à l'âge apostolique* (Lex Orandi, 10), Paris, 1949.

totally modified, it was adapted to the newness of the teaching and doing of Christ.[24]

Much earlier, Edmund von der Goltz, in a work that apparently enjoyed limited circulation, had already investigated Jewish influences on the Eucharistic Prayers.[25] In his essay, von der Goltz took as a hypothesis that, if the Eucharistic liturgies as well as the forms of the Christian table blessing have their common origin in the form of the sacred meal in the Apostolic Age, whose own structure is connected to the Jewish family customs, then elements in both lines of development must have been preserved which point to that original identity of Eucharist and sacred meal.[26]

Starting with the Jewish table prayers and comparing them to the prayers in the *Didache,* in the *Apostolic Constitutions* (Book VIII), and in the older Greek anaphoras, von der Goltz concluded:

> To the oldest component parts of the Eucharist belong the festive summons to give thanks, the so-called Preface. It takes its pattern obviously from the responses to the introduction to the table blessing: "Let us pronounce the blessing—the Name of the Lord be praised—Let us praise the Lord." The content of the great thanksgiving prayer is, as its train of thought reveals, a clear parallel, only that the old schema is filled with a new content in the Christian worship.[27]

Comparing the Jewish and Christian thanksgivings, he concludes that the latter depend on the former. He finds traces of Jewish prayers in the anamnesis, the intercessory prayers and the command to go in peace.[28]

These traces and influences were more easily seen in the Oriental anaphoras than in the Roman canon. Jean Paul Audet, by drawing attention to the Jewish prayer form called the Beraka, gave liturgists a fresh point of view from which to consider the canon. In a first article, he showed that the cult benediction was composed of three fundamental literary elements: (1) the "benediction" properly so-called, always brief, generally stereotyped, and calling for the praise of the divine; (2) the remembrance of the *mirabilia Dei,* a longer de-

---

[24] *Ibid.,* pp. 179-182.
[25] Edmund von der Goltz, *Tischgebete und Abendmahlgebete in der altchristlichen und in der griechischen Kirchen,* Leipzig, 1905.
[26] *Ibid.,* p. 18.
[27] *Ibid.,* p. 25.
[28] *Ibid.,* pp. 27-28.

velopment of the motive for praise; and (3) the return to the opening "benediction" as a kind of inclusion or doxology.[29]

Later, applying the idea of benediction to the Roman canon, Audet argued that the *Unde et memores,* while depending directly on the cult command given by Jesus: Do this in memory of Me, is also an implicit reference to the "benediction" pronounced by Jesus for the bread and wine, and more explicitly to its liturgical implementation conserved in the Preface, which is the true descendant of the old "benediction." Thus, he concluded, in spite of appearances, one remains faithful to this liturgical command as well as to the example of Jesus himself to give the name "anamnesis" to the motive, or the body, of the old "benediction," the prototype of our "eucharist." [30]

It was with the influx of the gentiles from the second century on that the literary forms of the old Eucharistia began to break down and be modified from its original form. As a result, the "benediction" properly so-called moved progressively toward a "thanksgiving," and little by little a slew of literary forms, inspired by the psychological and cultural dominant of gratitude, accompanied it, at the expense of the more theological admiration and rejoicing over the *mirabilia Dei* which it had up until then. At the same time, the functional relationships of the anamnesis to the "benediction," at the heart of the Eucharistia, tended to be loosened while recalling less the *mirabilia Dei* as such, and more the benefits received from God. At the end of a few centuries, the Roman "Preface," which in the West still kept in its very name the trace of the value of Exomologesis (the proclamation of God's name) of the old Eucharistia, was able to lose here and there every trace of anamnesis without anybody apparently being surprised at its absence.[31]

Recently, a fellow exegete, Henri Cazelles, has said that Audet's identification between the Jewish Beraka and the Christian Eucharistia has to be challenged.[32] Also, in a thesis that was very well received, Robert Ledogar contested Audet's theory that the source of the Christian anaphora is in the Jewish Beraka, in the sense of admiration in the face of the *mirabilia Dei.* Ledogar says that Eucharistein must

[29] J. P. Audet, "Esquisse historique du genre littéraire de la 'bénédiction' juive et de l'"eucharistie' chrétienne," *RB* 65 (1958), pp. 379-380. This article is based on his "Literary Forms and Contents of a Normal eucharistia in the First Century," *Studia Evangelica: Papers Presented to the International Congress on "The Four Gospels in 1957"* eds. K. Aland *et al.,* Berlin, 1959, pp. 643-662.

[30] *Ibid.,* "Genre littéraire et formes cultuelles de l'eucharistie," *Eph. Liturg.* 80 (1966), p. 366.

[31] *Ibid.,* "Esquisse historique. . . ," pp. 397-398.

[32] Henri Cazelles, "L'anaphore et l'ancien testament," *Eucharisties d'Orient et d'Occident* I (Lex Orandi, 46), Paris, 1970, p. 13.

be understood in the sense of a sacrifice of acknowledgment before
God. In this perspective, the primitive theme, conqueror of death, was
little by little enlarged into the diverse anaphoras in order to
englobe also the entire history of salvation from the creation on.[33]

Ledogar has made the following serious criticism of Audet:

> This beraka-doxology is something quite different from the
> "literary genre" which Père J. P. Audet calls a "Benediction"
> and sees to be the forerunner of the Christian Eucharistic Prayer.
> Among other things, it generally does not contain the "anamne-
> sis" of the *mirabilia Dei* which he considers an essential feature.
> Audet's analysis cuts across the lines that distinguish prose and
> poetry and other literary forms in the Old and New Testaments,
> but selects in each of them only that which fits the patterns he
> describes. This is legitimate and useful for the sake of isolat-
> ing the trends that will eventually crystalyze into the fixed
> beraka of the Talmudic period, but it does not justify fitting all the
> praise formulae of the first century into a single mold. And,
> most important of all, it does not justify translating the word
> Eucharistein as "to bless." The fact is that there were numerous
> forms of praise being used in New Testament times and that verbs
> used often retained their particular nuances. . . . The one thing
> they all have in common is the basic notion of praise as a pub-
> lic proclamation of God's qualities or deeds in history, and this
> notion is quite sufficient to account for the elements of "anam-
> nesis" often encountered.[34]

However, in our perspective, it is not so much whether Audet's
propositions are right or wrong at their starting point. The Roman
canon, for all practical purposes *sui generis,* was hardly thought of in
terms of a literary genre. Indeed, the very name canon would almost
preclude such a thought. There was only one Roman canon, a more or
less sacred text. To see the canon as a literary genre, to uncover the
structure around which it was built, was to open up the possibility
of many species of this genre and then to ask oneself why one element
cannot dominate over other elements. Thus, despite the reservations
legitimately made, Audet must receive credit for popularizing for a
large audience of Catholics the idea that the Beraka as a literary form
was the antecedent of the Eucharistic Prayer of the Roman Church.

[33] Robert Ledogar, *Acknowledgment: Praise-verbs in the Early Greek
Anaphora,* Rome, 1968, pp. 162-168.
[34] *Ibid.,* p. 124.

When Bouyer came to write his book on the Eucharist, he gave suitable but not unconditional recognition to Audet.[35]

To accept the canon as a literary genre is only to say that it is a human work, made with human words and human thoughts. However, it is also an action, in which words accompany a rite. Something happens that our words will always be inadequate to express. The Eucharistic Prayer is a special kind of language, one that seems for now best described as performative, that is, the issuing of an utterance is the performing of an action. Suffice it to say for now that the application of the idea of literary genre to the Roman canon had its role to play in leading to the development of several canons.

Finally, a study of the roots of the Eucharistic Prayer was important insofar as it shed light on the continuity of our canon with the past; it also heightened the long cultural distance that the Prayer had traveled in the Roman world until the time it became a fixed formula, the canon. Its very Jewish roots would greatly reduce for our contemporaries its right to be the unique Eucharistic Prayer for the Latin Rite of the Catholic Church.

Western Liturgical Tradition

Meanwhile, within the Western liturgical tradition itself, many other factors were at work that hindsight permits us to see as so many pressures that would lead to a reconsideration of the Roman canon's absolutist reign. We shall consider only those which we believe had the greatest impact on changing a fixist mentality.

First of all, there is the text which gives us a date in historical time from which to measure a before and an after. This text is the *Apostolic Tradition* of Hippolytus.[36] Dated toward 220 A.D., it is a witness of one person's belief of what Christian practices at Rome at that time should be. Before that date, we have hints and glimpses for which we are appreciative, but here, in a sober and clear text, we have an authentic witness to a vocabulary that has become more fixed and a religious practice that clearly resembles our own.

The *Apostolic Tradition,* popularized in the 20th century in the

---

[35] Bouyer, *op. cit.,* p. 35.

[36] We place Hippolytus under the heading of Western Liturgical Tradition for his *Apostolic Tradition* was written in the West and any study of the mass in the West must take it into account. That in no way takes away from its role in the Eastern Liturgical Tradition nor does it enter into the debate of what tradition the Eucharistic Prayer of Hippolytus more truly reflects.

English speaking world by Dom Connolly [37] and Dom Dix [38] and in the French speaking world by Dom Botte,[39] will have three important contributions to make toward our conception of the Eucharistic Prayer. It is not that any of these contributions could not have been arrived at in a scholar's study or a monk's cell, but here they are in an authentic text vested with antiquity and enjoying authority even though the work of a schismatic.

The first important contribution is that the Eucharistic Prayer of Hippolytus was a model. He tells us so clearly:

Let the bishop give thanks as we said above. In giving thanks to God, he does not have to use the same words as we gave before, as if he were studying to say them by heart, but let each one pray according to his own ability. If someone is capable of sustaining a solemn prayer, that is good. But if someone, when he prays, says a moderately long prayer, no one shall prevent him. Only let his prayer be correct and right.[40]

It seems clear that we should avoid the word improvised, whether in French or in English, in referring to Hippolytus' Eucharistic Prayer. "Improvised" and its noun "improvisation" are words that only with the greatest difficulty escape being pejorative. This is true despite an honorable tradition in Italian poetry and Arab poetry of today. However, this latter supposes a wedding of improvisor and listeners that our present Christian assemblies (except perhaps black Baptists) are not yet ready to imitate.

Hippolytus, then, presents us with a model and, in doing so, he minimizes the fixed form of a single canon. At his time, the movement from liturgical variety to liturgical unity had not yet been fully achieved at Rome. However, what is possibly more important is that it is no mean model that Hippolytus gives us, and yet, for all that, it remains a model developed along a simple structure.

In fact, stated simply, this is the second contribution of the Eucharistic Prayer of the *Apostolic Tradition* to a mentality that will

---

[37] R. H. Connolly, *The so-called Egyptian Church Order and related Documents,* Cambridge, 1916.

[38] Gregory Dix, *The Treatise on the Apostolic Tradition of St. Hippolytus of Rome,* London, 1937.

[39] Bernard Botte, *La Tradition Apostolique de Saint Hippolyte,* (Sources Chrétiennes, 11), Paris, 1946; *La Tradition Apostolique de Saint Hippolyte: Essai de reconstitution, LQF 39,* Munster, 1963.

[40] Botte, *LQF 39,* p. 29. My translation. Cp. Gregory Dix, *The Apostolic Tradition of St. Hippolytus,* London, 1937, p. 19.

envisage a variety of Eucharistic Prayers in the Roman Church: its parts are clearly joined together. The text has not been the plaything of historical additions but is the coherent composition of an ecclesiastic concerned with the correct ordering of Eucharistic assemblies.

The third contribution that the text makes is that it is Christological in the sense that, while it is addressed to the Father, from beginning to end it develops the work of Jesus Christ. Unlike the Roman canon, the idea of offering or sacrifice is not unduly emphasized. The contrast with the Roman canon is striking. Hippolytus' prayer was no doubt proclaimed aloud in the language of the people (Greek) and had a coherent structure based on a simple outline. The Roman canon, recited in a low voice in Latin with a loose structure emphasizing sacrifice, was obviously in the eyes of many of our contemporaries a poor second to this Eucharistic Prayer of Hippolytus.

It might be asked why the Roman canon retained for such a long time its place as the sole Eucharistic Prayer of the Roman Church. Aside from reasons of authority or unwillingness to change, one might say that it also enjoyed the protection of a mentality that wished to be loyal to it. Later, when new canons would be prepared, liturgists would suggest that once the Roman canon would be recited aloud in the vernacular its deficiencies would be quickly noticed, that is, it could only with the greatest difficulties then pass as the Eucharistic Prayer of contemporary man. Until then, the Roman canon was protected by such words as venerable or noble, even though such epithets rarely found their way into the writings of specialists discussing the origin and development of the canon. The language of historians of the cult, as the simple reading of the articles devoted to the canon and its parts by Dom Cabrol in the *DACL* will show, is generally as precise and free of emotional overtones as that of surgeons describing a lobotomy. In fact, the first major reflex action a Roman Catholic specialist would be most likely to have when confronted with the deficiencies of the Roman canon would not be to create new ones but to correct or improve the old one.

When Dom Eizenhofer called for a revision of the Roman canon on the grounds that its order had been interfered with and we no longer have the original one,[41] Dom Botte answered in the following words:

Let me add that [such a proposal] is dangerous for it means nothing other than modifying the canon by putting the Me-

[41] L. Eizenhofer, " 'Te Igitur' und 'Communicantes' im römischen Messkanon," *Sacris Erudiri* 8 (1956), pp. 14-75.

mento in another place. Some years ago a theologian suggested serious changes in the name of theology. Are we now going
to assist at an analogous offensive in the name of literary criticism? Dom Eizenhofer has done so, and he gives his reasons. I
am able to respond in my turn that his reasons seem to me clearly
insufficient and that his brilliant reconstruction has no more
consistency than a house of cards. To propose a reform of the
canon on such a weak base seems to me imprudent. The structure of the canon was fixed, in my opinion, at the end of the
4th century. Its text was definitively established by St. Gregory.
Let us not touch this venerable text, neither out of a theological
pretext nor a literary one.[42]

Later, Dom Botte will show himself as critical toward what he regarded as anarchical creations outside of Rome and as prudent
toward the creations by the Roman Consilium.[43]

Because of their great erudition, the liturgists of the 19th and early
20th centuries would not be so impressed by the *Apostolic Tradition*
that they would challenge the preeminence of the Roman canon. The
former would find its place in the vast synthesis of their knowledge,
but it would receive increased importance when knowledge of it
leaves the specialists' domain and the climate for proposing new
canons bcomes more favorable.

Other elements tending to relativize the fixed form of the Roman
canon were the rich liturgical pluriformity of the Roman Church as
found in its Sacramentaries, especially the extraordinary number of
Prefaces formerly used, the fact that non-Roman Catholic Churches
which broke away from the Roman Church would often construct
their own Eucharistic Prayers, and finally the practice of different liturgical traditions within the Western tradition itself. All of these elements
in themselves provide no reason for the creation of new Roman
anaphoras. There was obviously something else at work. It was something other than an increased recognition of the Eucharist as for the
community and a de-emphasis of the worship of the Eucharistic host.
It was other than a greater emphasis being given to the local or particular Church vis-à-vis the universal Church. If it must be summed
up, it was no doubt the dynamics of the pastoral concern of the
Church to reach contemporary man.[44]

[42] Bernard Botte, "Communication," *QLP* 38 (1957), pp. 122-123.
[43] *Ibid.,* "Où en est la réforme du canon de la messe?" *QLP* 49 (1968), pp.
140-141.
[44] Cf. Jungmann's remark: It is characteristic of the Liturgical Reform
of Vatican II that the pastoral consideration is decisive and that thus from
the outset the mass celebrated with the people was envisaged as the object

H. Wegman, writing on the changes taking place in the Dutch Church, has tried to sketch the causes of the evolution; among them he lists the concern of liturgists after World War II to link liturgy to life.[45] He sees the Eucharistic Congress at Maastricht (1946) as a kind of starting point, at least for the Dutch Church. He cites Doncoeur's impassioned address to the assembly as an important contribution in this direction.[46]

Obedience to Rome would gradually give way to liturgical experimentation in order to arrive at a living liturgy. The touchstone became the "man of today" who has his own needs and must pray in his own language and about his own concerns. If this criterion was true of the Roman prayers, it was also seen as true of the Roman canon. The Dutch were suddenly surprised to find themselves the cynosure of the Church. They had to explain themselves, and their reasons were various and of unequal value: we are a practical people; our bishops gave us the liberty to work; we had to restore a more biblical language; our ecumenical situation set us off on the path of renewal; the French pastoral effort to fight dechristianization spurred us on, and so on.[47]

It is certainly not our purpose to evaluate any of these reasons, but it does seem clear that running like an underground stream through all of them is the desire to reach today's man, to have his liturgy grow out of his life. As the post-war ideas began to take hold, they would be given a vital thrust by the Second Vatican Council. Armed with the Constitution on the Sacred Liturgy and the Constitution on the Church in the World, the pastoral zeal of the Dutch Church gave itself wholeheartedly to the renewal of the liturgy. Lucas Brinkhoff, summarizing the situation for German readers, has shown that gradually the Dutch were led to create Eucharistic Prayers inspired from the Scriptures while at the same time the Roman Liturgy together with its symbols was increasingly regarded as something foreign.[48] Later

---

of the reform of the Mass. This is in contrast to the reform of Pius V where the normal case appears to be the celebration of the Mass by the individual priest with a server. "Konstitution über die heilige Liturgie," *Das zweite Vatikanische Konzil: Dokumente und Kommentare,* Teil I, *LTK,* Freiburg, 1966, pp. 52-53.

[45] H. Wegman, "Monde d'aujourd'hui et liturgie d'hier," *Communauté Chrétienne* 44 (1969), trans. by K. Vanderheyen, pp. 117-130. See also the other articles in the number.

[46] Paul Doncoeur, "Comment se pose le problème de la liturgie populaire?" *QLP* 27 (1946), pp. 173-183.

[47] H. Wegman, *op. cit., passim;* Leo Bakker, "Holland, Versuchsfeld der Kirche Gottes?" *Orientierung* 5 (1968), pp. 59-63.

[48] Lucas Brinkhoff, "Die Liturgische Situation in Holland," in *Deutsche Liturgie? Sind wir auf dem Weg dahin?* Theodor Bogler, ed., Maria Laach, 1967, pp. 59-63.

Dutch Jesuit Leo Bakker explained that many in the Netherlands felt it to be their pastoral duty, not just to translate, but to shape new texts and to seek new forms by which true communication could take place, by which the Eucharist could be experienced by priest and faithful as a celebration in joy coming out of the Good News.[49]

More than a decade earlier Joseph Jungmann had written on "today's man":

Today's man has become level-headed; he is no longer the naive man of the Middle Ages nor the pathetic man of the Baroque period. And not only in his religious life. A sharp wind blows through the century, the air of a critical philosophy, the air of empirical scholarship, the air of technical progress. And it blows not only in the city streets, but also in the farthest mountain valley.

And yet the man of today knows, at least the Christian, the limitedness and contingency of his existence, and that he cannot escape God, that he needs Him, and he must seek Him, not to draw Him down into the small horizon of his foolish desires, rather to insert his life into God's plan and in His design— in short to worship Him. The religious life of today's man is either something essential or it is nothing.

And here comes the Liturgy to meet him, the correctly understood and correctly performed Sunday worship, the lively celebration of the Eucharist. In worship, as the Liturgy teaches it, the Christian, who in life is knocked about here and there, always regains a solid place on which to stand in this world; here the Christian conscience is renewed; here are those spiritual vitamins, which keep the religious life, the Christian life healthy. We only need to cast a few glances on the arrangement of the mass and what has been said will be yet clearer.[50]

Here, we see the same concern as noted in the Dutch Church, but, in a sense, the movement is in a totally different direction. Jungmann looks at today's man and then, as it were, brings him to the Eucharistic celebration and says, "Here are the answers to your problems." The approach permitted after Vatican II is to view today's man and then say, "Let us construct our Eucharistic celebration together so that we can bring your needs into it and not cut

[49] Bakker, op. cit., p. 63.
[50] Joseph Jungmann, "Eucharistie und Frömmigkeit," LJ 5 (1955), p. 99.

your needs to fit it." It is no accident that Jungmann himself would
contribute greatly to this change in approach.[51]

Despite the fact that in the Constitution on the Sacred Liturgy no
indication of any change in the Roman canon or the creation of new
canons was given, it was this Council document itself that would be
used as the justification for the new canons. As Monseignor Jenny,
Archbishop of Cambrai and member of the Liturgical Conciliar Commission remarked:

> No one will ever know the amount of words exchanged and the
> volume of pages written on a simple little paragraph. But
> the consequences will be considerable for certain principles
> adopted: this morning I told my neighbor that I had the impres-
> sion that, under the seemingly harmless expressions of a para-
> graph, we could be laying time bombs.[52]

Such "time bombs," insofar as the Roman canon was concerned,
were articles 21, 23, 33, 34, 48, and 50.[53] These are the very articles
that Vagaggini, a peritus at the Council and a member of the Consilium (the Postconciliar Commission), will cite in presenting his
project for a reform of the canon.[54] In a sense his book was the
Roman response to all the voices calling for new Eucharistic Prayers.
On June 20, 1966, Pope Paul acceded to Cardinal Lercaro's request
for permission to create new Roman canons. Thus the passage from
the old mentality to the new was made. Change and experimentation
on a scale hitherto unknown were possible.

[51] Especially with his *Missarum Solemnia,* Vienna, 1948; in English, *The
Mass of the Roman Rite,* Francis A. Brunner, trans., New York, 1951-1955;
and *Das Eucharistische Hochgebet,* Wurzburg, 1954; in English, *The Eucharistic Prayer,* Robert Batley, trans. Notre Dame, Indiana, 1960.

[52] "Le travail de la Commission conciliaire de Liturgie," *QLP* 44 (1963),
p. 239.

[53] E. J. Lengeling tells us that the Conciliar Commission of the Sacred
Liturgy, through its relator, declared expressly against a certain Father that
article 50 of the Constitution "Sacrosanctum Concilium" concerning the
revision of the ordinary of the mass ought to be extended also to the second
part of the mass "because also in the second part of the mass are some
things, even though of minor importance, which may be said to need revision,
e.g., certain signs of the cross." Then, to the "modum" of three of the
Fathers that the form of the canon itself always remain intact, the Conciliar
Commission through its relator answered, "This second 'modum' is indicated
by the schema's words, 'due care being taken to preserve their [the rites']
substance.' But we shall send all this on to the Postconciliar Commission."
"De Precibus Eucharisticis," Notitiae 8 (1972), p. 132. Cp. Jungmann's remark in his commentary on the Liturgical Constitution, p. 54.

[54] Cypriano Vagaggini, *Il Canone della Messa e la Riforma Liturgica,*
Torino, 1966; in English *The Canon of the Mass and Liturgical Reform,*
Peter Coughlan *et al.,* trans., New York, 1967.

2
THE THREE ROMAN
EUCHARISTIC PRAYERS

The first prayers that we propose to study are the three Roman Eucharistic Prayers.[1] These are the ones against which we shall measure the others in a sense that we must now immediately specify. Written to make up for a lack that even a revision of the canon would not fulfill, but also to counteract the unbridled creation of EPs by small groups, the Roman ones were the work of the best liturgists that the Latin Church could assemble, were promulgated for use in the Latin Rite, and were based on models that dated as far back as the earliest centuries of the Church. Hence, because these Prayers hold such a preeminent place, other EPs are to be set alongside of them, not that the former are the sole measure of orthodoxy or the model for writing an EP today, but the simple study of the same elements in the different groups of EPs is of great value in our continuing understanding of the way the Church addresses itself to God in the heart of its Eucharistic celebration.

In this chapter we intend to give a summary introduction to the immediate background of the Roman creations. Then, we shall analyze the following elements: (1) the structure of the prayers, (2) the way in which the praying community addresses God, refers to Jesus Christ, and refers to itself, (3) what the praying community finds significant to say about Jesus Christ, (4) what the praying community says about the elements (the bread and wine) that it uses and the action that it is accomplishing, and (5) what place is given to the role of the Holy Spirit.

Our choice of the elements to be studied has been guided by the concerns of today's Christians. By examining the structure of the EPs from one group to another, we shall see how the different elements entering into an EP are put together, which are considered necessary, and whether or not a change in the understanding of a given element may be detected in moving from one group of EPs to an-

[1] From now on Eucharistic Prayer will be abbreviated EP.

other. Thus we shall not rule out any Prayer on the grounds that it does not have the canonical structure of an EP. In a sense, the multiplicity of Prayers shows that a modern EP may be in search of a structure. Our next area of concern—the way the community refers to God, to Jesus Christ, and to itself—arises from our belief that these references will reveal significant differences in the EPs created by various groups. In fact, as we shall see in a later chapter, the very idea of naming God becomes a problem in one group of EPs. We have centered our next question around Jesus Christ for this will enable us to see how the faith of the Church in Jesus Christ is expressed in the various EPs. In every age there is a tendency to evacuate the human or to evacuate the divine in the person of Jesus Christ. Thus, our question will show us the way each group tends to establish an equilibrium in its understanding of the Person Jesus Christ. The next question concerning the praying community's understanding of the action it is accomplishing is important for the present-day confrontation of varying ideas on what the Eucharistic celebration is: reunion of fellowship, fraternal banquet, sacred meal, sacrifice of praise, etc. One's idea of what one is celebrating will regulate his choice of words with regard to what he is doing. This question will not lead us to talk about transubstantiation, but it will direct our attention to what the community believes about the elements of bread and wine. Our final question relative to the Holy Spirit is prompted by the theological restoration and the ecumenical advance it represents insofar as the Roman EPs are concerned. Little space was given to expressing the role of the Holy Spirit in the Roman canon whereas the role of the Spirit, not only in the anaphoras, but also in the whole liturgy of the oriental Churches, was quite noteworthy.

Summary Background to the
Roman Eucharistic Prayers

There is no need to write the history of the events that led specifically to the new Roman EPs.[2] Such a detailed account would distract us from our main concern, namely, to study the new EPs themselves. Besides, we would run the risk of not avoiding the merely anecdotal. However, a few words of background will not be

[2] A good recent work for background to the EP is that written by a student of Joseph Jungmann. We refer to Luis Maldonado, *La Plegaria Eucaristica: Estudio de teologia biblica y liturgica sobre la misa,* Biblioteca de Autores Christianos 273, Madrid, 1967.

out of place for, sooner or later, to understand the EPs better some
of the immediate background to their creation should be known.

Two important steps toward the creation of new EPs were the call
for the end of the silent recitation of the canon and its translation into
the vernacular. In our perspective, it is the advocation of something
that is important, not the actual date when it is put into practice.
Once an increasing demand to change something is made, the important shift in mentality is already present whether or not the object of the advocacy is ever actually approved. The significance of
the recitation of the canon aloud was that it was a return to the
practice of the early Church, long neglected and even forgotten to
such an extent that the silent recitation was considered to extend almost back to the origins. The burden of proving otherwise fell to
the opponents of such a proposition. Historical research, however,
was able to show the evolution in space, time, and thought that led
to reciting the canon in a low voice.[3] Nevertheless, the silent recitation was maintained in the Church as stemming from the developed understanding of the Eucharist [4] and, no doubt, because the
faithful had access to books with paraphrases or pious prayers and,
comparatively recently, translations of the canon. The silent recitation was associated with a religious sense of the sacred and, as such,
was a strong argument in preserving the *status quo*. When pastoral
considerations prevailed, the next step was to recite the canon in
the vernacular. This step effectively removed the sense of a sacred
language in which one publicly prayed to God at the most solemn
moment. However, what is more, not a few people found serious
liturgical and pastoral problems arising from the text. So much was
this true for some liturgists of note that they needed no other justification for creating new texts.

With the calling of the Second Vatican Council, it became obvious
that the thrust of the liturgical movement would receive a new im-
petus on a global scale. However, the first person to break into print
with a proposal for a new canon was the "enfant terrible," Hans
Küng.[5] It was almost in the logic of things that a non-liturgist would

[3] Charles A. Lewis, *The Silent Recitation of the Canon of the Mass,* excerpt
from a dissertation in the Gregorian University theology faculty, Bay Saint
Louis, 1962.

[4] Joseph Jungmann, "Ende der Kanonstille," *LJ* 17 (1967), pp. 220-232.

[5] Hans Küng, "Das Eucharistiegebet: Konzil und Erneuerung der römischen Messliturgie," *Wort und Wahrheit* 18 (1963), pp. 102-107. For
suggestions before Küng see F. X. Arnold, "Subjekt und Gestalt christ-
licher Liturgie," in *Kirche und Überlieferung, Frieburg,* 1960, pp. 263ff. Cp.
E. J. Lengeling, "Dis Messfeier als Eucharistie," *LJ* 11 (1961), p. 77.

put forth at that time a proposal that the most informed liturgists would hesitate to speak about in public.

Küng's project, published in 1963 in a Catholic review devoted to contemporary problems, has been amply studied by Vagaggini, dispensing us from any need to analyze it here. There are, nevertheless, two things worth mentioning. First, Küng's justification for a new canon is a specious one: since Pope John XXIII introduced the name of Saint Joseph into the Roman canon, this latter is not untouchable and can be changed! To touch the sacred text is no longer a violation. Such a reason may strike us as ludicrous, but it must be remembered that Küng was working within a system whose logic can only be explained within the interior of that system, which, as we have suggested, was in the process of changing.

What is more important than Küng's reason *why* the canon can be changed are his reasons *for* changing it. He wished particularly that a new canon or a reworked one emphasize that it is the community's prayer—not just the priest's—and that the sacrificial aspect be deemphasized in favor of the idea of Memorial. In point of fact, very little of what Küng wrote in this article was original with him for practically all justification for what he says can be found in Jungmann's works. It is Küng's reading of the latter and the assimilation of his thought that led him to propose a new canon.

The Austrian Karl Amon, who preceded Küng in calling for a reform of the canon but published a specific project only after Küng, at first advocated the use of Hippolytus' canon.[6] Like Küng, influenced by Jungmann, he was mainly interested that the EP fulfill its prayer and proclamation function, that the idea of sacrifice be deemphasized, and that the deprecatory parts cease to be in the canon.

We single out these two authors for they tried to work within the same framework as the Consilium did later, and, in fact, the criticism of their projects aided in deciding what a Roman EP should and should not be. In both cases, the reasons given for new EPs were never substantially under attack, but the projects proposed did have their weak points as Vagaggini clearly pointed out.[7] It is in this sense that the work of the Consilium on the EPs, begun in the autumn of 1966, already was immediately alerted to its task and

---

[6] Karl Amon, "Reformwünsche zum innersten Bereich der eucharistichen Feier," *Bibel und Liturgie* 35 (1961/62), pp. 107-109; "Wünsche an die künftige Messliturgie," *Bibel und Liturgie* 38 (1964/65), pp. 208-217; and "Gratias Agere: zur Reform des Messkanons," *LJ* 15 (1965), pp. 79-98.

[7] Vagaggini, *op. cit.,* pp. 76-83.

was beginning to form opinions on the possibility of revising the Roman canon, of utilizing the anaphora of Hippolytus, and of adapting or adopting oriental anaphoras.[8] It was decided that each of the new EPs would have its own particular richness. Prayer II, which although a new creation takes Hippolytus as a model, placed its emphasis on a thanksgiving that is christological. Prayer III, which owes so much to Vagaggini's projects, begins with the *Vere Sanctus*, emphasizing the holiness of God, the call to holiness of His people, and the holiness of the offering made. Prayer IV, composed with great awareness of biblical theology and the oriental tradition, tries to preserve all that is best in the Eastern anaphora. This prayer is striking for its presentation of the divine economy, that spiritual vision of God and his dealing with men. It is not our intention to study these prayers in and for themselves for we cannot do this in the same way for the other contemporary prayers. Nevertheless, we do hope to put to use here and there our greater knowledge of their composition.

The Structure of the Roman Eucharistic Prayers

In deciding the structure of the new EPs, the task presented to the committee was to choose what elements should be included as well as how they should be assembled while at the same time not departing too far from the structure of the Roman canon. Thus, the committee was faced with the problem of new creations or taking over purely and simply oriental anaphoras. Bouyer tells us that the Consilium considered adopting the anaphora of St. Basil, especially in its primitive Alexandrian form. This would have been a decisive ecumenical

---

[8] The new EPs have received a great deal of commentary, sometimes critical about certain steps taken, sometimes theologically or spiritually oriented. The following works have been most instructive for the present author: J. D. Crichton, "The New Eucharistic Prayers," *Liturgy* 36 (1968), pp. 89-101; Aidan Kavanagh, "Thoughts on the New Eucharistic Prayers," *Worship* 43 (1969), pp. 2-12; Bruno Kleinheyer, *Erneuerung des Hochgebetes,* Regensburg, 1968; Thierry Maertens, "Les nouvelles prières eucharistiques au service de l'assemblée," *Liturgie et Vie chrétienne* 65 (1968), pp. 194-202; Jacques Ménard, "La restauration de la bénédiction eucharistique," *Liturgie et Vie chrétienne* 65 (1968), pp. 180-193; A-M Roguet, "Les prières eucharistiques," *Vie spirituelle* (1968), pp. 70-87; Theodore Schnitzler, *Die drei neuen eucharistischen Hochgebete und die neuen Präfationem: in Verkündigung und Betrachtung,* Freiburg, 1968; G. G. Willis, "The New Eucharistic Prayers: Some Comments," *The Heythrop Journal* 12 (1971), pp. 5-28; the entire issue of *La Maison-Dieu* 94 (1968); and *Assemblées du Seigneur,* 2 ème série, No. 2, *Anaphores nouvelles,* Paris, 1968.

step, but it was one whose time had not come, and the Congregation for the Doctrine of the Faith judged it inopportune when the Consilium proposed it. This decision was not totally unexpected, and Bouyer says that the novelty of adopting an oriental anaphora would be such a great departure from the only kind of EP familiar to the great majority of Catholics that the necessity for an adapted anaphora was seen.[9] This was EP IV. It had been decided that the structure of the Roman EPs would be the same for all three, even though the manner of moving from one part to another part is sometimes varied. We propose to see this structure in terms of blocks. The first major block is the Dialogue–Preface–Introduction to the Sanctus–the Sanctus–the *Vere Sanctus*. The traditional opening dialogue is kept in all three prayers but their prefaces differ. Prayer II's Thanksgiving has a short christological development singling out the great acts in the life of Jesus while Prayer IV has a proclamation of the attributes of God. Prayer III does not have a Preface of its own and may adopt any one from the collection of Prefaces, provided it be consistent with Prayer III's own rhythm. The Introduction to the Sanctus links the earthly liturgy with heavenly liturgy and flows into the traditional Sanctus. The *Vere Sanctus* is found properly in Prayers II and III. In Prayer I it is little more than a brief addition while in Prayer III the development is somewhat longer. Prayer IV presents a lengthy development of the history of salvation from creation to the Pentecost event continued into our own time. Its attachment to the Sanctus is made through its initial address to God as *Pater sancte*.

The second major block is composed of different literary forms: Invocation–Narration–Acclamation–Anamnetic Offering–Invocation. The first Invocation is composed of two parts variously expressed in the three Prayers: God is asked to sanctify the offerings through the Holy Spirit so that they become the Body and Blood of Christ. In each Prayer, this Epiclesis is linked to the *Vere Sanctus* in different ways. In Prayer II, it is to the *fons omnis sanctitatis* of the *Vere Sanctus* that the request to sanctify is made. In Prayer III, the connection is made between the *oblatio munda offeratur* and *haec munera*. Prayer IV links up the *Spiritum Sanctum* of the *Vere Sanctus* and the *idem Spiritus Sanctus* of the Epiclesis. The Institution Narrative is essentially the same in all three although each one is introduced differently and other minor variations can be found. All three

[9] Bouyer, "The New Eucharistic Prayers of the Roman Rite," in Patrick McGoldrick, editor, *Understanding the Eucharist*, Dublin, 1969, pp. 169ff. See also Pierre Jounel, "La Composition des Prières Eucharistiques," *La Maison-Dieu* No. 94 (1968), pp. 39-40; also Emil Lengeling's Report, "De Precibus Eucharisticis," *Notitiae* 8 (1972), pp. 132-134.

have a link with the Epiclesis through the name of Jesus Christ in Prayer II and Prayer III and the expression *Filium tuum* in Prayer IV. In addition, Prayers III and IV both refer to the mystery to be celebrated in the Epiclesis and thus the transition to the Institution Narrative is facilitated. The Acclamation follows in all three. Addressed to Christ, it breaks the unity of address to the Father, even though precedent for this is found outside the EP in the Kyrie and Agnus Dei. The proclamation of the memorial offering, traditionally called Anamnesis, is then made. Each of the Prayers keeps the link between the act of remembering or celebrating and the act of offering. From Prayer II to Prayer IV, there is a progression in the redemptive events recalled. The wording of the offering is also varied in each Prayer. This block is completed with the second Invocation. In all three Prayers the assembly requests to be united through the Spirit and through participation in the reception of the Eucharist. Prayers III and IV ask God to look favorably on the offering. The Latin formula is somewhat varied as is customary in these Prayers even when the ideas are exactly the same.

The third part of the Prayers is formed by the Intercessions, which include the communion between the earthly and heavenly Church as well as Intercessions for the living and the dead, variously ordered and expressed from Prayer to Prayer.

Each Prayer concludes with the traditional doxology.

Analyzing the theological structure of the EPs, Max Thurian has presented another way of looking at them.[10] He sees them divided schematically into two parts, each of which follows a similar movement:

First Part: Benediction for the wondrous works of God in the eucharistic proclamation: Thanksgiving (Preface, Sanctus, *Vere Sanctus*).

Invocation of the Holy Spirit upon the bread and wine: First Epiclesis.

The Realization of the Body of Christ by the words of the Lord: Institution.

The sacramental Body of Christ is accomplished by his word: Christ and the Kingdom of God are present in the mystery.

Acclamation.

[10] Max Thurian, "La théologie des nouvelles prières eucharistiques," *La Maison-Dieu* 94 (1968), pp. 77-78.

Second Part: Benediction for the wondrous works of God in the sacramental anamnesis: Sacrificial memorial (Anamnesis-offering).
Invocation of the Holy Spirit upon the community: Second Epiclesis.
Realization of the Body of Christ by the prayers of the Church: Intercession.
The ecclesial Body of Christ is developed by prayer: Christ and the Kingdom of God will be manifested in glory.
Conclusion.

Communion: The ecclesial Body communicates in the sacramental Body.

This outline is quite fruitful for any theological considerations of the EPs for Thurian is one of the best commentators on the theology of the EPs. However, this theological structure, which will be found with variations also in contemporary non-Roman EPs, calls for some commentary.

First of all, the schematic division into two parts can obscure the fact that the whole prayer is one of thanksgiving and praise, that within this whole various elements enter in that are not properly thanksgiving or praise because, at the same time that the community is making a discourse, it is also very much aware that it is accomplishing an action. Thus, the thanksgiving extends from Preface to Doxology. The movement is to praise God by recalling his deeds and to return to praise. Only for the sake of complete clarity should it be noted that the invocations of the Holy Spirit are not properly invocations of the Holy Spirit, but invocations of the Father to send the Spirit, which is only natural since the EP is traditionally addressed to the Father.

Thurian's placing of the Anamnesis properly so-called at the beginning of the second part obscures the fact that it is not to be separated from the Institution Narrative on which it depends and that such a division accentuates too much that Christ is present by the words of Institution when the modern tendency is to regard the whole prayer as consecratory.

The paralleling of the Acclamation with what is called the conclusion is a forcing of the outline. In the first place, to refer to the Doxology as conclusion should require that the opening dialogue or the Preface itself be designated as introduction. Secondly, the Acclamation is addressed to Christ while the "conclusion" is addressed to the Father. Thirdly, the Acclamation is said by the whole community while the Doxology is said by the celebrant, even though in actual practice the congregation often joins in.

The realization of the sacramental Body of Christ is put in parallel with the realization of the ecclesial Body of Christ. This latter is attributed to the Intercessions when it should be properly attributed to the working of the Spirit in the community and to the reception of the sacramental Body of Christ.

No doubt, Thurian is well aware of the limitations of his outline. It is, in fact, a good device for developing an understanding of the structure of the EP. However, in presenting the structure of the Roman EPs, we have preferred another point of view, one that does not obscure the theological structure in attempting to explain it and does not neglect to take into account the whole movement of the EP.

The role of the variable Preface in the Roman EPs must not be forgotten in any consideration of the new prayers. Not to consider even briefly the corpus of 82 Prefaces is to ignore the full richness of the EPs, to continue the dichotomy that for so long separated the Preface from the EP (regarding the former as a simple introduction rather than an integral part), and to put aside what constitutes part of the genius of the Roman Rite.

Since we cannot study all the Prefaces in themselves, we propose to call attention to the principles on which they were constructed, thereby showing the continuity existing between the variable Prefaces and the three new EPs.

The 82 Prefaces found in the New Roman Missal are divided as follows: 41 are for the Proper of the season, 14 for feasts and mysteries of Our Lord, 16 for the feasts of saints and 11 for diverse celebrations. The Preface for Prayer II is found among the second group. The committee which worked on these Prefaces regarded them as essentially thanksgiving prayers at the outset of the EP. Thus, in contrast with some of the Prefaces in the Missal of Pius V and many in the Sacramentaries, the committee wished to eliminate those that were purely narrative, catechetical, or prayers of supplication. In the various Prefaces, the motive for thanksgiving was found in a particular deed or an aspect of the mystery commemorated in the celebration or in the history of salvation in general. Brevity of expression and focus on a given important aspect of the feast or season was taken as the rule. In this way, a more complete synthesis would be found in the ensemble of the texts. Furthermore, these Prefaces were to be composed with a certain lyricism and elegance of style capable of inciting the participants to praise and joy.[11]

For the vast majority of these Prefaces, antecedents were found in the Sacramentaries. At times some were combined with others to form a new one, or certain expressions were eliminated or changed. In the composition of new Prefaces not having models in the Sacramentaries, Scripture and rather felicitous phrases of the Council documents were employed. Thus, in the same way that the EPs went back to centuries old liturgical sources, so the Prefaces drew their inspiration from the rich treasury of the Church. However, the committee was quite aware of the need to modify and exercise a critical judgment in the composition of the Prefaces.

As is to be expected, there is in the Prefaces a much wider variety in addressing the Father or in referring to the Son than one finds in the post-Sanctus part of the EPs. For example, in the Prefaces for Easter, Christ is referred to as *Agnus, Sacerdos,* and as he who *nos apud te advocatione defendit.* The theology found in the corpus of Prefaces supplements greatly the theology—already rich—found in the EPs, but the theology is there, obviously not for its own sake, but as motive for praise and thanksgiving or remembrance of the mighty acts of Christ, which in itself is an indirect way of rendering praise or thanksgiving. The community also refers to itself by different names, for example, *fideles, imitatores, grex tuus,* etc. This must be remembered as a possible corrective to what we say later when we analyze the EPs in and for themselves.[12]

We must now turn our attention to the naming of the parts of the EPs in order to be quite clear about any possible ambiguities. As far as possible, the indications that follow are not based on historical or extrinsic judgments, but arise from the EPs studied. In presenting its EPs, the General Norms used the following vocabulary to describe the elements that went into their make-up.[13] There is an

[11] See the fine article of the late Placide Bruylants, "Les préfaces du Missel romain," *La Maison-Dieu* 87 (1966), pp. 111-132. For a commentary on the new Prefacees as well as the new Roman EPs, see Louis Soubigou, *A Commentary on the Prefaces and the Eucharistic Prayers of the Roman Missal,* John Ott, trans., Collegeville, 1971.

[12] Antoine Dumas, "Les nouvelles préfaces du Missel romain," *La Maison-Dieu* 94 (1968), pp. 159-164.

[13] See the "Institutio Generalis Missalis Romani," *Missale Romanum: Editio Typica,* Typis Polyglottis Vaticanis, 1970, Article 55.

initial Dialogue, a Preface, Sanctus, *Vere Sanctus,* an Epiclesis, Institution Narrative, Anamnesis, Offering, Intercession, and Doxology. These are not the elements to be found in every EP, but they are the ones found in the three Roman Prayers.

The word Preface curiously enough presents some difficulty because it is still sometimes regarded by certain authors as the introduction *to* the EP and not more properly as the opening part *of* the EP. The idea of its being an introduction comes not only from the ambiguity of the word but from its very variability, the fact that as a part it can be detached from the rest and interchanged. It is in this element, that begins rather than introduces the EP, that the idea of thanksgiving is especially expressed. The Sanctus is not regarded as an exterior acclamation but as an integral element in the EP, one uniting the earthly with the heavenly liturgy. The Epiclesis is a petition that God send the Holy Spirit on the gifts so that they become the Body and Blood of Christ and on the community so that when it receives communion it will be profitable to its salvation. The word thus covers two different purposes for the sending. In the Roman EPs, as we have seen, the two are divided while in Oriental anaphoras of the Antiochene tradition they are generally together or the one that in the Roman EPs precedes the Institution Narrative usually follows it in the Oriental anaphoras, where it articulated the implication in the anamnesis of the Institution. The introduction of an Epiclesis is an ecumenical gesture toward the Eastern Liturgies. Its division into two parts allows for the first Epiclesis to explicitate what the *Quam oblationem* left unexpressed and to maintain the eucharistic theology of the West with regard to the moment of consecration. The Institution Narrative itself represents what happened at the Last Supper, where Christ instituted the sacrament of his passion and his resurrection and left his Apostles the command to perpetuate this mystery. The expression Institution Narrative perhaps puts too much emphasis on the narrative form in which are found the words of Institution to the detriment of the *verba Domini* themselves. However, historians of religion would find little difficulty with a narrative holding the central place of a rite. The Anamnesis cannot be separated from the offering which follows it, and the two elements are distinguished in order to unite them. In the Anamnesis properly so-called the idea of offering is included for it is the subject making the memorial of the mystery who offers. Two remarks are called for here. First of all, this memorial is not purely subjective for it is endowed also with a sacrificial sense expressed in the offering. Secondly, we say "Anamnesis properly so-called" for other parts of the EP include anamnesis or remembrance of the mighty deeds of God or of His Christ. The difference is that in the beraka the Anamnesis was the motive for blessing God (as in the Preface) while in the "Anamnesis properly so-called" we have a liturgical cult act that actualizes and offers. The authors of the Roman EPs chose next to incorporate the Intercessions within them. Others have regarded Intercessions at this point as intrusive or doubling the prayer of the faithful. Vagaggini argued in favor of keeping them since their omission would remove the whole idea of the Eucharist as a *propitiatory* sacrifice.[14] In the Norms, the Intercessions are described as expressing that the Eucharist is celebrated in union with the whole Church, heavenly and earthly, that the offering is made for it and for all its members living and dead who have been called to participate in their redemption and salvation acquired for it by the Body and Blood of Christ. What is important to remember, then, is that the Intercessions found in the Roman EPs are regarded as intimately linked to the Eucharist. They also make a point of uniting the earthly Church to the heavenly Church by referring to the Blessed Virgin Mary and the saints. That is what distinguishes them from the intentions found in the Prayer of the Faithful. A new element also is that non-believers are included in the Intercessions. The Church's concern is for all men, those within and those outside its visible membership. The closing Doxology expresses the glorification of God. It depends more on the beraka form of the EP than on the Intercessions to which it is grammatically attached.

The major changes from the Roman canon consist, then, in the introduction of the explicit Epiclesis into the new EPs and the position of the Memento and intercessory prayers in a block after the Anamnesis. At the same time, the major change from the structure of the anaphora as found in Hippolytus' EP and the Antiochene tradition is the position of the Epiclesis before the Institution Narrative whereas its traditional place is after the Anamnesis. That this Epiclesis split into two is actually thought of as a unity is evident from the General Norms which treat both at the same time. Finally, the introduction of the Acclamation after the Institution Narrative is like that found in the Antiochene Anaphora of the Twelve Apostles and in the Alexandrian Rite. Normally, in the Roman canon, the Acclamation "Amen" came only after the final Doxology.

14 Vagaggini, *op. cit.*, pp. 111-113.

*The Way in Which the Praying Community
Addresses God, Refers to Jesus Christ,
and Refers to Itself*

The community has two preferred ways of addressing God in the EPs, as *Pater* or as *Domine*. Naturally in the Sanctus this becomes *Sanctus sanctus sanctus Dominus Deus Sabaoth* and in the Doxology, which is the same in all three prayers, *Deo Patri omnipotenti*. Not counting these two instances, the form of direct address is as follows: in Prayer II *Sancte Pater* is found in the Preface while *Domine* without any modifier is in the *Vere Sanctus,* Anamnesis, and the Intercessions. In Prayer III, *Domine* is found in the same three parts as Prayer II with the addition of a *Clemens Pater* in the Intercessions. Prayer IV makes a wider use of the vocative form, using it in the first sentence of each of its parts and clearly favoring the expression *Pater*. In the Preface, it uses *Pater Sancte;* in the *Vere Sanctus, Pater Sancte* and *te Pater;* in the Institution Narrative, *Pater Sancte* again; and in the Intercessions *Clemens Pater. Domine* is found in both Epicleses and in the Anamnesis and Intercessions.

The titles given to Jesus are consistent in the three EPs. The following chart will readily illustrate this: [15]

	2	3	4
Christus	E²	E²	AnE²
Christus tuus			I
Christus Dominus noster		I	I
Unigenitus tuus			VS
Filius tuus		AnE²	
Filius tuus Jesus Christus	I		
Filius dilectionis tuae Jesus Christus	P		
Filius tuus DNJC		VS E¹	
DNJC	E¹		E¹
Domine	Ac	Ac	Ac
Deus	I	I	I
Verbum tuum	P		
Salvator	P		
Redemptor	P		VS

This chart calls for several comments. First of all, the *Domine* is

[15] P=Preface, VS=Vere Sanctus, E¹=Epiclesis One, Ac=Acclamation, E²= Epiclesis Two, and I=Intercessions.

found only in the Acclamation and is thus not typical of the way the community refers to Jesus Christ in the EP, but it is a title that is used when addressing Him directly or in combination with other expressions when referring to Him. The title *Deus* appears in all three EPs for it is used in relation to the Virgin Mary's being the *Genetrix Dei*. The remainder of the titles reveal two main clusters: a Christ-cluster and a Son-cluster with the expression *Dominus noster* added on, particularly to the title Jesus Christ taken as a single name. The titles are all traditional and at their origin have theological overtones. Perhaps the titles that strike us as most theological are *Unigenitus tuus* and *Verbum tuum. Salvator* and *Redemptor* are used in the christological parts of the salvation history accounts of Prayers II and IV. Thus, in these three EPs, the community generally considers Jesus in terms of His relationship to the Father or in His messianic condition, elevated in glory as Lord.

The praying community rarely concretizes itself. Some form of *nos* without any further qualification or the third person plural ending of the verb is consistently used to designate the group. There are only a few variations from this rule. In Prayer II's Preface, a reference is made to *populum sanctum,* but this refers to a much larger group than the assembled community. Later, in the second Epiclesis, the community calls itself, whether by past practice or by looking forward to the reception of the consecrated elements, *corporis et sanguinis Christi particeps*. Finally, it asks to become *aeternae vitae consortes* in the Intercessions. The only self-descriptions of the assembled community that Prayer III has are references to *populum* in the *Vere Sanctus* and *ecclesiae tuae* in the second Epiclesis, both of which go far beyond designating the local community. At the head of the Intercessions, the community asks to become *munus aeternum,* a sentiment that in one way or another will be taken up by most of the other contemporary EPs. Finally, the reference to the assembled community as Church is taken up once more in the Intercessions by the expression *Ecclesiam tuam, peregrinantem in terra.* It is precisely this aspect of a Church in this world, a pilgrim Church as it were, that we shall see appear more frequently in subsequent chapters. Prayer IV also has the broad *ecclesiae tuae* reference as well as a desire to become a *hostia viva*. Both are found in the second Epiclesis. In the Intercessions, it refers to itself as *nobis omnibus, filiis tuis*. Here we should point out that the Intercessions in all three Prayers give the sense of a vast family which does not hesitate to include all men in its embrace. This universalist conception of the Intercessions is a great gain that has cast into the background the original discussion as to whether or not Intercessions should be in the EP at all on the grounds that they duplicate the *Oratio fidelium* or are not primitive. Both Bouyer and Vagaggini argued for the Intercessions: Bouyer on the grounds that, once the liturgy of the word and the liturgy of the table were united, the Intercessions found their normal place in the EP; Vagaggini that, although they were introduced later into the EP, the Intercessions developed in close connection with the emphasis on the idea of offering the gifts and the rites of oblation. Hence their omission would greatly change the structure of the overall theological signification of the EP. Most recently Emil Lengeling, relator of a special commission constituted in 1971 to study the problem of unofficial EPs, argues for a place in the EP for the expression of the communion between the local Church and the universal Church. Lengeling sees this as an element that, while not being indispensable, is integrated naturally into the EP. As for the Memento of the living and the dead, its frequency may be limited but not lacking in principle.[16]

What the Praying Community
Finds Significant To Say
about Jesus Christ

Prayer II (based on the EP of Hippolytus) begins by saying that it is right and just to give thanks

per Filium dilectionis tuae Jesum Christum

---

[16] Bouyer, "The New Eucharistic Prayers . . .", pp. 171-172; Vagaggini, *op. cit.,* pp. 108-114; and Emil Lengeling, "Le Problème des nouvelles prières eucharistiques dans la liturgie romaine," *Questions liturgiques* 53 (1972), p. 251. Lengeling defines the literary genre of the EP as a presidential prayer with the participation of the faithful, a prayer of thanksgiving and supplication with an anamnetic character and a trinitarian structure. He then divides the elements into those that are indispensably constitutive, those that are easily integrated into the Prayer without being indispensable, those that cannot in principle be lacking but whose frequency may be limited, and those that are possible and even desirable to have in an EP. He places the communion with the local Church and the universal Church in the second category and the Mememto for the living and the dead in the third. On the whole question of Intercessions, see W. Jardine Grisbrooke, "Intercessions at the Eucharist II. Intercessions at the Eucharist Proper," *Studia Liturgica* 5 (1966), pp. 20-44 and 87-103. A summary article on this question has been written by P. J. Leblanc, "A Consideration of Intercessory Prayer within the Eucharist," *The Dunwoodie Review* 8 (1968), pp. 115-132.

and then it goes on to select certain pertinent information concerning Jesus Christ:

Verbum tuum per quod cuncta fecisti, quem misisti nobis Salvatorem et Redemptorem, incarnatus de Spiritu Sancto et ex Virgine natum. Qui voluntatem tuam adimplens et populum tibi sanctum acquirens extendit manus cum pateretur, ut mortem solveret et resurrectionem manifestaret.

In effect, what we have here is a condensed salvation history seen from a christological point of view. It is also the motive for thanksgiving and includes the traditional motives of creation and redemption. The language here receives its density from the mighty deeds of Christ and from its allusiveness. The use of an expression such as *Verbum tuum* calls to mind Old Testament and New Testament, from Genesis to John, from "And God said" to "the Word was made flesh." Or, to take another example, the expression *extendit manus cum pateretur* refers not only to the position of Christ on the cross but brings to mind Isaiah 65,2: "Outstretched these hands of mine, all the day long, to a nation of rebels." If that reference is obscure even to the well-educated Christian, it at least brings to mind certain passages of John's gospel where Christ speaks of being "lifted up" (John 3,14; 8,28; 12,32-33).[17]

The community next desires that the gifts that it has brought become the body and blood of our Lord Jesus Christ. It immediately moves into the narration of what he did on the night he was handed over *voluntarie,* an adverb that received its original force from a former period which wished to counteract a tendency to see Jesus as a passive instrument in the hands of God but an adverb which still has something to say to us today. The Institution Narrative is simple and clear: For Jesus the bread is His Body, the wine is His Blood, and His Body is *pro vobis tradetur* and His Blood is *pro multis effundetur in remissionem peccatorum.* Thus, the retelling of the Last Supper event shows the Christian specificity of the act accomplished by Christ: His passion and death are done for somebody and for a reason; they are "for you" and "for many" and "for the forgiveness of sins."

At this point the whole community proclaims its *Mysterium fidei* in an acclamation *ad libitum,* but the first one suggested is: *Mortem*

[17] Bernard Botte, "Extendit manus suas cum pateretur," *QLP* 49 (1968), p. 307; E. J. Lengeling, "Hippolyt von Rom und die Wendung 'Extendit . . .'," *QLP* 50 (1969), pp. 141-144.

tuam annuntiamus, Domine, et tuam resurrectionem confitemur, donnec venias. Although, as we have pointed out earlier, the unity of the discourse is broken at this point, it may be justified by the Christian consciousness of the change that has taken place. Jesus is now present in a special way. The unity of the discourse is sacrificed to another dynamic just as vigorous applause or shouts of agreement interrupt the great orators. Here the community acclaims what is significant for it: Christ has died, Christ is risen, Christ will come again; but death, resurrection, and coming are not just limited to events past and future, they are also present ones. It is this idea that is taken up in what immediately follows in the discourse resumed by the presiding minister: *Memores igitur mortis et resurrectionis eius, tibi, Domine, panem vitae et calicem salutis offerimus. . . .*

However, before continuing our analysis of what the praying community finds significant to say about Christ, we must enter directly into a problem that is not only methodological but also theological. It is methodological because we must determine what weight we are going to give to the vocabulary in the EPs, especially in any comparative study of prayers written in different languages by different mentalities. Who is to determine what weight to give a word like *memores?* This is a problem that poses itself not only for the Roman Prayers but for the contemporary non-Roman ones. The Roman Prayers are inheritors of age-old traditions and an age-old language, which often owes much to Greek and Hebrew. Hence, the problem: In attributing a certain theological weight to a word in Latin are we to deny the same theological weight to its translation into a modern language when, for example, it is used in a contemporary non-Roman EP without an explication of the word's deepest meaning?

Let us see what this means with regard to the word at hand: *memores.*[18] The word cannot be separated from the command of Christ in the conclusion of the Institution Narrative: *Hoc facite in meam commemorationem.* The community is conscious of fulfilling this command in what it does, but it is not simply commemorating a past act, it is reactualizing something in the present. The word *memores* (and its variant forms), related to the Greek *anamnesis* and the Hebrew *zikkaron*, receives its full force from a knowledge of its antecedents and how the word was employed either in the

---

[18] Max Thurian, *The Eucharistic Memorial*, J. G. Davies, trans., Richmond, Part One: The Old Testament, 1960; Part Two: The New Testament, 1961; Brevard S. Childs, *Memory and Tradition in Israel*, Studies in Biblical Theology No. 37, London, 1962.

everyday language of the period or in the cult language. To put it succinctly, to call to mind in the present context is to reactualize, and the reactualization is always accompanied by an offering. The Anamnesis is no simple recall.

No doubt the Roman Prayers, as the immediate inheritors of this cultic-language tradition, do not have to be more explicit in their language and the burden of fuller clarity is on the creators of new prayers in the vernacular. However, in this work, we feel under no obligation to plumb the depths of a word nor do we consider it any fault in vernacular creations when they do not develop at all the meaning latent in the vocabulary used. We prefer to concentrate on the larger context of a sentence and to limit ourselves to the understanding that the well-informed Christian lay person could have of the discourse called the EP.

Thus, simultaneously, the community remembers the death and resurrection of the Lord and offers *panem vitae et calicem salutis* or the Body and Blood of Christ, specified in the Epiclesis immediately following as it looks forward to the reception of the sacrament. The community then makes its intercessions in the name of Jesus Christ and *per ipsum et cum ipso et in ipso* renders honor and glory to the Father.

In Prayer III, beginning at the *Vere Sanctus*, we are told that God vivifies and sanctifies *univers per Filium tuum, Dominum nostrum Jesum Christum*. In both the Epiclesis and the Institution Narrative there are no essential differences from Prayer II. However, in the Anamnesis properly so-called, the community calls to mind *eiusdem Filii tui salutiferae passionis necnon mirabilis resurrectionis et ascensionis in caelum, sed et praestolantes alterum eius adventum.* Aside from the addition of the Ascension and the Second Coming, we should remark the descriptive adjectives accompanying the nouns. Max Thurian in his commentary on the EPs finds the addition of the Ascension significant:

> The mystery of the ascension is essentially the affirmation that the Son, God and man, continues his work of salvation by an intercession that makes his one sacrifice on the cross present. The Christ, as the Epistle to the Hebrews shows us, is comparable to the Jewish High Priest who, at the time of the liturgy of expiation, after having completed the sacrifice on the altar, went into the holy of holies of the temple in order to make the propitiatory aspersion with the blood of the sacrifice. The Epistle to the Hebrews makes this liturgy of expiation an

image of the mystery of the ascension. Christ, having accomplished once for all the expiatory sacrifice on the altar of the cross, has entered "beyond the veil," where he is "still living to make intercession on our behalf" (Heb. 7,25; 9,1-24). Thus, the mystery of the ascension reveals the perpetual sacrifice of Christ, the unique High Priest, continuing by his propitiatory intercession the work of redemption accomplished in the expiatory sacrifice of the cross.[19]

Has the mere mention of the word "Ascension" in Prayer III and its lack in Prayer II really changed anything insofar as the listener to the discourse is concerned? In both prayers one intercedes through Christ. For the Christian, the Ascension is already implicit in the word Resurrection, just as *in caelum* is really implicit in *ascensio*. In fact, one could argue against the expression *in caelum* on the grounds that it continues the idea of a three-storey universe. The reference to the Ascension does not need its justification by a theological sounding, no more than the Resurrection does. Theologizing on it in a commentary on the EPs is more a sign of its neglect in traditional Christian teaching and/or its importance in Calvin's understanding of the Real Presence than the fact that it is mentioned in Prayer III. It is true that Vagaggini, the principal author of Prayer III, had based himself on the Epistle to the Hebrews in his variant project for a second Roman canon, where he cited: *semper vivens ad interpellandum pro nobis.* If the phrase had been kept in the final revision, no one could object to Thurian's theologizing on it to show its great significance in the EP, but the phrase was not kept.

It is appropriate here to mention another problem that arises in analyzing satisfactorily the theological content of the Roman EPs. Their creators are deeply conscious of their choice of words vis-à-vis tradition. These prayers are composed in Latin, and thus antecedents for the vocabulary used must be found as often as possible (except when Latinists will object to the turn of a sentence or can substitute a more refined word for one they find objectionable). Thus, Vagaggini in his notes to his project refers us to the Leonian Sacramentary, No. 1137, and the litany of the saints in the Roman missal for the expression *mirabilis ressurrectionis et ascensionis in caelum.*[20] It seems strange to us now that someone should resort to the *Leonian Sacramentary* to justify the adjective, but at the time of the composition of these Prayers such historical

---

[19] Thurian, "La théologie des nouvelles prières eucharistiques," p. 88.
[20] Vagaggini, *op. cit.*, p. 167.

as well as biblical references helped get them accepted.[21]

Returning to the community's references to Christ, we next see the offering of *hoc sacrificium vivum et sanctum,* immediately followed by the request to look upon *oblationem Ecclesiae tuae et, agnoscens Hostiam, cuius voluisti immolatione placari. . . .* This avoids the modern antithesis of the sacrifice of the cross and the sacrifice of the mass so that the unique sacrifice remains unique while the sacrificial aspect of the action being performed is also preserved. As in Prayer II, the community looks forward to participation in the Body and Blood, and they wish to be *unum corpus et unus spiritus in Christo.* What is interesting to note here is that the community wishes to become what they already are. It is the tension existing between what they know they should be and what they realize they never quite succeed in being perfectly. Already one body by previous communions in the Body and Blood of Christ, they wish to be this one body.

Prayer III, like Prayer II and Prayer IV, makes reference to Mary as *Dei Genetrix,* honoring her with her greatest title rather than insisting on the divinity of Jesus. In the prayer for the dead, the community asks that the departed be received into the Kingdom, *ubi fore speramus, ut simul gloria tua perenniter satiemur, per Christum Dominum nostrum, per quem mundo bona cuncta largiris.* It is not only Christ who crowns us in glory in the next world, but He is also the one through whom the Father gives every good thing in this world. This latter idea reminds us of the *Verbum tuum per quod fecisti* of Prayer II and the *Vere Sanctus* of Prayer III itself *per Filium tuum . . . vivificas et sanctificas universa.* There may be evil in this world, but the community concentrates squarely on the goodness of God and the goodness of His world. It was created good and man fallen into sin was redeemed. There is an equal confidence when the community looks forward to the future.

In Prayer IV, we have a totally different approach than in the preceding two prayers. Prayer II plunged almost immediately into the Mystery of Christ in the Preface and Prayer III in the *Vere Sanctus.* Prayer IV, however, adopts another pace and seems almost to delay over its praise of God. It is an account of salvation history, a great gain for an EP of the Latin Rite, with an emphasis on the Father's role. When the Son enters into this account, the community

---

[21] Although the historical method deepens the knowledge of tradition, Kavanagh, *op. cit.,* has remarked, "Antiquity has nothing to do with insuring against a static outcome, nor does easy documentation have anything to do with tradition as such: were it otherwise, tradition would not have existed prior to the invention of historical method," p. 6.

singles out His being sent by the Father, His quality of Savior, His conception by the Spirit and birth from the Virgin, and His assumption of our manhood. His work consisted in *salutem evangelizavit pauperibus, redemptionem captivis, maestis corde laetitiam.* This is good biblical usage (Isaiah 61,1; Matt. 11,4-6) for it shows by His actions rather than by a statement that He was the Messiah. In fact, in this whole section the various scriptural passages are linked together in what appears to be a very natural way.

The Prayer continues:

Ut tuam vero dispensationem impleret, in mortem tradidit semetipsum ac, resurgens a mortuis, mortem destruxit vitamque renovavit. Et, ut non amplius nobismetipsis viveremus, sed sibi qui pro nobis mortuus est atque surrexit, a te, Pater, misit Spiritum Sanctum primitias credentibus, qui, opus suum in mundo perficiens, omnem sanctificationem compleret.

Here we have a kind of anticipation of what comes after the First Epiclesis, to which these words lead: Institution Narrative, Anamnesis and Epiclesis. Its justification may be that it completes the history of salvation from the creation to the sending of the Spirit. However, it is difficult to avoid the impression that the cloth was not cut sufficiently to fit the finished product, since everywhere else any kind of "doubling" is avoided. As in Prayer II, we have a specific mention of Christ's cooperation in His passion and death: in *mortem tradidit semetipsum* to fulfill *tuam dispensationem,* for even here the Father's role is primordial, and the Spirit is sent *a te, Pater.*

For the community, Christ is the one who has destroyed death, renewed life and sent the Spirit. In the Epiclesis that follows, we are told that the great mystery that the community is celebrating *ipse nobis reliquit in foedus aeternum.* This is also an anticipation of the words of the Institution Narrative. As such, it underlines the fact that the present celebration is linked to the celebration at the Last Supper in a special way. The Institution Narrative, unlike the other two prayers, continues to place a certain emphasis on the Father: *ipse enim, cum hora venisset ut glorificaretur a te, Pater sancte. . . .* This introduction to the Last Supper event also insists on Christ's relationship with His followers: *ac dilexisset suos qui erant in mundo, in finem dilexit eos: et cenantibus illis. . . .* This is one of the few places, if not the only place, in the three Roman Prayers where the "human-ness"—not humanity—of Christ is allowed to enter in: He loved His own, He ate a meal with them. It is worth pointing out for other contemporary EPs will take these two phrases to speak in a more intimate way to Jesus or about Jesus, thus avoiding the more dignified kind of language represented in the Roman prayers.

In the Anamnesis that follows, the community is mindful of:

> Mortem Christi eiusque descensum ad inferos recolimus, eius resurrectionem et ascensionem ad tuam dexteram profitemur, et, exspectantes ipsius adventum in gloria, offerimus tibi eius Corpus et Sanguinem, sacrificium tibi acceptabile et toti mundo salutare.

This Anamnesis is longer and more explicit than the others. As such it is quite close to the expression of the Apostles Creed and presents clearly the whole pascal mystery. The offering of the Body and Blood of Christ is a sacrifice that is worthy of God and is for the salvation of the whole world. As we noted at the end of the *Vere Sanctus,* the community is aware that its celebration is a sacrifice, one with the Last Supper and the crucifixion.

The community then prays that those who eat the bread and drink from the cup may be themselves in *Christo hostia viva, ad laudem gloriae tuae.* The action just accomplished, the reactualization of the presence of Christ leads into another action, the eating of the sacrament which results in the union *in unum Corpus* just as in the other two Prayers.

In the Intercessions that follow, the death of Christians is described as *qui obierunt in pace Christi tui.* In the other two Prayers, death was referred to as *qui in spe resurrectionis dormierunt* and *fratres nostros defunctos . . . ex hoc saeculo transierunt.* These expressions are almost too soft or too nice toward death. As we shall see, other contemporary EPs will not be so phlegmatic in the face of this event. This is merely part of the serenity of the praying community as reflected in its EPs. There is no intention of placing any kind of value judgment on this serenity. The EP is only part of the whole celebration. It is quite possible that other parts will use a language that is less serene, for example, a reading from the book of Job.

*What the Praying Community Says about
the Action It Is Accomplishing
and the Elements (Bread and Wine) It Uses*

Since it is responding to what God has done for it, the community makes use of a great deal of "You-ness" in these Prayers. It is very conscious that it is talking to someone who is infinitely good, loves man, and has done everything to bring about his salvation. It responds in thanksgiving and confession of the glory of God (Preface and Sanctus, Doxology). It asks for the sending of the Spirit (Epiclesis). It proclaims the death, resurrection, and coming of Christ (Acclamation). It celebrates, brings back to mind, and offers (Anamnesis). It intercedes and returns to praise (Intercessions and Doxology). Its most common verbs are *praedicamus, confitemur, quaesumus, deprecamur, detulimus, celebremus, annuntiamus, recolimus,* etc. As we have already noted, there is a certain serenity in these Prayers. Having earlier confessed their faults, the worshippers are not overly conscious of themselves in their EPs. In one sense, they represent a kind of ideal "We," a community whose relationship to God is well-balanced. It is humanity at its best praying to God, responding to God for all that He has done.

Insofar as the bread and wine are concerned, we do not wish to repeat what we have just said in the section on what the praying community has to say about Christ. However, the relationship we there pointed out between Christ and the elements of bread and wine applies here. We shall now concern ourselves with how the community refers to the bread and wine as well as the overall action of the celebration. In the first Epiclesis, the bread and wine are called *haec dona* (II) and *haec munera* (III and IV); the wish is expressed that they become *Corpus et sanguis Christi.* In the Anamesis, they are called *panem vitae et calicem salutis* (II), *hoc sacrificium vivum et sanctum* (III), *Corpus et Sanguinem, sacrificium* (IV); in the second Epiclesis, *oblationem Ecclesiae tuae* (III), *Corporis et Sanguinis Christi* (II), *Corpore et Sanguine Filii* (III), *Hostiam, quam Ecclesiae tuae ipse parasti* and *uno pane . . . et calice* (IV). In the Intercessions, we have *haec hostia nostrae reconciliationis* (III) and *haec oblationem* (IV). The whole action that is taking place is called in the first Epiclesis *haec mysteria* (III) and *hoc magnum mysterium* (IV). Finally, in the Anamnesis of IV there is a reference to *memoriale celebrantes.*

Thus, the bread and wine are referred to as gifts or offerings that become the Body and Blood of Christ and thereby a sacrifice, an oblation, an offering. There is no doubt that for this community Christ is present in the elements and that there is a link between the Last Supper, the Cross, and the present Eucharistic celebration. None of the Prayers spends time in talking about the bread and wine as bread and wine, that is to say, there is no sentimentality for these elements as such nor any romanticizing about their being the simplest elements for a meal. The authors of these Prayers are not taken up with the bread and wine as things to be considered in themselves for their own worth nor for their symbolic value, leaving this to be expressed by the gestures of the celebrant. These Prayers do not encourage a Eucharist-as-meal point of view. For those who like to be reminded of the immediate natural link of the bread and wine to man, they must go back to the Offertory prayers which preceded the EP, where the bread is referred to as the fruit of the earth and the wine as the fruit of the vine and both as the work of man.

The community takes itself into this sacrificial language when it wishes to be a *munus aeternum* (III) and a *hostia viva ad laudem gloriae tuae* (IV).

Thus, the EP is the cultic offering of the Son's sacrifice by the Church to the Father. The Church participates in the offering which the Father has prepared and which it asks Him to accept. Finally, it offers itself to the Father when it looks forward to being united with Christ in the communion. This network of relationships is accomplished around the bread and wine become the Body and Blood of Christ and the thanksgiving memorial which the Church carries out. In the Prayers this is expressed in a liturgical vocabulary different from that used for theological concepts seeking to explain what happens at the Eucharistic celebration.

*The Place Given to the
Role of the Holy Spirit*

In comparison with the Roman canon, these new Roman EPs give a more explicit place to the Holy Spirit. We do not intend to repeat here what we have already said about the double Epiclesis except to recognize again that its inclusion overcomes a certain neglect and that it is not without ecumenical value.

Prayer II, apart from the two Epicleses and the Doxology, makes only one reference to the Holy Spirit: *Jesum Christum . . . incarnatum de Spiritu Sancto et ex Virgine natum.* Prayer III, in the *Vere Sanctus,* praises God for *per . . . Jesum Christum, Spiritus Sancti operante virtute, vivificas et sanctificas universa.* Prayer IV has the *incarnatus de Spiritu Sancto et natus ex Marie Virgine* reference in its *Vere Sanctus,* but also closes with the thought that the Son sent from the Father *Spiritum Sanctum primitias credentibus, qui, opus suum in mundo perficiens, omnem sanctificationem compleret.*

The Holy Spirit is never considered isolated from the Father and/or the Son. The community never addresses Him directly and never elaborates on His work. The phrase *opus suum in mundo perficiens* is one that other creators of EPs will expand on, but here the community, as is its custom, merely mentions the broad principles of the Spirit's role without entering into details. The Epicleses make evident the role of the Spirit in the carrying out of the action and the uniting of the community.

3
AMERICAN EUCHARISTIC PRAYERS

Like their Roman counterparts, the American EPs are a result of the renewal initiated by Vatican II and of the encouragement given to the Roman Consilium to create a variety of EPs. However, it was pastoral concern for a particular group that provided the needed push for these authors to compose prayers or adapt prayers for the specifically American situation.

The typical American EP first grew out of a college or university experience, whether on a Catholic or a secular campus. Thus, while the EP is addressed to the Father, the authors had to keep in mind that the audience "overhearing" the presidential discourse and saying Amen to it was a well-educated group of young men and women who, as worshippers, were looking for a meaningful expression of the Eucharistic celebration. This search for meaningfulness extended to all parts of the Mass, and the EP was not regarded as an exception. Several well-known international figures had called for a revised canon and the influence coming from centers like Amsterdam and Louvain, where the Dutch experimentation was impressing Americans studying theology there, prepared the psychological background for creative initiative for EPs in English.

We propose to study the American EPs immediately after the Roman ones for, in comparison with the two groups to follow, they are more dependent on the traditional anaphoric structure. Frankly experimental, these American EPs make no pretense to be the last word in EPs. Having once determined the basic components of an EP and generally using Scripture and Christian teaching as a source, the authors have tried to write EPs that would find a resonance with an American audience. Generally these authors are specialists in fields other than the liturgy or, sometimes, theology, although several have studied in liturgy programs. A brief profile of the authors of these prayers would look something like the following. At the time of the composition of the prayers, ten of the authors were students and/or seminarians, one was an assistant pastor and one was an assistant director of novices. Nine of the twelve authors were Jesuits (some have since left the Society), one was a Benedictine priest, and two were lay women. Most of the authors were from the East Coast or resided there, engaged in graduate studies at universities. The book from which we have selected our prayers is edited by Jesuit Father Robert F. Hoey, a former university chaplain at Boston College and, at the time of his book's publication, a graduate student in theology at the University of San Francisco. Thus, the background of the book is essentially Jesuit for even the lay women were students at Jesuit universities. It is the work of young adults made possible by the greater liberty for experimentation that the university campus affords. Their efforts are attempts that have met with a certain amount of success in community situations. There is no doubt that to many members of small communities these EPs are more meaningful than the Roman EPs. This is true in spite of the fact that some of the American EPs are not always completely successful and "meaningfulness" is not the ultimate criterion of an EP.

The Experimental Liturgy Book was the first and the most ambitious American collection of EPs. In fact, it was more than this as it was also concerned with revitalizing the texts of other parts of the Eucharistic service, from Entrance Rite to Dismissal. In his introduction to the collection, Father Hoey emphasized that the genesis of the book was the desire to make available to all interested persons some of the experimental liturgical adaptations that had appeared. It was then hoped that experts would be able to evaluate them and point out what their merits or faults might be. Two basic norms were used in selecting the material for the book: (1) the liturgies should be worshipful and reverential, and (2) the liturgies should be responsive to the needs of various congregations in our times.[1]

Father Hoey's collection was not an amorphous one. A selection was based on the two norms just stated, and some of the prayers had already undergone a revision after actual use. In other words, a refining process had already taken place at the time of publication. Our main concern is with the part of the book devoted to Eucharistic Prayers, pages 130-177. In the study that follows we shall concern ourselves only with those EPs that are complete (from Preface to Doxology) and strictly American. By "strictly American" we mean those EPs that are not translations with minor adaptations of Roman or Dutch prayers. In point of fact, the American EPs are greatly

[1] Robert F. Hoey, *The Experimental Liturgy Book,* New York, 1969, p. xi.

influenced either by the four Roman EPs or by the same sources that these latter used.

In addition to Hoey's book, we must mention a publication by a fellow Jesuit, John Gallen's *Eucharistic Liturgies.* The greatest part of this book is made up of texts of greetings, prayers over the gifts, and dismissals. However, in the Fourth Part, we have four EPs written or collected by John Hogan, S.J. These Prayers, according to Peter Fink, S.J., who wrote the Preface to the book, are seen as a concrete application of the principle that the liturgical prayer of a culturally-historically defined people must take place within the historical and cultural dimensions that constitute the human life and history of the people who are gathered to pray.[2] Thus, we see clearly enunciated the principle which has led our authors to elaborate their EPs. In other words, the American EPs should not only be American by reason of their authors' nationality but also by reason of the cultural-historical experience of a particular people. Naturally part of the historical-cultural experience of American Catholics, at least up until the time of this writing, has been a strong Roman influence. This influence makes itself felt time and again in the EPs we will study in this chapter.

A third publication that has enjoyed limited success is called *The Underground Mass Book,* a rather pretentious title for a delightful little collection of texts.[3] Like the previous two works, *The Underground Mass Book* contains much more than EPs. It has a selection of contemporary readings drawn from many sources together with hymn texts. It has ten EPs but it does not always have the sources completely identified. Thus, one of Oosterhuis' most famous EPs does not bear his name nor the name of his translator. The editor has assembled texts actually in use but often these must have been without any indication of their author or even their origin. The impression one receives is that of a rather hastily put together collection, whose one criterion was the fact that the texts were actually in use. Unlike the previous two publications, the editor does not show interest in feedback or in a refining process. His work is more like a photograph of the times, but, all too frequently, insofar as the EPs are concerned, one without any indication of date, place, or author. It is for this reason that *The Underground Mass Book* is of very limited use for our study.

Because of the large number of texts with which we are con-

---

[2] John Gallen, *Eucharistic Liturgies,* New York, 1970, p. 5.
[3] Stephen W. McNierney, editor, *The Underground Mass Book,* Baltimore, 1968.

cerned, we cannot proceed exactly in the same manner with them as with the three Roman EPs. However, the method outlined in the previous chapter remains substantially the same here. We shall look at the structure of these American EPs, only noting where they are at variance with the Roman ones; next we shall see how the praying community addresses God, refers to Jesus Christ, and refers to itself. We shall then study what the praying community considers significant to say about Jesus Christ, what it says about the bread and wine together with the action being accomplished, and finally what role it gives to the Holy Spirit.

Thus, while still considering the same five elements we studied in the Roman EPs, we are less interested here in detail than we are in significant variations not found in the Roman EPs. This means that similarities between the two groups will be treated in a more rapid and general manner whereas their differences will occupy the center of our attention. These Prayers want to be modern presentations of tradition and quite frequently they want to express a certain American characteristic.[4]

The Structure of the American EPs

The elements that make up the structure of the American EPs are generally the same as in the Roman EPs. Unlike the Oosterhuis EPs, which gradually eliminate the assembling of elements in favor of a prolonged meditation-type discourse, the American EPs use the "assembly line" approach. The chart on page 54 gives an overview of the elements that make up these American EPs.

Each Prayer begins with a Thanksgiving, has an Institution Narrative-Anamnesis in the middle, and closes with a Doxology. There often are Offerings, Petitions, and Epicleses before or after the Institution Narrative. Generally the structure varies according to the model chosen. A Prayer such as 629, modeled mainly after the Roman Canon (EP I), will have a slightly different structure than those —the majority—modeled after either the Roman EPs II, III, IV, the Eastern anaphoras or that of Hippolytus.

It is not just the order of the parts (or elements) that creates structure, although this has traditionally determined the type of structure in distinguishing the Eastern anaphoras from one another,[5] but

---

[4] We shall refer to the American EPs by the numbers assigned to them in Hoey's collection, *op. cit.*

[5] Alphonse Raes in the Introduction to the *Pars Tertia: Anaphorae*

the elements themselves are structured differently. For example, in Prayer 635, the Thanksgiving leading up to the Institution Narrative is so structured that there are five short Thanksgivings alternated with five Acclamations. In Prayer 625, there is an address to the Father, followed by an address to the Son, followed by an address to the Holy Spirit. It is easy to include the traditional elements in this triple address, but the very fact of a triple address in this Prayer has determined the basic structure into three parts, each of which has its own structure. The author, a Benedictine, is perhaps influenced by the three vows of monastic profession. This Prayer introduces the distribution of the bread and wine after the Institution Narrative and Acclamation. Since the EP is more than a discourse (it is also an action), the introduction of the particular action of eating into its midst alters radically its structure.[6]

Another thing that affects the structure of these American EPs is the habit of introducing Petitions or similar elements at different moments. In the three Roman EPs, the Petitions are gathered together between the second Epiclesis and the Doxology; in the American EPs they are likely to be anywhere. Thus, in 620 they are attached to the Offering, in 621 to the Epiclesis, in 625 to the Acclamations; in 627 there are a number of these Petitions and even a "pledge." It is one thing to discuss whether or not Petitions should be in the EP at all and another to sprinkle them around liberally. Prayer 627 has Petitions attached to the Thanksgiving immediately following the Acclamation; for added measure, the "pledge" appears after the Petition; there is also a Petition after the Epiclesis to which is added a sort of "apology":

We are far from perfect but with the Spirit of love we can learn to live the life that we are called to live.

Orientales in Anton Hänggi and Irmgard Pahl, *Prex Eucharistica,* Fribourg, Switzerland, 1968. We read: "Typus definitur non secundum numerum aut indolem orationum sacerdotalium quas anaphorae continent neque secundum diversitatem actionum ritualium personarum quae in sacrificio celebrando cooperiunt, sed unice secundum ordinem diversum quem orationes sacerdotales in anaphora occupant." P. 99.

[6] See Bard Thompson, editor, *Liturgies of the Western Church,* Cleveland, 1961. Many Christians have wished to have the Eucharist distributed immediately following the Institution Narrative or after each of its two parts. Martin Luther suggested it in his Preface to *Deudsche Messe und Ordnung Gottis Diensts* [sic], in Thompson, p. 134; and it was recommended in *The Westminster Directory,* the Puritan worship service of 1644, in Thompson, p. 370. At this time it was not realized that there was an EP at the Last Supper, viz., the blessing pronounced by Jesus.

Novitiate Library

It is said that one critic of unofficial EPs has referred to them as a mixed salad of personal piety. We have here, perhaps, such a well-intentioned salad.

In Prayer 616, we have the following "response":

And in response to the great love You first showed us, we dedicate ourselves to follow Christ by dying to sin and selfishness and by living out the two great commandments which he gave us: to love You, Father, above all things and to love one another.

This is the kind of thing generally associated with the private thanksgiving after communion. The EP does not seem to gain by its introduction. However, it is no accident that it finds its way in here. People generally are more at home with prayers of Petition than with other kinds of prayer. The introduction of a "pledge" or a "response" may be an effort to be more than mercenary. Even the Petitions tend to be worded (structured) so that there is an involvement of the persons in what they are asking for. 618 illustrates this as well as any of the other Prayers:

So we ask You, Lord God, to send us his total power and love, your Holy Spirit, so that, full of hope, we can get on with our tasks on earth, arm in arm, all the while taking care that no one of your people walks alone.

The community, seeing itself as responsible for others, rarely asks for things for itself but generally its members wish to have certain gifts in order to be able to share them with others. There is here none of a *quid pro quo* spirit although that is a danger to be avoided in these prayers.

Several of the canons under study try to develop a theme (620, 624, 630, 631, and 635). It is true that practically every EP develops the theme of thanksgiving. However, here we mean a specific aspect of God's graciousness that is selected for particular attention. Thus, 624 chooses to articulate its thanksgiving with the idea of "the Word of God"; 630 chooses "human unity"; 631 the "Love of God" and 635 the "Lord of Love." 620 articulates its thanksgiving through the notion of the "Pilgrim Church." These "theme" EPs can make use of the same elements as found in the

Roman EPs, but the wording of the elements is generally influenced by the particular theme chosen. One of the advantages of a "theme" EP is that it can easily be related to a similar theme developed in the Liturgy of the Word. This is, in fact, a satisfactory way of relating the Liturgy of the Word to the Liturgy of the Eucharist.

If we now look at the chart which shows the structure of these Prayers, we shall note several tendencies. First, the Thanksgiving frequently follows a salvation history pattern, several of the Prayers containing what the Eastern anaphoras consider an *oratio theologica, oratio christologica* form, that is, a substantial part is devoted to God the Father or God in Himself and a substantial part to the role of the Son. However, we do notice also that in some of the Prayers the Thanksgiving, as we have earlier remarked, is not free of Petition. The Sanctus is not present at all in four of the Prayers; it is modified in several others. The Epiclesis on the gifts is rare and never occurs before the Institution Narrative. There are cases where the Epiclesis is vaguely stated, and, of the two cases where the Epiclesis is omitted entirely, one of the two Prayers is a rewording of the Roman canon. In general, however, the chart shows that the structure of these EPs is basically traditional.

The Way in Which the Praying Community
Addresses God, Refers to Jesus Christ,
and Refers to Itself

The preferred address to God in these Prayers is the single word "Father" (26 times) or with a qualifying adjective: "Holy," "heavenly," "eternal," "merciful," "almighty," and so forth. Most frequent is "almighty" (11 times). The second most frequently found form of address is that of "God," which appears alone four times, always in the English vocative form "O God," and is joined with other words such as "Lord God" (5 times) or "God our Father" (3 times).

The preference for the term "Father" is no doubt the result of the wish to have the most meaningful and intimate form of address that the community can employ. God the Father is consistently thanked for His gifts. Like the Roman EPs and unlike the Oosterhuis EPs, there is never any difficulty on the part of the community to name God. On the other hand, the community is not very inventive in naming God. Its source for naming God is the Roman

616	618	620	621	624	625
Thanksgiving from Creation to the Spirit at Pentecost	Thanks Christo-logical	Thanks for Creation Sanctus Thanks for the Son	Thanks for Creation Sanctus Thanks for Son and Salvation history	Thanks for Creation Salvation history	Thanks for Creation Acclamation (with mod-ified Sanctus) Petition Salvation history
					Address to Son
I.N. Acc-Anam	I.N. Acc-Anam	I.N. Anam	I.N. Acc-Anam	I.N. Anam	I.N. Acc Petition
	Offering	Offering (Petition)		Offering	
	Anam				
					COMMUNION
	Epiclesis² Petitions	Epiclesis²	Epiclesis¹,² Petitions	Petitions	Anam-Offering Anam
Response (sort of Epiclesis)				(sort of Eplicesis)	Address to H.S. Petitions Epiclesis
Offering					Closing
Doxology	Doxology	Doxology	Doxology	Doxology	Blessing

627	629	630	631	635
Thanks Petitions	Thanks Sanctus Offerings Petitions Mementos Petitions Thanks for the Son	Thanks Sanctus Thanks for Salvation history	Thanks Sanctus Thanks for Salvation history Petition Epiclesis² Offering	Thanks Acclamation (5 x) Sanctus
I.N. Acc Thanks Petition Epiclesis²	I.N. Acc- Anam Offering Petitions	I.N. Anam Offering Epiclesis² Petitions	I.N. Acc- Anam Offering Petitions Offering	I.N. Thanks Anam Offering Petitions
Adoration Doxology	Doxology	Doxology	Doxology	Doxology

I.N = Institution Narrative
Acc-Anam = The Anamnesis is in the form of an Acclamation
Epiclesis² = On the community
Epiclesis¹,² = On the gifts and on the community

liturgy, and it seems content not to be innovating. This is in striking contrast to the Oosterhuis EPs, as we shall see in the next chapter.

While there are three Prayers that omit the address "O God" in any of its forms, none omit using the expression "Father" in one of its forms.[7]

The most frequent expression used to refer to Jesus is "Your Son" (31 times). This expression is found in every one of the EPs. It is also found in combination, such as "Jesus Christ Your Son" (5 times) or "Your Son Jesus Christ our Lord" (3 times).

The other outstanding title used is "Jesus Christ our Lord" (13 times). "Jesus" is found alone once, "Lord" twice, and "Christ" five times. Individual Prayers try to introduce other formulae, such as, "friend and brother" (618) and "Word of Love," "Wisdom," "Alpha and Omega," "beginning and end"—piled one upon the other (624).

The preference for "Your Son" would seem to indicate the community's desire for an intimate way of talking to the Father about His Son. To the extent that it does this, it is not appropriating Jesus to itself. Unlike the Oosterhuis EPs, there is very little emphasis on Jesus the *human* mediator. Jesus in the American EPs is consistently either *Your* Son or *Our* Lord, although once he is called "that unforgettable man" (618).[8] Jesus' mediatorship is quite clear, but these Prayers do not insist on naming Jesus in such a way that the community can easily identify with His humanity. There is a tendency nowadays on the part of many Christians to see Jesus as many of His contemporaries saw Him, that is, prior to the knowledge that He is Jesus Christ the Lord. Yet here in the American EPs this tendency rarely breaks through, for example, "Jesus your Son and our Brother" and "friend and brother."

Popular piety never feared referring to Jesus as "Jesus," whereas Church prayers always employed post-Easter formulae such as "Lord" or "Jesus Christ our Lord." The introduction of the more popular formula into the American EPs is, as we have seen, slight. However, there is a de-emphasis of the post-Easter formulae, which perhaps are seen as making Jesus less accessible to the community. This is an interesting phenomenon since prayer groups in America are eager to praise Jesus precisely as Lord. Even in using the simple

[7] The hypercritical age in which we live has led some to dispute even the use of the word "Father" on the grounds that Freud has thrown the Father image into disrepute. For the limitations of Freud's understanding of God as Father see Antoine Vergote, *The Religious Man,* Sister Marie-Bernard Said, trans., Dayton, 1969, pp. 167-187.

[8] Prayer 618 borrows this expression as well as the wording of its offering ("this sign of our faith") from Oosterhuis EP 1. A comparison of the two Prayers would reveal other similarities.

expression "Jesus," these prayer groups use it with the post-Easter recognition of the name as a saving name. No one will deny that there is a big difference between "Jesus" considered as a saving name and "Jesus" considered as the name of a man who lived in the days of the Caesars.[9] However, the prayer context ought to indicate that the former is meant.

The "we" of the American EPs uses different expressions to talk about itself:

the people you made in your own image (616)

Your children; brothers; Church of Jesus Christ (629)

masters of the earth; brothers to all men (630)

your children; Your sons in Christ Jesus (631)

Unlike the Roman EPs, there is a desire on the part of the "we" of the American EPs to concretize itself by its relationship to God, Jesus Christ, or its fellow man. It feels the need to talk about itself: "Still in pilgrimage upon this earth, we trace in trial and under oppression the paths he trod" (620). The requests made show an outward thrust toward its fellow man and stress the virtues the community feels that it needs:

We may learn the true meaning of love we may find . . . an unquenchable thirst for justice and peace (624)

we pray that we may be able to bring all these things to their ultimate perfection in you. (625)

open our fearful hearts (625)

[9] See Irénée Hausherr, *Noms du Christ et Voies d'Oraison,* Orientalia Christiana Analecta, 157, Rome, 1960. Hausherr says: "To invoke the name of Jesus does not mean to say: 'Jesus,' especially for the Christians of the first centuries. The orthodox liked to confess their faith by saying: Jesus Christ, Jesus Messia, Son of God, and, especially, Lord . . . Among the titles of the Incarnate Word, the theological sense of the early Church, the fidelity of the Christians to the teachings of their Church, and also some of the magnificence of the Byzantine or Roman imperial customs preferred instinctively and voluntarily the most glorious, such as, Lord Jesus Christ Son of God and Jesus Christ Son of God Savior." Pages 118-119.

may [we] always have the courage to live the faith we believe. (627)

The American EP "we" takes up more space than the Roman EP "we" because it is trying to break out of the traditional restrained place assigned to the "we." It is an attempt to distribute, as it were, the *nobis quoque peccatoribus* a bit more generously throughout the whole EP, without necessarily accentuating the community's unworthiness. Because it has a deep desire of establishing contact with God, it keeps calling attention to itself to assure itself that, while it is taken up with addressing a "You," it itself is not forgotten. Furthermore, since the EP is an address not only to God but also a proclamation to the community, the frequent references to itself serve as a means of establishing contact between the celebrant and the congregation.

The "we" in these prayers is an idealistic one. Most frequently it asks for a gift in order that it may do something with it in the world; for example, "May we share in this Your gift of Love by giving ourselves to all Your creatures even to those who do not love us in return" (631). The "we" recognizes that it must do what it can to bring about healing in this world, that it is not enough to ask God to do the healing. In short, it sees its relationship to the world as a "helping" relationship. There is little doubt here that this is a characteristic of the American idea of itself.

As is quite common in public prayer and easily possible in EPs, the "we" is a double "we." That is to say, there is a "we" that embodies the assembled community as a particular Church and a "we" that identifies itself with man throughout the ages. When referring to this second "we," the Roman EPs prefer to use nouns that substitute for the first person plural whereas the tendency on the part of the American EP is to use the pronoun. It is in this way that the "we" of the American EPs keeps intruding itself whereas the Roman EP "we" remains discreet. We may illustrate this by taking the three passages in the Roman EPs that refer to the creation and passages in some of the American EPs that refer to the same event:

Roman EPs	*American EPs*
Jesus Christ is the living word for whom you created all things (II)	You made the universe *for us,* the people You made in Your own image (616)

You are truly holy, God of the universe and all creation proclaims Your Praise for it is You who give life, it is You who sanctify all things by your Son Jesus Christ (III)

By the power of your touch you gave *us* life and raised *us* to a dignity far beyond all that *we* deserve (621)

You brought *us* into Your world (627)

You are the God of goodness, the source of all life who made the world so that every creature be crowned with Your blessings (IV)

Blessed are you, gracious Father, for from the beginning you made *us masters* of the earth (630)

Sometimes by inserting this "we" with abandon, an author can come up with confusing juxtapositions:

> Together with Christ Jesus and in Him, *you raised us up and enthroned us* in the heavenly realm, *sending down upon us* the Spirit of adoption. (616)

Nevertheless, this concentration on the "we" evidences a certain shift of emphasis and interest from the Eucharist as sacrament to the assembled community.

What the Praying Community Finds Significant To Say about Jesus Christ

As we have already seen, the American EPs are by and large modeled on the Roman EPs insofar as their structure and the use of the elements found in that structure are concerned. Hence, what the Roman EPs found significant to say about Jesus Christ are also found here in the Thanksgiving, Institution Narrative, and the Anamnesis. There is no need to repeat that in detail.

In a recent article in *La Maison-Dieu,* Miguel Arranz has identified three major themes in the Post-Sanctus prayer of the anaphoras of the Antiochine type. These three themes are: (1) the theme of the mission of the Son of God made man, (2) the theme of the love of God going so far as to give his Son, and (3) the theme of the revelation of God through his Son.[10] It is possible to take these three themes and incorporate them in a single sentence such as "God so loved man that He sent His Son to reveal this love to man." This sentence is intrinsic to the message of Christianity, and it is only natural that some aspect of it be elaborated in the great Thanksgiving Prayer. The American EPs are no exception for, time and again, they thank the Father that he sent his Son. This is the most significant statement that the American EPs can make. All of them find the Son's leaving behind a memorial and his Passion (including his Resurrection) his most significant actions. This is also true of the Roman EPs.

Where some of the American EPs differ from the Roman EPs is in the tendency of the former to make Jesus more human. Thus, 616 says, ". . . that He might experience the agony of death for the sake of every being." 618 reminds us, "He did the great human things." The American EPs are concerned with making Jesus' life recognizable as a real human life. There is a reaction against the stylized Jesus, which tended to place him above the reach of man or to make him not fully human. The human Jesus is an American tradition that found its flowering in the Negro Spirituals. Furthermore, collections of private prayers encourage a man-to-man talking with Jesus. As the Episcopalian minister, Father Malcolm Boyd, said, when asked why he didn't call his book *Am I Running With You, Jesus?* rather than *Are You Running With Me, Jesus?*, "This is where I am at this moment." [11] What might be called the flesh and blood Jesus has had a great attraction for large segments of American society; hence the success of Kazantzakis, *The Last Temptation of Christ* or D. H. Lawrence's *The Last Man,* and more recently in film, Pasolini's *Gospel According to Saint Matthew* or on the stage *Godspell* (a retelling of the parables in Saint Matthew's Gospel in modern song styles) and the British-written, American-produced *Jesus Christ Superstar.* What reinforces all this in America is man's quest to find himself and others more human in a technological society.

The tendency is also, no doubt, a reaction against a major religious problem—the emphasis on Jesus' divinity at the expense of his humanity. Before accepting Jesus as Lord, he must be accepted as man.

[10] Miguel Arranz, "L'Economie du Salut dans la prière du Post-Sanctus des anaphores de type antiochéen," *La Maison-Dieu* 106, 1971, pp. 46-75.

[11] Malcolm Boyd, *Are You Running With Me, Jesus?*, New York, 1965, p. 7. Some find Boyd's "buddy-buddy" approach to God distasteful even in private prayer; this is why they have a horror of any of it creeping into the Liturgical prayer of the Church.

This is merely another way of saying that what he assumed he redeemed and what he did not assume was not redeemed. The implicit rejection of Jesus' humanity is part of the whole natural-supernatural, human-divine separation that has been part of the Catholic catechetical scene for centuries. From this background, it becomes significant that in one of the American EPs (perhaps influenced by Oosterhuis) Jesus can be named simply "Jesus" without any qualifying titles (616).

The human Jesus, like all of us, is a man who has friends (616, 624, 630). His world is also our world (618), and we trace . . . the paths he trod (620). It was when he was "at dinner" that he took the bread into his hands (621). He is God's Son and "our brother" (627).

The choice of the expression "at dinner" is a good one to illustrate the kind of shift we are talking about here. In American English, we have, among many others, the following choices for describing men getting together over food in the evening: at dinner, having a meal, eating supper, having a repast, or at chow. If the word "supper" were chosen in 621, there would be no step back from a sacral language, for the meal which Jesus took with his disciples is called in English, "The Last Supper." If the word "meal" were chosen, we would simply have the more generic term for men getting together to eat food during the day. "At chow" (army slang for a meal) would clearly smack of an attempt to put the gospel into the language of the barracks. The word "repast" would be stilted. However, "at dinner" suggests that like millions of Americans who sit down every night to dinner so did Jesus, and while he was "at dinner" he took bread. . . . Immediately, Jesus as a person with whom the assembled community can identify is subtly made to seem closer because of the level of the language.

What the Praying Community Says about
the Action It Is Accomplishing
and the Elements (Bread and Wine) It Uses

Just as in the Roman EPs, so in the American EPs the community thanks, remembers, offers, and asks. The thanksgiving in the form of praise is generally for the work of creation and redemption. What is said to be offered changes from Prayer to Prayer and even within Prayers. The following offering is found in Prayer 616:

And in response to the great love You first showed us, we dedicate ourselves to follow Christ by dying to sin and selfishness and by living out the two great commandments which He gave us to love You, Father, above all things and to love one another.

And, guided in our task by the Holy Spirit living in the Church, we offer our entire lives for the spreading of the Gospel among men of every class and nation, until the designated time, when all men will enjoy the freedom of the children of God and You gather all creation under one head, Jesus Christ, our Lord. (616, following the Anamnesis in the form of an acclamation and extending to the Doxology)

The wording of 616 shows that the offering is in response to a past event. Because of what Christ did in the past the community wishes to do something in the present. The language is heroic: the community is going to die to sin and selfishness and it offers its whole life to the spreading of the Gospel. As we shall see, this same kind of offering will be taken up in some of the other Prayers, but they will not limit themselves to the offering of themselves. For the moment we prefer to follow the Prayers in their numerical order.

All: Christ has died. Christ is risen. Christ will come again.

Celebrant(s): That is why, Lord God, we are offering this sign of our faith and that is why we now recall his sufferings, his crucifixion, his death, his burial. (618, the Offertory-Anamnesis)

The next Prayer, 620, explains this "sign of our faith" and sees it as a sign of communion:

And so we offer you, most merciful Father, through your beloved Son, this sacrifice of praise and thanksgiving, in union with our Pope, with ————, our Bishop, and with all your people. May it be a sign of our communion in the one perfect sacrifice of your Son. (620, after the Anamnesis)

This sign of communion in the one perfect sacrifice of the Son becomes in 624:

And in the everlasting power of his command, we offer you this sign of our belief and of his saving presence in our midst. (After the Anamnesis)

There is ambiguity in the expression "sign of our belief" for it could mean that the belief is that Christ is present. Then the second phrase governed by the noun "sign" would mean that Christ is actually present. In other words, the bread and wine would be a sign that, first, we believe Christ is present and, second, he *really* is present. On the other hand, the sign is "offered," and this in response to the command, "When you do these things do them in memory of me." Does this mean, then, that the sign of our belief is that the community believes that since it is doing what Christ did, it is doing it in memory of him? One wonders if this ambiguity as to what the belief refers to is better than the ambiguity of 618 which did not explain at all.

The offering of 625 is in much the same style as that of 616:

Mindful of your great love and of your complete gift of self to us on the Cross, we offer you in return, O Lord Jesus Christ, our entire lives with all that we do and have. (Anamnesis-Offering)

On the level of expression, the offering of 625, as that of 616, is a *self-offering* made in memory of a past event. Here we have a twofold insufficient balance, first, between an event that is past but "re-presented" and, second, between the offering of Christ by the Church and the offering of the Church itself. It is, of course, difficult for a modern language to give full due to the idea of memorial, but when 625 attempts to expand the *memores offerimus* of the Roman canon, it moves in the direction of recalling a past event, namely, Christ's death on the cross, rather than the sacramental "re-presentation" of that event.

In Prayer 629, immediately following the Sanctus, we have, "We offer you this sacrifice of praise" and "We wish to offer you ourselves in this your Son's most holy sacrifice." Then, after the Anamnesis, we have a clearer expression of the sacrifice:

We pray that this perfect sacrifice of your Son which we offer to you in humility and love may be the sign of our surrender to you.

Yet here the offering is actually cut off from the Anamnesis for it finds itself the first of three petitions, the second of which is really a development of the self-offering already made in the Post-Sanctus:

> We pray that before the eyes of all men we may live your Gospel and witness to Christ's presence, that we may support one another in love, that our hearts may be open to the poor, the sick, the unwanted, to all who are in need.

The first petition, however, requests that the offering of the Son's sacrifice in humility and love may be the sign of the community's surrender to God. This request is so worded that it asks that the sacrificial sacrament be the sign of man's self-giving to God when in reality it should first be the sign or sacrament of the Son's total self-giving to the Father. The liberal use of the word "sign" leads to sacramental imprecision. The next Prayer, 630, expresses this idea without ambiguity:

> Placing here, then, this sign of his sacrifice, we unite ourselves to him, who gave his life that we may be one, even as you and he are one.

This offering is put in the framework of unity for the Prayer has taken as its theme "Human Unity."

Prayer 631 speaks of offering three times. The first time is just before the Institution Narrative: "Bless and accept these gifts of bread and wine and of ourselves which we offer to you now." This is the kind of expression found in the Roman canon but not in the new Roman Prayers. Since an offering of this type is found at the Offertory when the bread and wine are acknowledged as gifts, it might be omitted in an EP preceded by an offertory rite. Oftentimes, writers of unofficial EPs tend to forget the wider context of the Eucharistic celebration and use the EP as if it were a container into which everything may be put. This first offering of EP 631 may not represent an example of this, and at any rate it could justify its practice by the opinion of Dix that the primitive meaning of the EP is to express the totality of the action (offertory, consecration, and communion).[12] The second offering of Prayer 631 is found after the Anamnesis:

> We offer you this act of praise and thanksgiving and the service of our lives in love and gratitude for your great gifts to us.

[12] Dix, *The Shape of the Liturgy*, p. 120.

The word "act," which certainly finds its justification from the expression *canon actionis,* is nevertheless substituted for the word "sacrifice," which would be the more traditional noun for designating the kind of praise and thanksgiving offered by Christians. The self-offering, which forms the second part of the whole offering, is developed in a petition that follows it:

> May we share this your gift of love by giving of ourselves to all your creatures, even to those who do not love us in return.

The third offering expressed in Prayer 631 corresponds to the offering that the Roman EPs express in the Anamnesis-Offering. However, in the former, it is placed just before the Doxology as a kind of culmination of the whole central part of the Prayer:

> Therefore, in joy and confidence, we offer you, Father, the body and blood of your Son. For through him and with him and in him . . .

Prayer 635, the last Prayer of our group, expresses its offering succinctly: Joined with His mother, His disciples, and with the faithful through the centuries, we rejoice in offering you this sign of your love. Once again it is the theme here, "The Lord of Love," that shapes the expression of the offering. In the context of the Anamnesis which precedes the expression of the offering, this sign is seen to be the sign of the Father's perfect love for us since it commemorates the Son's redemptive Passion.

Only two Prayers omit any explicit offering of themselves or the bread and wine. These are 621 and 627. This may be simply because it is taken for granted rather than as a result of any anti-sacrificial idea. Prayer 621, for example, puts its offering in its opening Thanksgiving when it acknowledges, "We alone, of all your creation, can call you Father, and offer you praise that is pleasing to you." It continues, "We join now in prayer about the table of your Son and offer you thanks at his request." The word "offer" here is the synonym of "give." Now, when we study the sentence immediately following the Institution Narrative, we find the words, "Heavenly Father, we give you thanks for the gift you have given us in Christ Jesus your Son." Since such words could be a prayer at any time during the day, their significance here must be linked with the bread and wine and the Institution Narrative. It is at this point that the

Roman EPs offer the gift to the Father whereas 621 puts the accent on the gift it has received.

Prayer 627 is similar to Prayer 621 in that, after the Institution Narrative, it too thanks God for the gift of his Son. In return, the community renews its dedication to God. 627 concentrates more on Jesus' presence than the idea of sacrifice.

In the passages just studied, where the offering is made explicit, we see—and it is only to be expected—that this explanation is quite varied. Sometimes the community is offering a sign, but this sign can be a sign of "His sacrifice," "our faith," "Your love," and "His saving presence in our midst." Once the Body and Blood are offered, once the bread and wine, and once the sacrifice of the Son. Three times the sacrifice of praise (and thanksgiving) is offered. Three times the community offers itself. What perhaps is noteworthy is the hesitancy to apply the word sacrifice directly to the offering or to use the word sacrifice without any qualification. In fact, not a single one of the American EPs studied speaks with the same clarity as the Roman EPs. EP IV expresses this most clearly but in a manner not customary in the Roman tradition:

We offer You his body and blood as a sacrifice acceptable to You. (Roman EP IV)

The American EPs are more at home with the "sacrifice of our lives" or the "sacrifice of praise." When Prayer 629 speaks of "Your Son's most holy sacrifice" and "this perfect sacrifice of Your Son which we offer," we have the most direct sacrificial references. This is due to the fact that 629 is a rewording of Roman EP I, the Roman canon.

The American EPs avoid any confusion between one sacrifice and many sacrifices. Generally they do this without diminishing the idea of a reactualization of the Calvary event. It is precisely the central location of the Institution Narrative that accomplishes this. The community always makes the link between what Christ did the night before He died and what it is doing here and now.

Let us now examine the references the community makes to the bread and wine and to the action, considered as a whole, that it is accomplishing. Prayer 616, just before the Institution Narrative, gives as its motive for coming together, the eating of the Lord's Supper. Such a designation is not found in the other Prayers, and only 635 uses the theological term "memorial": "Find acceptable this memorial we now perform in union with the whole Church." More often, the action as well as the bread and wine is a thanksgiving or a sign (of love, of belief, of His presence). It is also, in Prayers 627 and 631, a gift. Thus, there is a variety of terms to refer to the action and/or the bread and wine, but there is not really any felt need to designate the whole action. One simply performs it.

It is also to be noted that for these Prayers there is no hesitation to refer to the bread and wine as bread and wine even after the Institution Narrative. Here is their practice:

eat this bread	drink the chalice of the Lord	(616, Acc-Anam.)
eat of this bread	drink from this Cup	(627, Acc.)
eat of this bread	drink of this cup	(629, Acc.)
sharing our bread	drinking from the same cup	(630, Epi[2].)
eat of this bread	drink from this cup	(631, Acc.)
eating this bread	drinking this cup	(635, Anam.)

Yet the context generally shows that this bread and this cup has undergone a change. First of all, the text of St. Paul, 1 Cor 11:26, is the decisive influence on the manner of expression. This alone explains the practice. Secondly, there is the link that each of these expressions makes back to the Institution Narrative by use of the demonstrative pronoun "this" and/or the ritualistic word "cup." Only 635 has anything as explicit as "May this bread become His Body to make us one and this wine His Blood to join us to Him who is our Savior," which occurs just before the Institution Narrative. Finally, Prayer 625 has the following expression: "nourished by the Body and Blood of your own glorified Body," which creates more problems than it solves.

The Place Given to the
Role of the Holy Spirit

The Holy Spirit is mentioned in all the Prayers but not necessarily in an Epiclesis. More frequently the reference to the Spirit is made in the salvation history accounts of the Thanksgiving or in the Doxology. Only six of the Prayers have Epicleses properly so-called. None of them have Epicleses both before and after the consecration. When the Holy Spirit is invoked, it is more often for his descent upon the community rather than upon the gifts. It happens too that this invocation of the Holy Spirit is just one among many Petitions instead of being a Petition significant enough to be separated from the others. Unlike the Roman EPs, where the sending of the Spirit on the community is linked to the reception of the Eucharist, the American EPs ask for the Spirit "so that":

> so that, full of hope, we can get on with our tasks on earth, arm in arm . . . (618)

> that he may make of us yet more perfectly a royal priesthood empowered to proclaim before all men your saving name . . . (621)

> that we may learn from him and from his memory the true meaning of love . . . (624)

> that we may be able to see the needs of God's developing kingdom around us. (625)

> so that whoever speaks the truth in love will be heard by each man in his own tongue. (630)

There is a genuine concern in these Prayers that the power of the Spirit work in the members of the community. This wish *to do something* is probably a typical American characteristic for it appears frequently in the American EPs.

One thing seems to be certain insofar as the choice of expression to refer to the Spirit is concerned: Holyghost would be clearly an archaism. It is always printed Holy Ghost, but where it does survive orally, it is no doubt due to its being thought of as a one word term, such as, for children, "adamaneve" or "sannaclaus."

4
THE OOSTERHUIS
TABLE PRAYERS

Among the many people involved in creating a Dutch vernacular liturgy, Huub Oosterhuis is undoubtedly the best known to English readers. His first book, *Your Word is Near*,[1] containing the most popular of his EPs, has been translated into English, French, and German. A former Jesuit, Oosterhuis is still active in the Amsterdam student parish community although he remains something of a controversial figure. In February 1971, for example, he presided at the Eucharist despite the fact that since his marriage he had been asked to cease his ministerial activities.[2] To understand his EPs and the spirit from which they are written requires some acquaintance with his thought. Indeed, this might be said about any author of EPs, but it is particularly necessary for this intensive, introspective, profoundly concerned Dutch poet.

There is probably no better place from which to start than Oosterhuis' latest book *In het Voorbijgaan,* translated into English in two separate slim volumes.[3] If we search out his understanding of man, God, and Jesus Christ as expressed in his prose, we shall have an easy access to understanding his EPs without in any way detracting from the complexity and profundity of their thought.[4]

Let us first see what Oosterhuis has to say about man. When he speaks about man, Oosterhuis is constantly aware of man's infirmities, injustices, and his greatness. He asks, "But what is a man? He is tremendous, puzzling and almost nothing at the same time. He is

[1] Huub Oosterhuis, *Your Word is Near, New York,* N. D. Smith, trans., 1969.

[2] This was widely reported in the press, Dutch and foreign.

[3] Huub Oosterhuis, *In het Voorbijgaan,* Utrecht, 1968. The first half of this work appears in English under the title, *Prayers, Poems & Songs,* David Smith, trans., New York, 1970; the second half under the title, *Open Your Hearts,* David Smith, trans., New York, 1971.

[4] In the following pages devoted to Oosterhuis' thought, the references shall be to the English translations, I referring to *Prayers, Poems & Songs* and II to *Open Your Hearts.* The page reference follows the Roman numeral. The ten table prayers studied are found in II, pp. 6-39.

divided, a stranger to himself, riveted to his body and nailed to his origin and shortcomings. A doubtful identity. A man is only half-known in his own name and soon forgotten" (I, 160). It is this double tension of man—fallen yet something mysterious—that finds voice in the writings of Oosterhuis. Having taken a hard look at man, he finds no cause for optimism, but his religious faith gives him an illumination. Thus, commenting on the passage in Luke:

> If you then, who are evil, know how to give your children what is good, how much more will the heavenly Father give the Holy Spirit to those who ask him! (Luke XI, 13)

Oosterhuis says that we find there a proclamation that people, for all their shortcomings, are still good enough to be the image of God. The dimension of man's oridinary life is illuminated and people are encouraged and strengthened in what they are (I, 49).

Faith has its role to play in all this. Believing is intimately related to growing and maturing (I, 35), and not believing is no longer seeing anything in sharing and communication with other people, not expecting anything more from them, no longer listening to them. Not believing is thinking that nothing means anything to you anymore (I, 36). Here we see faith being defined in terms of man's ability to reach out to other men and not to withdraw into isolation. It is not something acquired once-for-all. Oosterhuis says, "Faith is not a constant in your emotions or in the thoughts at the back of your mind. It is not a possession. It is a to-and-fro between yes and no" (I, 38). This faith-dialectic—seen most clearly when confronted with world events—is no mere acceptance of something called God's will. In fact, it is a process in which man himself is tried as he finds himself questioning or crying out against the crimes of the 20th century.

Oosterhuis, then, is well aware of the ambiguity of man in our present age, and the "we" of his table prayers does not hide this ambiguity, this elbowing with belief and unbelief, hope and despair, love and hate. The tensions within man are not denied. That is why when this man uses words to speak about God, he says in all honesty:

> There have been centuries when men boldly took on God, radiantly and simply, and dared to adorn his name, in all sincerity and in glowing faith, with mighty epithets like omniscient and omnipresent. Centuries when people were able to fill great words such as this with their faith and to express themselves and recognize themselves in them.

No one is called upon to judge the centuries or to set them off
one against the other. All we have to do is to live in our own century—and our century does not get on easily with such radiant
epithets for God. Perhaps all words applied to him are too great
for us (I, 24-25).

Despite difficulty in using the traditional words to speak about God,
man is not reduced to silence (although the temptation is great), but
he is forced to speak with brutal honesty to and about God. To do
this, man makes use of what Oosterhuis calls a "second language,"
the language of what cannot really be said. The language that you
speak so as not to have to be completely silent. The language of emotion and ecstasy. This is the only language which is really daring
enough for people. It is not a language of having and understanding,
but a language of groping and naming. It is the language of protest
and freedom. And not the language of a pretentious Church system
of thought, with its dogmas and categories and formulas about God
and man, salvation, the soul, truth, and the natural law, but the
language of preaching and the liturgy, of witness and singing, the
birth language of faith (II, 104-108).

This second language that Oosterhuis is talking about is the language of myth.

What people believe is true and meaningful, what they think is
eternal and original, what they see as reality—however terrible
this may be—and what they hope is going to happen—all this
they express as images in their myths. Not the historically verifi-
able facts of our existence, but the hidden meaning or the
feared absurdity of those facts, our burning inner life—that is
what we want to express in the second language (II, 108).

Praying, bearing witness, speaking the language of faith, calling
people and imagining them is going by fits and starts, becoming
less and less certain with every word and preferring to remain
silent. But you cannot go on being silent. You have to go on.
You have to listen and be heard. It is somewhere between or
past words that people find each other and understand each
other (II, 112).

For Oosterhuis, only this second language is good enough for God.
This is the language of poetry and prayer. Not that there is a
reserve of a poetic language or a prayer language that one taps.

This second language is primary in comparison with ordinary, every-day language. It is forged in the midst of a creative act whose result, when seen or heard by reader or auditor, elicits the response, "Yes, that is poetry, that is prayer." However, one who tries to use a so-called poetic language or a so-called prayer language, that is, a stock language, is probably doomed to failure if there is no intensity or existential struggle (breaking through to tranquility on occasion). As Oosterhuis says, there is no special language for prayer, sacred and sublime, no standardized jargon, consciously simple or formally polite (II, 44). It is God as revealed in the Old Testament that serves as Oosterhuis' model for speaking about Him. The Bible shows that the God of Israel is different from all other gods, not a god who compels and makes demands and uses force, not a "mother earth and Father heaven" to whom we bring our sacrifices with our backs bent and our eyes cast down. He is space and freedom and you can say anything to him. No word is too uncouth or too spontaneous for him. You can play with him, flatter him, overcome him, or go as far with him as you want to and as you have to, just like Abraham when he bargained with him about Sodom and Gomorrah. You can pour out your heart to him and rage against him, as Job did (II, 44). And later on, Oosterhuis says, "Incomprehensible, daring words are born in the ecstasy and despair of prayer" (II, 49). To put it briefly, looking at the models of Old Testament prayer, Oosterhuis con-cludes that man must not cease to be himself when speaking to God, that is, he must not try to adopt attitudes toward God as he wears clothes, exterior things with no interior content.

What is praying? Praying is speaking God's name, or rather, seek-ing God's name . . . Praying is trying to turn that empty, fleeting little word "God" into a name that means something to me, to us, now (II, 49); and praying is blessing, praising, giving honor to God . . . calling God by his name, giving him the chance to become him-self, "our God" (II, 50). It is obvious that Oosterhuis' concept of prayer has not only grown out of his personal experience, but also his reading of the Bible, particularly the Psalms. The Psalms in all their variety teach us how to talk to God. It is Oosterhuis' frankly biblical approach that makes his texts so living and . . . so shocking.

Here then we have, as it were, one of the two poles in the com-munication process called prayer: a man who dares to speak, not simply in any manner whatever, but in a language that comes from the heart. Oosterhuis' conception of man, his place in this world, and his relationship with God determines to a great extent not only what man says to God but also what tone and depth of language he uses to talk to him. This, of course, is not determined in isolation from Oosterhuis' conception of God, which is the second of the two poles we must take into account. As we saw above, in talking about man's relationship to God, it is the same biblical approach that dominates in Oosterhuis' conception of God. The God of Abraham, Isaac, and Jacob is a God, who can be moved, who is made public by the people who bear witness to him (I, 16), who is liberation (I, 22), a God of people (I, 21 and II, 51).

Nevertheless, Oosterhuis is aware that the word "God," the moment that it is uttered, gives rise to a variety of reactions on the part of those who hear it. That is why he cannot take the word for granted, as something known and agreed upon, for behind the word "God" lies a variety of understandings of its meaning, and this is true even among believers. The God of the philosophers, the God of an institution has done enough damage and sometimes the preacher "will have to free people from every recollection of the word 'God' so that they will depart greatly relieved and 'no longer believing' " (I, 53). It is clear, then, that man must strip himself of false images of God, images that not only destroy God but destroy man, in order to return to a conception that lets God be God and man be man.

The God of the Old Testament is no less a God of love than the God of the New Testament. In fact, such a separation makes no sense and does more harm than it does good. However, the New Testament is the revelation of God in Jesus Christ, and it is the New Testament that gives us access to Oosterhuis' understanding of Jesus.

Oosterhuis tells us that God makes his will and his intentions, his ideas of peace and his name fully known by becoming the God of Jesus. Jesus, a son of men, is one of many men, without form or splendor. He lives a long way away and fails, falling into the hands of men. But we no longer feel the scandal that this crucified man was to his followers and to strangers. He dies—because of a foolish misunderstanding (I, 23). However, it is in Jesus and in his glorified body that we read what lies ahead for us and who is waiting for us. This vision of hope has been handed down to us in the Gospel that there is, in the whole cosmos, no other truth to which we have to turn than the humanity and the human form of Jesus of Nazareth. We have no one else to expect (I, 118). It is in true biblical fashion that man reminds God of what he has done to Jesus, his faithfulness to him, that man knows God will also be faithful unto man (II, 51). That is why, behind every cry of "how long yet" and "why"—words that Oosterhuis says characterize the freedom and abandon of almost every Jewish prayer (I, 67)—there is still an anchoring of faith that returns when the breaking of bread is recalled.

Thus, now knowing something of Oosterhuis' thinking, we have every reason to expect that in his EPs the "we" will be a man not afraid to express his every thought to a God whom he hopes to move and to remind of his faithfulness to Jesus and, finally, that the expression of this man's prayer will be in that so-called second language that allows the poet to reveal his deepest thoughts in a language that men can understand.

The Structure of the Oosterhuis Table Prayers

Although there is a clear distinction between the elements included in EPs 1 to 6 and those in 7 to 10, the common structure of all ten prayers is an address to God with a reference to Jesus Christ and the bread. The Oosterhuis EP, reduced to its minimum content and form, could be summarized thus: God, we speak to you because of Jesus who left us this bread.

In Prayers 1 to 6, Oosterhuis includes the same elements as are found in the Roman EPs. Thus, we have an opening exhortation to the people gathered together. It may or may not be cast in the form of a dialogue. This is followed by an address to God usually to thank or bless Him. In Prayers 1 and 2, there is an Acclamation in the form of a Sanctus following this thanksgiving. The thanksgiving is continued, but this time it is centered on Jesus Christ, the mediator between God and man. This mediating role is always clear in the prayers.

The second thanksgiving contains the Institution Narrative. In Prayers 1, 2, and 4 it is followed by an Acclamation. An Offering and Anamnesis (or inversely) is then made (only in 4 is the Offering omitted).

Prayers of Petition follow. An Epiclesis generally heads the list of Petitions. This Epiclesis is always an invocation of the Spirit on the community. Unlike the Roman EPs, there is never an invocation of the Spirit on the elements. There is a Doxology or at least the traces of one. Thus, in 1, 2, and possibly 3, there is a true Doxology, that is, God's glory is proclaimed; sometimes only the mediating formula "through him with him and in him" is used at this point; and sometimes it is used as a transition to the Our Father. Oosterhuis, it should be remarked now, generally integrates the Our Father into the Eucharistic Prayer and follows it immediately with the reception of the Eucharist.

Prayers 7 to 10 depart greatly from the pattern set by Prayers 1 to 6. Prayer 7 is essentially a string of petitions following questions asked by the choir. In one of the petitions a reference to the Institution of the Eucharist is made.

Prayer 8 gives more space to talking about the Son than about the Father's deeds (as in REP II). It is only after the Institution Narrative that the celebrant says, "we bless you now and we admire you." It has some of the core words of the traditional Institution Narrative: this is my body, living bread; this is my blood, my soul for you—do to each other what I have done.

Prayer 9 returns more to the use of elements as found in 1 to 6, but it rearranges some of them. The Petitions follow immediately upon the initial address to God. The Epiclesis for the community makes its return in the Petitions. The Our Father, which usually followed the Doxology in Prayers 1 to 6, is recast and forms part of the Petitions. There is then a thanksgiving for the Son, in which an Institution Narrative—not just a short reference as in 7 and 8—is included. A Benediction, Anamnesis and Acclamation follow in rapid succession.

Prayer 10 [5] may be said to be at the other end of the scale from Prayer 1. It is a monologue addressed to a God who does not answer. References to "that man from Nazareth" and to "this little piece of bread" are the only hints given to indicate that this is not a bedside prayer but a table prayer. One feels that this is the kind of EP a priest would employ in an Ingmar Bergman film. While it is not the kind of prayer that would please a man seized with a "living faith," it remains the prayer of a man of faith striving not to equate God with any conception he may have of Him.

We can readily show the shifts that take place in Oosterhuis' uses of the Doxology. Let us first of all consider the Roman EP Doxology as normative: Through him, with him, in him, in the unity of the Holy Spirit, all glory and honor is yours, almighty Father, forever and ever. Amen. Not once does this Doxology appear in the Oosterhuis Prayers. The difference is significant. The Roman Doxology is formed, not only from a Trinitarian perspective, but also from one that sees Christ *presently* giving glory and honor to the Father. The first two Oosterhuis Prayers adopt an eschatological perspective,

---

[5] In the German translation of *In het voorbijgaan*, Prayer 10 is eliminated from the corpus of Table Prayers and is found under another heading.

when the new creation will be established and men, who now do not live in peace, will be reconciled:

Then your name will be made holy on earth, through Jesus Christ, with him and in him, for ever and ever. Amen (2)

In Prayer 3, this becomes:

Through Jesus Christ, with him, and in him, we are your people and you are our Father now and for ever and ever. Amen.

Here the praying community, which has emphasized God's desire that men be a "new people," uses the traditional place as well as some of the form of the Doxology to sum up this understanding of the new people related to the Father. Prayers 4 and 5 change this to a final Petition, the kind that concludes an *oratio:* "We ask you this through Jesus your Son, with him and in him, now and forever. Amen." (5) In Prayer 6, the Doxology survives only within the Petition:

Bear us up in your hands and give us your peace, so that, through Jesus, with him and in him, we shall become your sons, born again.

The shift represented in Prayer 7 is even greater for the traces of the Doxology are found in a paraphrased Our Father. Furthermore, the agent through whom God's name will be made holy is the people who represent Jesus in this world:

Give us, around this bread and this cup, the strength to be him, and that, through us, in us, your name may be lived, made holy . . .

Finally, in Prayers 8, 9, and 10, the Doxology as such disappears in favor of some kind of profession of faith.

It may be interesting to single out how Oosterhuis changes the form of the Our Father to give it a new significance. In Prayer 7, he weaves it into the string of Petitions and links it up with the reception of the bread and wine:

If, then, that is life for this world,
give us, around this bread and this cup,

the strength to be him,
and that, through us, in us,
your name may be lived, made holy,
your kingdom of peace will come,
bread of justice,
people for people,
your will be done,
new heaven, new earth—
open that door
that no one can close.

Again, in Prayer 9, the Our Father is condensed and applied first to the community and then to Jesus Christ:

Jesus of Nazareth,
who made your name holy,
accomplished your will,
became bread and wine for us,
food and joy
and the forgiveness of sins.

May we not chase after emptiness,
run away from truth,
forget your name,
May we hasten the coming of your kingdom
and accomplish your will,
share the bread of this world with each other
and be quick to forgive all the
harm that is done to us.

This technique of taking a prayer form and rewording it or using it in a new way is a favorite one of Oosterhuis. In fact, he has an EP not found in this collection that draws its inspiration from Psalm 80.[6]

In these ten Prayers, we see a change in Oosterhuis' understanding of the EP with a gradual movement from a structure assembling elements to a more unified address to God making few references to Jesus or the bread and wine. This movement may also be described as one from proclamation to interior monologue. The EP that is proclaimed stresses what God has done as creator and through Jesus the redeemer. It is easily rounded off with a Doxology. The EP that is like an interior monologue teases thought and is

<hr>

[6] *Prayers, Poems and Songs,* pp. 70-72.

preoccupied with working out the relationship between God, man, and the world. The EP that is proclaimed is in the tradition of the solemn prayers of Israel. The EP that is like an interior monologue owes its origins to the Book of Job and the complaint Psalms. In this way, Oosterhuis moves further and further from the traditional understanding of the EP.

The Oosterhuis Prayers give a greater role to the entire assembly and the choir. Anyone who has assisted at the Amsterdam community's service or has heard the EPs on tape knows that it is a religious experience to hear these hymns of praise, these cries of worship lifted up to the Father. In fact, when the EP is sung well by priest, choir, and people, there seems to be something necessary in the very singing, almost as if the EP—considered as a hymn of praise and accompanying word of the community's action—is most fittingly done when sung.

It is also to be noted that the entire assembly sings the Institution Narrative in certain Prayers. This is contrary to Eastern and Western tradition, where the Institution Narrative is reserved to the celebrant alone. Of course, any text may be set to music and we even have evidence that the Roman canon after the Preface was sung by the Pope.[7] However, it is quite another thing to think of the EP as something to be sung by priest, choir, and celebrant. If one starts off with that idea, the structure may be shaped accordingly. In fact, some of the Oosterhuis EPs are reminiscent of the dramatic role of the Greek chorus, which was to comment on the action and express the feelings of the people.

Three of Oosterhuis' Prayers (4, 7, and 8) have their parts apportioned to the celebrant, the choir, and the whole congregation. It is the celebrant who wishes peace to the community (4), directs its attention to God (7) or invites it to pray (8). It is also the celebrant's role to invite the community to partake in the Body and Blood (4, 8) or sum up their final request (7). Apart from that, it is not clear on what basis the other parts are assigned. The choir has some kind of role of introducing the discourse; in Prayer 4 it begins the Preface:

> It is our honor, it is our safety to speak your name and stand before you, listening, waiting, praying, Lord our God.

In Prayer 7, this introduction is put in an interrogative form:

---

[7] Jacques Froger, "The Chants of the Mass in the Eighth and Ninth Centuries," *The Gregorian Review,* Jan.-Feb., 1956, pp. 13-15.

Whom shall we worship and believe and who is worth our words
and greater than our hearts? If there is a God who loves men,
what is his name?

The task of the celebrant and the whole congregation is an attempt
to address this God who loves men. The beginning of Prayer 8 appears abrupt enough. After the celebrant invites to prayer, the choir
sings:

You speak to people throughout all ages in many languages in
visible things and what cannot be seen. You look for us in
heaven and earth.

Of all these Prayers it is Prayer 7 that is the most original. If we
were to present this Prayer in outline form, it would look something
like the following:

First Part: The Religious Situation of Man

Choir: xxxxx *   If there is a God who loves men, what
* each x equals one line of poetry.
                                 is his name?
Celebrant: xxxxx   You see how restless we search for
                                 You.
All: xxxxxxxxxx   Open the doors of your light. Let us
                                 see you.
Celebrant: xxxxxxxxx   Open the doors of our hearts.

Second Part: God's Mystery of Salvation

All: xxxxxxxxx   If there is a city of hope.
Celebrant: xxxx   If there is a man to lead us to you.
Choir: xxxxxx   If that man is Jesus of Nazareth.
All: xxxxxxxxxxx   If his body and blood gives strength,
                                 give us it.
Celebrant: xxx   If you are the God who loves men,
                                 open us then to you.

The whole Prayer is cast in the form of a search leading to dis-
covery and conversion. In the First Part, which we have called "The
Religious Situation of Man," the choir proclaims the search for a God
who loves men, someone who is greater than man, capable of greater

love. What is the name of this God? The celebrant, summing up the feelings of the choir, addresses a You who knows the thoughts man expresses feebly in his restless search of this You. Then the whole congregation (including choir and celebrant) addresses this You with many epithets and asks him to "open the doors of your light and let us see you." The celebrant immediately reverses this desire by singing, "Open the doors of our hearts," acknowledging man's inclination to evil and hate.

God's Mystery of Salvation forms the second part of the Prayer. God has not abandoned man to himself. A promise has been made to man concerning a place, a city that is peaceful. The whole congregation wishes to go to that place and to set up a table and distribute bread "that feeds like a body." The celebrant introduces the idea that there is a man through whom the congregation can find a way to the You. It is the choir that takes up this thought and names the man, Jesus of Nazareth, who became "a piece of bread broken, a cup of wine drunk." All then sing together that, if that is the way to bring about "the kingdom of peace," then, around the bread and the wine, they wish to do what Jesus did. This is a door that once opened cannot be closed. The celebrant ends the Prayer by taking up the original question and making a final request: If you are the God who loves men, open us then to You. Thus, a change has taken place from the beginning which announced the search. Here, at the end, God is acknowledged and man awaits in simplicity his initiative while at the same time desiring greatly to welcome this God.

This is a highly original EP, and a striking way of representing the importance of the Eucharist in man's relationship with God. Yet, one must ask whether or not the technique of "suspension of belief"— proper in other literary genres—may be used in the EP, which from its very outset is celebrated in the light of the Resurrection by a people baptized who, when assembled for the memorial meal of the community, exercise their priesthood of believers. They come together because they have already been called together; they already are the new people they are called to become, and they know this.

The Way in Which the Praying Community
Addresses God, Refers to Jesus Christ,
and Refers to Itself

In Prayers 1 to 6, the designations of God by the praying community are rather consistent: Lord our God, God of people, source of all that exists, our hope, our light, our Father, one and trustworthy God, I-shall-be-there-for-you.

The titles or names applied to God in Prayer 6 are taken from Psalm 91, which precedes the Prayer. Thus, God is called friend, most high, shield, trust, refuge, shadow of safety and also stranger. This last appelation is interesting since it introduces the first hint of the ambiguity of the relationship between the Christian and God. The word itself is not found in the Psalm, but it arises from the ever-present problem for Oosterhuis to name God. The Prayer begins with the words: "We thank you, God almighty, and we bless you. You cannot be thought of or named. You are a stranger. . . ."

In the remaining Prayers, the difficulty in naming God becomes even more evident. In 7, Oosterhuis makes an effort to name God by building up a series of images:

> You, with your name unnamable, God,
> word, incalculable,
> dream folly power freedom,
> you who go your way unseen,
> God of strangers no one,
> God of people running fire
> you unheard of in this world—

This effort to name the unnamable is very much like the apophatic approach of some of the Eastern anaphoras. It is different from the great Eastern EPs in that it makes use of the poetic technique of rapidly juxtaposing images that sometimes seem contradictory. Not that the speaker is content with contradictions, for he cries out at one point: "You who are called liberator, why must we be slaves. . . ." The Prayer closes, not with an affirmation, but with a grammatical conditional: "If you are the God who loves men, open us then to you."

In Prayer 8, although he is the God who speaks to people and looks for us, he is never addressed by celebrant, choir, or congregation. It is through Jesus we know he became "our Father." This is a far cry from the abundance of ways in which God is addressed and referred to in Prayers 1 to 6.

In Prayers 9 and 10, it is the pronoun "you" that dominates. It is almost as if God can only be named in the most simple terms, his otherness, his you-ness. It is only after the Institution Narrative that the speaker says in 9, "Blessed are you, living God, because of him the son of man. . . ." In Prayer 10, God is referred to simply by "you" or by what he is not; in this latter case, Oosterhuis makes use of one of his favorite poetic devices, the piling up of images that serve as likenesses or approximations:

You are not a man,
not a hand, not eyes
blind in the sea,
stone in the water,
no god, no spirit,
no power—

Here we see Oosterhuis trying to strip away false approaches to God in order to leave a more purified one. It is almost the same thing as saying: You are not a Greek God, you are not changeable, you are not limited, and so forth.

These different forms of addressing God result from the difficulty of words to circumscribe the uncircumscribable. In this way, we see Oosterhuis striving to do what the Eastern anaphoras do. However, there are two differences. The first is that even when there is an admission that God is unnamable, he is nevertheless consistently named in the anaphoras, whereas with Oosterhuis we see in Prayer 10 the disappearance of any attempt to name God other than by the second person pronoun. The second difference is that the whole tone of the Oosterhuis Prayer seems to smack of subjectivism or agnosticism. Although we must hasten to add, it is not agnostic in any anti-religious sense. Any idea of discussion of the philosophical stance of the speaker or his present existential situation is not included in an oriental EP or for that matter in the new Roman EPs, where the faith stance taken is generally one of serenity or resolved conflict. This is not true with these latter EPs of Oosterhuis. The speaker is very self-conscious and spends a great deal of time articulating his difficulties and doubts or uncertainties.

It is in this kind of God-talk that the question naturally arises, "What place do personal problems have in the EP?" The tradition of the Church has always been to relegate such problems outside of the EP although, to counteract errors, EPs have been used to affirm dogmatic statements. The novelty of Oosterhuis' EPs are that the faith expressed therein is admittedly sometimes a groping one. The question is, then, should the faith expressed in an EP be a faith purified of all doubts—as, for example, in the Church's creeds—or may an EP express itself in questions, conditionals, and personal difficulties, a sort of "I believe, help my unbelief," with some emphasis given to the latter. This question is not so easily answered if we remember that the EPs about which we are speaking were composed for a specific congregation.

It is worth examining more closely Oosterhuis' preoccupation with the importance of the "name" of someone. In Prayers 1 and 2, the Doxology is in the traditional form but with one significant change: Oosterhuis substitutes "your name will be made holy" for "glory and honor to you." It amounts to the same thing except that this manner of expression is more typical of Oosterhuis, who is influenced by the Semitic respect for the name of God and the understanding that the name of the person is the person. From a liturgical point of view, all that Oosterhuis says about the name is a gloss on the Benedictus, "Blessed is he who comes in the name of the Lord" as well as the "hallowed be thy name" of the Our Father. "To come in the name of the Lord" is, according to the context of these Prayers, to do things for people and/or to be the image of the love of God for us. In Prayer 3 this becomes clear where the Benedictus as such disappears in favor of the following extrapolation:

> Blessed are you, the God of the powers, and blessed is he who comes in your name, Jesus Christ, your Son in this world, our shepherd until we die, our example from day to day, so that we may do what he did, so that we may become new people, bread and peace for each other.

From a study of all the Prayers, we get a well-rounded view of Oosterhuis' understanding of the importance of the name. Thus, man's honor and safety is to speak God's name and stand before him in an attitude of expectation (4). God is called "God of people" by man (a shortened form of the "God of Abraham, Isaac, and Jacob), and he himself said that his name was "I shall be there for you" (5). This God calls all the living by their names so that they may rejoice in him (5). Since Jesus came "invested with [God's] name" and "inspired by [God's] name," it is *through this Jesus* that the community comes into contact with God: "we ask you this through Jesus your Son."

Although Prayer 6 tells us that God is incomprehensible ("You cannot be thought of or named"), he nevertheless sent Jesus of Nazareth, whom he called and predestined to be the *angel of his name*, that is, the messenger of his faithfulness. Of course, it is Jesus who taught us to say, "Our Father."

Prayer 7, which is a beautiful Prayer constructed around the theme of "opening," begins with the "philanthropos" concept (familiar to the Greek anaphoras) put in the form of a question by the choir: If there is a God who loves men, what is his name? The celebrant then addresses this God who loves men as "You, who know what is in us and understand what never can be said," substituting the explicative clause for the adjective "omniscient." The congregation also addresses God as "You," but continues "with your name unnamable" and then follows an attempt to name God with a string of epithets. As always, it is Jesus of Nazareth who leads men to God. Partaking of the bread and wine, the congregation hopes to act in such a way that God's name may be lived, made holy on this earth.

However, in Prayer 9, even though men are unable to achieve peace and justice, God still calls them by their names, that is, individually, to do justice and to be good. On their part, they do not want to "forget [God's] name." That is why they keep their eyes fixed on "Jesus of Nazareth, who made [God's] name holy" and whose promise to men is that "he will give us a new name. . . . He is our way through death."

The last Prayer, Prayer 10, which is special in the whole corpus and observes its own interior laws, has the interesting phrase "whatever your name is" with reference to God. This testifies to the experience of man when God seems to be silence to him. At moments like that man can only endure the silence.

There are, then, several constants in these references to the "name." First, there is the impossibility of naming God. Secondly, one is obliged to name him anyway. This one does through God's relationship to man seen in his dealings with the Jews and with Jesus, who came in his name and shows man how to name God, especially as "Our Father." In the third place, God calls men by their names so that their lives may hallow his name. Since God is unnamable man cannot possess him, but when God calls man by his name man's very existence is in play. This relationship between God and man reached its ultimate development in Jesus of Nazareth, the messenger of God's name, he who comes in the name of the Lord, he through whom men go to God.

In the Roman EPs, we saw that generally a "Son-cluster" or a "Christ-cluster" were favored when talking about Jesus Christ. In all cases, however, there was no time when the simple pre-Easter event name "Jesus" was employed.

It is significant that in the Oosterhuis EPs the designation Jesus Christ appears only in Prayers 1 to 3 and "Lord" in 1 and 2. One of his favorite expressions is "Jesus of Nazareth" (2 and 5 to 10). Generally the references to Jesus Christ are varied, quite often taken from Scripture and frequently ear-catching. Oosterhuis' avoidance of the traditional designations is a result of his obvious desire to emphasize Jesus as our mediator and his wish to avoid such theological terms as "Savior" or the traditional "Our Lord Jesus Christ," especially in the latter Prayers. There is a definite penchant to use the word "man" in relation to Jesus:

this unforgettable man (1, 4)
image and likeness of your love of man (2)
taken from among men (2)
man of grace (2)
least among men (4)
this man (4)
your man (5)
son of men (6, 9)
a man (7)
that man (7)
God for all men (8)
this son of men (8)

This is perfectly in line with Oosterhuis' continual underlining of Jesus as man's mediator. It is Jesus who makes it possible for man to go to God.

What is interesting in the references to Christ is that there is no clear-cut difference between EPs 1 to 6 and 7 to 10. Prayer 10 is the only one that stands out by using a single reference to Jesus Christ, "that man Jesus of Nazareth," which in its own context is perfectly consistent.

Sometimes Oosterhuis builds up references to Jesus drawn from Scripture, e.g., in Prayer 4:

the beginning and end
first to be born from the dead
light of the world
first born of all creation
least among men

In Prayer 6, Jesus is "the angel of your name," "messenger of your faithfulness," and "servant without form or distinction." These references arise from the context of Psalm 91 where Yahweh says:

Yes, if he clings to me I will rescue him,
I will make him great, for he holds on to my Name.
If he calls, I will answer. In anguish and need: I with him,
I will make him free and clothe him with glory.

He shall live to be full of years.
He shall live to see my rescue. (II, 25)

"Angel of your name" corresponds to "I will make him great for he holds on to my Name." "Messenger of your faithfulness" corresponds to the whole thrust of Yahweh's pronouncement and, in particular, to "if he clings to me I will rescue him." "Servant without form and distinction" corresponds to the promise to "clothe him with glory" so that he is no longer "without form or distinction."

In Prayer 7, where the speaker sees that the way to the peace of God is through suffering, Jesus is referred to as "he who gave his whole soul,/ was poured out like water,/ a lamb slaughtered,/ piece of bread broken, cup of wine drunk. . . ." The piling up of image upon image, each with its own nuance, holds in the air for a measured moment Jesus' terrible suffering and emptying of himself.

So it is that Oosterhuis' references to Jesus are constantly justified by their context; their frequency and variety are explained by his poetic practice of "piling up images" and by the different situational viewpoint the praying community is adopting.

In the Roman EPs we remarked the seeming serenity of the "we," the praying community. The "we" of the Oosterhuis EPs is considerably different. The praying community reveals itself particularly in two places: in its first address to God and in its Petitions. The community is aware of its solidarity with all men in the world of here and now: "You have made us great and small, each one of us different in heart and face, but all of us your people" (5). Oosterhuis has commented on this solidarity in a sermon:

But at the same time we also admit in this gesture [of the breaking of bread] that we hold to that vision of a future world where there is justice, where we do not tear each other to pieces, but do what is unthinkable and impossible and are what we cannot be yet—people living in peace. (II, 5)

If there is one feeling of guilt that the community shares, it is that man is not a man of peace. This is reiterated constantly:

Curb our passions that make us seek each other's lives (1)

build up peace (2)
we may become bread and peace for one another (3)

we may be your peace in this world (4)
keep the plague of war from us (6)
slaves, servants of war, caught in each other's hands/
people who beat and are beaten/ people who kill and die (7)

this world which is always the same of almost-
people and groping hands, world of deaf ears
slaves, servants of war, caught in each other's hands/
and of armed peace (8)
we are unable to achieve peace and justice (9)

The Amsterdam community is obviously not thinking of its own wars, but their solidarity with all men makes them responsible for all wars. Oosterhuis in other parts of his book makes it abundantly clear that the Vietnam war or the Arab-Israeli conflict are very real concerns of his community. In a sermon on guilt and forgiveness, he quotes Camus approvingly:

There are no just people. There are only people who are to some extent poor in justice. The worst criminal and the most upright judge stand shoulder to shoulder. Both are equally wretched and in this they are at one with one another. (I, 57)

Again in a sermon on Christmas, commenting on the Angels' greeting, "Peace on earth," he says:

We should not think of ourselves as being greater than we are. We are, here in this church tonight, no greater than we always have been, but we are people of good will. And we are impotent— too little for the problem of world peace and often too little, or too great, too high-handed, too stubborn for peace in ourselves. (I, 83)

So, in this war-shattered century, the praying community has uppermost in its mind a desire for peace while the witness of war is almost everywhere.
Even if there were no war, the community is still aware of the

ambiguity of life and characterizes itself as "thirsty with restless hearts" (1). It prays to be kept from anxiety and bitterness (2), that good will rescue this world from death (6), that "he will unravel the cords that bind us, powers of darkness, despair, violence" (7). And the depths of its feeling of helplessness are seen in Prayer 10 where the speaker says:

> Just name them then,
> countries and towns
> where life is not worth living.
>
> Then you do not
> take death off our shoulders
> and nobody
> is made better by you.
>
> Just like everyone
> who breathes and looks
> and has no defense
> against the things
> that just happen
> whether there is no God
> who sees everything.

These are strong passages. When they are isolated from their context, they may take on even greater force. It should therefore be remembered that the God of this prayer is not a God who relieves man of his responsibilities or gives man an easy way out. The cheerful optimist of "God's in His heaven, all's right with the world" would not be able to accept this prayer. Despite the movement of You–I it is no Buberian I–Thou that is at work here. It is a meditation on paradox, whose very last line attempts some kind of resolution:

> I should like to do
> something, understand you,
> sit down on your
> doorstep, endure
> the silence that you
> are, that we are.

The contrast of the you and the I is brought together in the "we" of the very last line. And then it is left hanging there.

While this may seem to accentuate negative aspects of life, there is room for a more balanced view in the other Prayers:

we exist, with difficulty, but full of joy
we have touched your heart
we are your heaven and your earth (2)

you have created us man and woman
as people standing shoulder to shoulder
in joy and sorrow, but always toward you (3)

you fashioned man and gave him life
and placed eternity in our hearts (4)

Admittedly these references occur in the earlier Prayers, but the tone of all the Prayers is one of men willing to assume the responsibility for their lives despite the self-destructiveness they see in themselves.

What the Praying Community
Finds Significant To Say
about Jesus Christ

In the section devoted to the praying community's way of referring to Jesus, we saw an attempt made to find meaningful ways of referring to Jesus. Oosterhuis chose images from the biblical tradition and presented them in a spare, precise imagistic way. As we have seen, one image needed another if human speech was to attempt to grasp the significance of Jesus. Here, however, we want to examine more closely what things the praying community is selecting out of all possible things to say about Jesus. More precisely, we want to see the things that the praying community keeps saying again and again about Jesus. These are things they almost have a compulsion to say very much like the iconographical images that painters kept repeating in early Christian art.

First of all, we note the things that are in common with the Roman EPs. The one idea found in all ten Prayers is that Jesus died. This is always stated explicitly although not always in the same way. Some of the synonyms Oosterhuis uses are "was slaughtered" (7), "broken" (7), "drunk" (7), "stripped" (8), "extinguished" (8), "emptied himself" (8), and "was killed" (10). In most of the other Prayers, there are always references to Jesus' suffering, rising, ascend-

ing, being seated in glory, and his coming to judge at a future time.
In Prayer 6, Oosterhuis paraphrases Psalm 91:

> Therefore, God,
> because he did this,
> because he became so small,
> even as far as the cross,
> because *he clung to you*
> and *called you, in anguish and need,*
> you answered him, *rescued him*
> and *made him great*
> and *clothed him with your glory.*
> *He will live to be full of years.*[8]

This use of a poetic language also enables Oosterhuis to take up
some of the key words and use them in reference to the community.
So it is that the community in its Petitions in Prayer 6 calls on the
Lord to "rescue us too."

In common with the Roman Prayers there is always a reference
to the memorial left behind by Jesus. This is done minimally in
Prayer 10; but, in most of the other Prayers, Jesus' taking of the
bread and the wine is done in a more explicit fashion. From the other
Prayers, we know that the community thinks of this taking of the
bread as a memorial (1), a sign of love (2), the body and blood
of Christ (5).

Oosterhuis likes to make Christ's humanity more explicit than
the Roman EPs do. No one who reads the Roman EPs can fail to
see the many explicit and implicit references to Christ's humanity in
them. That is not the point. The Roman EPs do not see any difficulty
with Christ's humanity. The Oosterhuis EPs, however, give the
impression that they do not want their community to forget that
Christ was human. It is very important that Christ's humanity be kept
in the forefront. This is no doubt a strong, some would say an overly
strong, reaction to an emphasis placed on the divinity of Christ, especially in some Eucharistic devotional practices.

Let us see how Oosterhuis stresses the humanity of Christ. First of
all, he insists on using the name of Jesus, a name never used without
some other qualifying title in the Roman EPs. Then, he likes to use
the words "man" and "from Nazareth" as means of describing Christ.
Jesus is "this unforgettable man who has fulfilled everything that is
human" (1), "one of us, taken from among men, Jesus of Nazareth,

---

[8] Emphasis added.

man of grace" (2), "this man" (4), "your [God's] man" (5), "a man," "that man" (7).

Of course, while this accent on "man" is important, it is by no means exclusive. The community has an abundance of expressions to use concerning Jesus. The epithets applied to Jesus and the actions ascribed to him are always in reference to the mission His Father confided to Him and/or His carrying out this mission in regard to man. The Son is the mirror of the Father. This is our expression to summarize those of Oosterhuis: the Son is "the likeness of God's love and goodness" (1), "image of God's love" (2), and "word and form of [God's] glory" (9).

For man, Jesus is the light-bearer, the kingdom-bringer, the redeemer (1), savior, man of grace, herald and giver of a sign of love (2), shepherd, example (3), servant, first-born, (4), messenger (6), everyone, Adam, fire and light, living water, a vine, a word (8), a new name-giver, and our way through death (9). This foregoing list is not exhaustive since we have already seen in other parts of this chapter those epithets or images that have been omitted. The list is rich, meaningful, and, what is more, often surprising, a quality that is not unimportant in any public discourse.

There is no reference in these Prayers to the fact that Jesus was born of Mary. These Prayers prefer to emphasize Jesus' relationship to God, who called and sent him (1), light of his light (2), who came in God's name, His son in this world (3), God's servant sent by Him (4), His Son invested with His name (5), the messenger of His faithfulness (6), the way to God (7), through whom God spoke and who was born of Him (8). Also, as we have seen above, they show what we have called a "mirror relationship" to God. Thus, the divinity of Christ is not neglected at the expense of his humanity, although in the latter Prayers clear references to this divinity are lacking.

Jesus' relationship to men is shown by choosing events in His life or by summarizing what He is for men as a result of what He did for them. The first Prayers speak of the messianic acts accomplished by Jesus: He brought God's kingdom to the poor and redemption to captives (1), gave sight to the blind and life to the dead (2). But the remainder of the Prayers concentrate on Jesus' fulfilling everything and giving Himself not only on the cross but also in the bread. Having emptied Himself for all men, "He can do nothing else but be our God, God for all men in this our world."

In its Anamnesis-Offering, Roman EP II refers to the death and resurrection of Christ. Every EP should have some reference to

Jesus' suffering and exaltation. Except for Prayer 10, which is a special case and refers only to Jesus' being killed, all the other Prayers have this balance, but the language employed is sometimes more poetic than credal, more connotative than denotative, precisely where the traditional EPs prefer a more denotative language. Thus Prayer 6, based on Psalm 91, sees Jesus' death and resurrection in terms of His becoming "so small, even as far as the cross, because he clung to you, in anguish and need, you answered him, rescued him and made him great and clothed him with your glory. He will live to be full of years."

Prayer 7 stresses the death of Jesus:

Jesus of Nazareth . . . who gave his whole soul, was poured out like water, a lamb slaughtered, piece of bread broken, cup of wine drunk

but insufficiently, because too implicit, expresses the Resurrection, even though it correctly links this Resurrection to the Eucharist:

If, then, that is life for this world, give us around this bread and this cup, the strength to be him, and that, through us, in us, your name may be lived . . .

Prayer 8 runs into the same difficulty:

And therefore he emptied himself for friend and stranger, for good and evil, and at his wits' end and for eternity could and can do nothing else but be our God, God for all men in this our world.

These passages obviously raise the whole question of the desirability of using a poetic language in the EP. We know Oosterhuis' position on this question, but we also know that it is not the practice of the Roman tradition.

In the preceding pages, it has been pointed out that Oosterhuis not only has evolved the form of the EP, but also has altered its content by giving more place to the expression of man's groping in the faith. This results in EPs that are far different from the usual expectation of a Catholic EP; for example, we have seen that the expression of Christ's divinity is less precise than that found in usual liturgical practice. In the section that follows, this same tendency will be noted with regard to the change of the bread and wine into the Body and Blood of the Lord.[9]

What the Praying Community Says about
the Action It Is Accomplishing
and the Elements (Bread and Wine) It Uses

In the Roman EPs, the community refers to the bread and wine in Epiclesis I and asks that it become the Body and Blood of Christ. In Oosterhuis' Prayers, there is never any similar clear formulation within the heart of the Prayer. Often there is only the minimum reference in the discourse to the elements or the action. Perhaps, this would not be noteworthy if the Institution Narrative were found in every Oosterhuis EP, but it is lacking in Prayers 7 and 10. However, rather than summarize our findings, let us look at each Prayer separately.

Prayer 1 refers to "this bread, this cup" after the Institution Narrative, the eating and emptying of which proclaims the death of the Lord until he comes. It is this "sign of our faith" that the community presents to God. At the very end of the EP as the community is about to receive, the discourse continues: This is the forgiveness of our sins. This is the body, broken for you.

Prayer 2 is similar but it adds before the Institution Narrative that what Christ did was a sign of his love, and at the reception we have the rhetorical question:

Does not the cup that we bless
give communion with the blood of Christ?
Does not the bread that we break
give communion with the body of Christ?

Prayer 3, after the Institution Narrative, simply refers to presenting "the sign of our faith." Prayer 4 uses the Pauline formula: 1 Cor. 11, 26. At the reception, the celebrant says to the people: "Come, for everything is prepared,/ The body of Christ will preserve you/ and may the blood of Christ come over us."

In Prayer 5, immediately after the Institution Narrative, the

---

[9] When Oosterhuis uses the words body and blood with reference to the Eucharist, he does not capitalize them. We have followed his usage when we refer to his Prayers.

celebrant says: "with bread and wine/ we remember, until he comes/ his death and resurrection."

In Prayer 6, once again immediately after the Institution Narrative, the community asks God to accept what "we are doing here in memory of him." This is the only reference to the action that the community is performing.

While there is no Institution Narrative in Prayer 7, the discourse does make clear the action it is accomplishing when it says:

> If there is a way to you/ a man/ direct our feet then,/ give us that man./ If it is he, Jesus of Nazareth,/ if there is no one else to expect/ than he who gave his whole soul,/ was poured out like water,/ a lamb slaughtered,/ piece of bread broken, cup of wine drunk,/ If, then, that is life for this world,/ give us, around this bread and this cup,/ the strength to be him. . . .

In Prayer 8, where there is a condensed Institution Narrative, the choir sings: "And in this bread/ here in our hands/ we receive him/ in groping faith—/ your name, your son,/ and our own life/ in joy and sorrow." The community then calls the bread "this small sign" that one day they shall speak of God as man speaks to man. The celebrant says to the people: "Open your hands/ and take this bread/ and peace/ be with all of you."

Prayer 9 has a short Institution Narrative before which it recalls that Jesus became bread and wine for us. At the end of the Prayer, it adds: "We recognize him/ and we proclaim him/ here in the breaking/ of the bread."

Finally, Prayer 10, the most laconic of all, has no Institution Narrative and simply refers to "this simple piece of bread that does not appease our hunger."

Besides the Institution Narrative, when it is included in the EP, the privileged moment for talking about the bread and wine as the Body and Blood of Christ is at the communion (1, 2, 4). But what is to be said of those Prayers that do not have an Institution Narrative? Another way of putting this question from our perspective is to ask, "What does the praying community feel necessary to articulate concerning the Body and Blood of Christ?" This much can be said. The community does not feel obliged to talk about a change taking place in the bread and wine. It calls the bread bread both before and after the Institution Narrative. In fact, in Prayer 8, it is said, "This is my Body, living bread," echoing John 6, 51-52 (see also Roman EP II, which "corrects" Hippolytus because after Hippolytus there has been a dogmatic development with regard to the eucharistic presence), so that the expression "living bread" or just "bread" can refer to the Body of Christ. In the context of:

This is bread,
This bread is my body,
My body is living bread,

where bread moves from bread as ordinary food to bread that is qualified by the word "living," the believer feels no need to articulate what has happened for any outside agency. The "shorthand" of the faith-community permits it to still use the word bread without necessarily calling it the Body of Christ. This is not the developed tradition of the Church, however, and the tendency has always been to make clear the belief as much as possible to avoid any possible weakened interpretation of it.

The Oosterhuis EP prefers to speak of "presenting" (*stellen,* in Dutch "to present") rather than "offering." Yet, in Prayer 5, we are given an inkling as to how we are to understand "present." The community prays, "Accept this sign of our faith . . ." Something is presented, that is, offered in order to be accepted. There seems here to be an attempt to purify the vocabulary employed of any crude idea of sacrifice or that an additional sacrifice is offered. Again, in Prayer 6, we have, "Accept what we are doing here in memory of him." This "what we are doing here" is vague in comparison with the Roman EPs *offerimus tibi . . . hoc sacrificium vivum et sanctum* (III) and *offerimus tibi eius Corpus et Sanguinem* (IV).

The idea of memorial is explicitly mentioned in the Oosterhuis EPs after the Institution Narrative in 1, 2, and 5. But more often the community remembers without designating their remembrance by a substantive such as memorial.

The Place Given to the
Role of the Holy Spirit

Although the place given to the role of the Holy Spirit is rather limited in these Prayers, it is nevertheless well-conceived where it is present. We have already pointed out that Prayers 1 to 6 form one group and 7 to 10 another group, one in which there is greater freedom of experimentation. Thus it comes as no surprise to learn that the Holy Spirit is mentioned in each of the first six Prayers whereas only Prayer 9 of the second group makes any reference to Him. The Oosterhuis practice is to invoke the Spirit, as the first Petition among several, on the community but not on the gifts. The expression "Your Spirit" is used with the exception of Prayer 4, which uses "Holy Spirit" twice.

Prayer 1, after the Anamnesis, asks: Send us your Spirit who is life, justice, and light. The three predicate nouns are not chosen at random for they bring to mind the Preface, in which the community voices the following thanksgiving to God:

> You called us and broke through our deafness, you appeared in our darkness, you opened our eyes with your light, you ordered everything for the best for us and brought us life.

Jesus also was "sent to serve us and to give us light" (Preface), his Resurrection from the dead is recalled and he will come to do justice to the living and the dead (Anamnesis). The role of the Spirit, then, is to continue to give life, justice and light to men for, as the Petitions that follow add, God wants man's well-being and not his death.

In Prayer 2, the Spirit is invoked as "God here among us, friend-ship and truth, life overflowing." Once again it is in the Preface that we find antecedents for these attributes. God is thanked for his friendship with man:

> We thank you that we have been born . . . that within living memory we have touched your heart and that we are your heaven and your earth.

Further in the Thanksgiving, the community prays: "You promise us freedom, life overflowing, and we keep you to your word, Lord our God." Friendship and truth are qualities that will help the community, which asks in the Petitions, to be free for "everyone who is our neighbor so that our hands may build up peace."

The invocation of the Spirit in Prayer 3, "Send your Spirit over us, sustain us and keep us alive, God, give us hope," despite the fact that it can be linked to the thanksgiving for creation and de-liverance in the Preface, is more properly to be seen as a reference to the community's witnessing through the Eucharist to the life of Jesus resurrected by the Father. Immediately before the Epiclesis the community prays: "Let us now share in his life." The form of the Epiclesis determines the petition that follows it: "Let it be seen in your Church that you are not a God of the dead and do not put our trust to shame."

The greeting of the celebrant to the people at the beginning of EP 4 wishes peace from the Father and from his Son "and from the Holy Spirit, who calls in us and breathes in us, who lives in us." This Spirit, the community believes, was sent so that it might do what Jesus has done (Anamnesis). That is why it prays:

Let your Holy Spirit move us so that we may become like this man and that we may be your peace in this world, justice, light of your light, a new beginning of love.

While it is true that there is no explicit reference to the reception of the Eucharist in this Epiclesis, such a reference is inescapable for on the level of discourse "to become like this man" is to partake in "the sign of his love."

Prayer 5 expresses the Anamnesis-offering-Epiclesis in a way that resembles more Protestant than Catholic Practice:

Therefore, Lord God, with bread and wine we remember, until he comes, his death and resurrection. Accept this sign of our faith and send your Spirit down over us.

The Petition that follows takes up the "us," showing that this "us" is made up of all kinds of people who want to be a "new people . . . who hear your voice with living hearts."

The influence Psalm 91 has on EP 6 extends to the Epiclesis, where the community prays: "Send your Spirit, who can protect this world in the dead of night." This echoes the Psalmist's confidence in God: "In the dead of night you have nothing to fear." Although many evils are enumerated in the Psalm and in the EP, the phrase "dead of night" is a good one to sum up all evil and every kind of darkness from which the Holy Spirit ultimately protects the world.

Both Petitions and Epiclesis are found before the Institution Narrative in Prayer 9. The Epiclesis, "Send us your Spirit, give us the power to become people, whatever it may cost us," has reference to the reality that in our world people are separated from one another by war, injustice, and suffering. To become people is to live at peace, establish justice and heal the sufferings of one another. The Spirit is invoked to this end but the community realizes that this will not come about without their cooperation ("whatever it will cost us"). Because of Jesus, recognized and proclaimed in the breaking of the bread, the community is sure that they will become this new people for "he will give us a new name. He is our way through death."

It is regrettable that the Spirit does not find a place in the other Prayers for his role is well integrated in the Prayers we have examined. As we have seen, often there is a preparation, on the level of expression, for the qualities attributed to the Spirit, which in their turn are carried over into the manner of expressing the Petition. The qualities attributed to the Spirit are not His exclusively for they are often attributed to the Father or to the Son, either in the same Prayer or in other Prayers. The community recognizes that it lacks these qualities, but it continues to ask for them with great faith and hope.

5
THE EUCHARISTIC PRAYERS
OF THIERRY MAERTENS
AND HIS GROUP

We have seen the Roman EPs as essentially traditional and the American EPs as trying to achieve a freer expression than the Roman EPs while remaining rooted in the tradition. These American EPs more or less followed the traditional structure and generally kept the traditional structuring of each element within the total structure. There was, however, an attempt to involve the praying community more actively in the EP. We saw also that there was a distinct tendency to express concern for others in terms of social justice and a desire to do something about the ills of this world. More discursive than the Roman EPs, the American EPs attempted to use a language that would recall the biblical events and at the same time allow the community to identify itself with them. The language tended to be simple, direct, and immediately accessible to the community.

The Oosterhuis EPs, the work of an individual and not a scattered group, were quite different from the Roman and the American EPs. First of all, we saw a distinct evolution in thought in the Prayers so that we had to speak of them in terms of two groupings. From his sermons, we were able to have a clear statement of his understanding of God, Jesus Christ, man and the language man uses. Oosterhuis' full involvement in an actual community as well as his vocation of poet afforded him a greater opportunity to elaborate and apply his ideas to the EP. His use of the tradition was much freer and less obvious than the preceding two groups. As we saw, his idea of the EP could be reduced to an address to a You with some reference to the man from Nazareth and the food on the table.

The Maertens EPs sound yet another note. They are influenced by the tradition and by the experimentation of Oosterhuis, but they go their own way. This chapter will study first the justification for

98

the EPs found in the *Livre de la prière* and then the Prayers themselves from our five-fold approach.[1]

Dom Thierry Maertens, who along with Marguerite De Bilde is responsible for the *Livre de la prière,* has long been interested in liturgical renewal, especially its pastoral dimensions. His association with the review *Paroisse et Liturgie,* as well as the series it publishes, and his active participation in the *Guide de l'assemblée chrétienne* have clearly shown his desire to make the liturgy a meaningful event in the lives of the laity. It is no wonder, then, that he should be bold enough to present for publication new EPs. He is a man unafraid to innovate and to provoke reactions. He prefers to do something rather than to hesitate. It is unnecessary to belabor the point: Maertens sees experimentation and evaluation as a necessity for responsible local communities.

In 1963, at the same time the Constitution on the Sacred Liturgy was being prepared, Maertens' *Pour une meilleure intelligence de la Prière Eucharistique* had a second edition.[2] His method in this work was to proceed by analyzing word-groups in the canon from a historical, linguistic and scriptural point of view. Like similar books, it was very informative, but nevertheless served to underline the fact that the Roman canon was very much an archaeological object. In his conclusion, Maertens pointed to the three fundamental elements of the Roman canon: (1) thanksgiving to the Father, (2) remembrance and offering of the work of the Son, and (3) the invocation of the Spirit on the offerings, the persons assembled, and the gifts.[3] He praised the fifth-century redactor of the canon for drawing his vocabulary from the primitive Eucharistic *fonds* and for using important words which had a rich doctrinal history. This led him to suggest that a particularly profound catechesis could be made by studying the principal doctrinal themes through the vocabulary of the canon.[4]

As we shall see, in the ensemble of the Prayers presented by Maertens, these three fundamental elements found in the Roman canon will be preserved (although not necessarily in each Prayer) but not without some adaptation. We would suggest here, however, that Maertens admiration for a vocabulary with a history and its use in catechetics through a thematic approach to the canon is a seed

---

[1] Jean-Thierry Maertens *et al., Livre de la prière,* Paris, 1969.

[2] *Ibid., Pour une meilleure intelligence de la Prière Eucharistique,* Bruges, (Paroisse et Liturgie 42), 1963.

[3] *Ibid.,* p. 149.

[4] *Ibid.,* p. 150.

that helps us to understand what he is doing in these new EPs, which develop word-themes in such a way that it may be said he introduces the catechetics into the EP itself. What the Roman canon suggested, the EP of Maertens makes explicit and develops. We shall return to this when we treat directly of the Maertens EPs.

In *Liturgie et Vie Chrétienne,* Maertens has given his own critique of the new Roman EPs. Some of his comments are revelatory for the EPs he himself has patronaged. He remarks:

> The first essential function of an anaphora is to guarantee the assembly gathered together that everything it is and does is really the actual "reliving" of what Jesus did and was, especially at the Last Supper. From another point of view, the Eucharistic Prayer, not only in its words, but also in the bread and wine and in the presidency, signifies the fidelity in which the assembly means to place itself in relation to the founding-event which Jesus, Christ and Lord, is. In this way, the anaphora does not start out in the first place as a theological discourse which would explain the founding elements of the Eucharist, nor as a simple proclamation of what Jesus does: it is more the profession of faith in which the assembly, by its president, says and carries out its communion with Jesus Christ, gives itself globally to the reality of the meal of the Lord, with all that it is and experiences today in the world.[5]

Thus, Maertens stresses the EP's function in regard to people rather than its function in consecrating the bread and wine. In guaranteeing the link of the present with the past—the fidelity of the community to Jesus Christ—the anaphora is not an explanatory theological discourse nor a proclamation of a past event. Rather, it professes the community's faith that it is in communion with Jesus Christ and that what the community is and does outside the memorial meal is related to the memorial meal. This description of the EP allows Maertens to introduce the everyday lived reality of the assembly into the EP. The movement is from the gift offered to the community's articulation of the gift's meaning, from the memorial of what Jesus Christ did to what the community did, does, and must do in its everyday world. Whereas popular spirituality taught that we bring our "everyday lives" to the sacrifice of the Mass and unite them *mentally* to the offering of the Church, Maertens is suggesting that we

5 Thierry Maertens, "Les nouvelles prières eucharistiques au service de l'assemblée," *Liturgie et Vie Chrétienne* 65, 1968, p. 195.

not only bring them mentally but that we make them explicit. This apparently assembly-centered approach is quite different from that of the EP of the Byzantine Rite as articulated in the *Hymn of the Cherubim:* "let us now lay aside all earthly cares, that we may welcome the King of all things who draws near amidst unseen hosts of angels." In the Maertens EPs, the earthly cares are part of the very material out of which the EP is created.

Maertens criticizes the new Roman EPs for lacking imagination in their thanksgivings, which give a large place to the work of salvation begun by God and its completion in Jesus Christ, but make no mention that God does not cease to act in the present world, within or outside of the Church.[7] His own EPs will try to avoid an emphasis on past events or a sort of static understanding of God's revelation and acting in history.

He finds that the thanksgiving for creation is sometimes formulated in terms of power and providence that the contemporary mentality, strongly impressed by the role man plays in God's creation and by God's humility in becoming flesh in the person of the Son for the service of men, finds difficult to accept.[8] God's power and providence are not denied, but, just as Oosterhuis remarked, today man is not comfortable with high-sounding titles applied to God.[9] Maertens is saying that omnipotence runs the risk of doing away with man's responsibility and that providence risks doing away with man's service to his fellow man. To reply that this is caricature would be to close the debate too rapidly. Maertens is not setting up an either/or; he is simply stating a present emphasis or understanding of the notions of omnipotence and providence. In suggesting that the authors of the new Roman EPs could have been inspired by *Pacem in terris* or *Gaudium et spes* as guides to following the working out of the history of salvation in the contemporary world, Maertens arrives at the heart of his criticism: whereas the Church took contemporary man into consideration in other areas of the Council's work, when it came time to write new EPs it looked backward for its models.[10]

We must now turn our attention, first of all, to the justification given fo the EPs presented by Maertens and Marguerite De Bilde in the *Livre de la prière*. There are five sections pertinent to our in-

[6] Cited in Irénée Dalmais, *Eastern Liturgies,* Donald Attwater, translator, New York, 1960.
[7] Maertens, "Les nouvelle prières eucharistiques. . . , p. 195.
[8] *Ibid.,* p. 197.
[9] *Supra,* Chapter Four.
[10] Maertens, "Les nouvelles prières eucharistiques . . . ," p. 198.

quiry: the Foreword, the Introduction to the first part, the Afterword, the Introduction to the second part, and the note introducing the literary genres (all of which are found in the first part of the book, Prayer in Community). We shall begin our inquiry with the note introducing the literary genres and then take the other four sections in order.

Of the eleven literary genres proposed, three are designated *Action de grâce, Agape,* and *Eucharistie.* These three are distinguished as follows: under *Eucharistie* are classed those prayers which appear closest to the inspiration and outline of the old benediction handed on from Jewish tradition; for *Agape* and *Action de grâce* (the former for meals and the latter for reunions) the authors have taken more liberty with regard to the fundamental eucharistic genre.[11] From these distinctions, it is not clear which correspond to what we would call canon, anaphora, or Eucharistic Prayer. A reading of all the Prayers under the three genre headings show us that it is sufficient for our purposes to study the ten Prayers under *Eucharistie* although there are EPs properly so-called in the other two genres.[12]

The Foreword states the authors' hope that their Prayers may serve as an attempt to find a contemporary liturgical prayer, that is, one completely faithful to the gospel and rich in tradition as well as in tune with everyday living.[13] In terms of the language used in the Prayers, this means wedding the biblical and liturgical language of yesterday with the language of the newspaper, not in an attempt to be modern but rather to be true.[14] Seeing itself as the interpreter of all humanity to God, the assembled group's Prayers have a universal

---

[11] *Livre de la prière,* p. 305.

[12] Those Prayers listed under the genre "Agape" are practically all EPs; those listed under "Action de grâce" are not. Some of the "Agape" Prayers have a similar structure to those under "Eucharistie." Others present differences; for example, "Nous qui n'avons pas vu Dieu," p. 105. In this Prayer, in a most peculiar fashion, the text attributes to Isaiah the Sanctus, which the assembly voices in traditional manner, and then the President says:

> But no angel has come to purify our lips. Heaven and earth are presently full of man's glory. Perhaps we would be worthy apostles of your holiness if we had seen your mighty throne and the cherubim who serve you.

This perhaps is what is meant by the note on the literary genres when it says that greater freedom was taken with the Agape Prayers than with those under the heading of *Eucharistie.* However, the group under *Eucharistie* raises the significant problems that our study wishes to treat. It is enough now to be aware of Maertens' desire to take a larger freedom with language and tone in the Agape Prayers.

[13] *Livre de la prière,* p. 10

[14] *Ibid.*

emphasis, embracing the history of the world and of salvation as well as the broad spectrum of the infinite solidarities of modern man.[15]

The desire to up-date language is not a new one, but the desire to consider the infinite solidarities of modern man and to be the spokesman for all humanity is a new one in the sense that these EPs wish to break beyond the bonds of the visible Church. In other words, what the new Roman EPs did in its Intercessions, these EPs wish to extend to the whole Prayer.

The Introduction to the first part informs us that some Prayers start from life to reach Christ, others start from Scripture, some attempt to be more lyrical than others.[16] The editors' greatest difficulty was to find an expression and a vocabulary that would permit modern man to situate himself before a God who is no longer one who confers social values on nature and history, but one who allows man to make his own discoveries in the very handing over of his liberty and love.[17] This statement recalls Maertens' earlier criticism of the new Roman EP thanksgivings.

It is in the Afterword by Paul Guerin that we have the most comprehensive statement and the best justification of the attempt to write new EPs rooted in the Bible, tradition, and contemporary events.[18] It will be necessary to present Guerin's argumentation at some length.

Guerin is convinced that EPs, "integrally modern and radically traditional," can be created. He begins by pointing out the heterogeneity of the EPs found in the tradition. His characterization of these groups is interesting for they argue not only for a plurality of form but also for a plurality of human approaches. He says that a Eucharistic world is made up of many things: Mozarabic verbosity and Romano-Ambrosian rigor, Gallican spontaneity and Antiochene classicism, Alexandrian simplicity and Ethiopian "letting go." [19] However, while the three new Roman EPs introduce plurality, they are not modern prayers except in their universalist Intercessions. Thus, acceptable as a necessary stage, the Roman EPs remain very far from our modern sensibility.[20] Before explaining this modern sensibility, Guerin sketches the older sensibility in which the authentic faith expressed itself: a sovereign God was "up there" with angels filling the gap between Creator and creature; heaven was everything

[15] *Ibid.,* p. 11.
[16] *Ibid.,* p. 15.
[17] *Ibid.,* p. 16.
[18] *Ibid.,* p. 177.
[19] *Ibid.*
[20] *Ibid.,* pp. 177-178.

and earth just a place of brief sojourn, where Jesus spent some time. The cultic reflex corresponding to this outlook was to adore God, offer to him, make expiation, bring human actions into the divine sphere. Jesus, the High Priest, was the bridge between God and man. The older prayers expressed the faith through this particular religious and cultic mentality. However, there was a tension between faith, which weakens the sacred-profane distinction, and religious sensibility which tends toward the sacred and the cult.[21] Guerin maintains that this tension was found in the older EPs, and he believes it is found in the EPs of Maertens. Religious sensibility, not faith, has changed; the EPs of Maertens echo our modern religious sensibility.[22]

Guerin indicates the "contours" of this modern religious sensibility with regard to faith in God, Jesus Christ, the Church, and the Christian.

The faith of today's man is a sorrowful one, having known and continuing to experience the erosion of unbelief. As in mystical experience, there is a certitude of the presence of God, at once personal but incommunicable. God is the luminous cloud: inaccessible *and* near, mysterious *and* real, incapable of being plumbed *and* knowable. He is in the midst of men. Modern faith thus assumes a sacred dimension, a religious sentiment—not that of cosmic nature but of the human. In this "human-sacred," we have not the sacred of terror but the sacred of giving. Modern Christian faith expresses itself through this latter sacred, the one of man, the one of personal relationship and collective engagement.[23]

Another characteristic of modern spirituality is the desire for an agreement between human experience and spiritual experience. The former is the experience of liberty and responsibility; the latter of the God who is at once wholly other and the source of our deepest being. He is the God of men who come together, a humble God whose transcendence is that of love. This God's glory is the success of man insofar as this success goes over toward the meeting with Him who is the source of this continual need of going beyond oneself. It is for this reason that the cultic sacrifice in its old form gives way to the offering of our entire life, always open to God's call to go beyond ourselves.[24]

Jesus Christ is He who reveals man to himself as responsible, avail-

21 *Ibid.,* p. 178.
22 *Ibid.,* p. 179.
23 *Ibid.*
24 *Ibid.,* p. 180.

able, and humble. Jesus Christ is He who is faithful to God and to His human condition. He is the sign of signs that our human interpretation uses to see God. By Him, we know in our faith that God speaks, acts, and loves. Jesus is the model of the believer, a sinful follower whose only rule is love. He has confronted the human condition in its double nature of life and death. He has shown us that death gives continual birth to life.[25]

The Church is seen as community and as sacrament, the meeting place between Christ and men. Its sinfulness cannot hide its true richness, namely, that it has received the Spirit at work in the assembly.[26]

The Christian's place is in the world, but he is no better than anyone else, being just as much at sea when it comes to choosing and interpreting his values. However, what is characteristic of the Christian is his certitude of *"sens,"* which Guerin extrapolates as "it signifies something is going somewhere"; in other words, there is in life a meaning directed toward an end. This meaning, Jesus Christ risen from the dead, is the center of our faith. We have to proclaim this sense to ourselves as well as to others, for relationship with a person is one of dialogue not one of possession. The Eucharist confronts us not only with a text but also with an event that the rite enables us to appropriate.[27]

Having sketched the contours of the modern sensibility, Guerin next answers possible objections. We may summarize these in a single sentence: Maertens' attempts are a "cultural liturgy," the mere amplification of the spontaneous religious desires of modern man rather than the expression of the central mystery of the faith.[28]

First of all, Guerin says in answer, there was an effort made to be open to all the forms of the modern religious sensibility, especially the binome: intimate/collective. Thus, a single form of sensibility is not absolutized. However, perhaps not enough space was given to other forms of modern religious sensibility: (1) the religiosity which creeps into modern scientific thought, (2) the spirituality of the desert, and (3) the mentality that sees the "need of God" and the "desire of God" in constant dialectical tension. This shows that we need several languages to speak to the same God.[29]

Next Guerin speaks of the problem of writing EPs as the same

25 *Ibid.,* pp. 181-182.
26 *Ibid.,* p. 182.
27 *Ibid.,* pp. 182-183.
28 *Ibid.,* p. 183.
29 *Ibid.,* pp. 185-186.

kind of problem of interpretation that bothers contemporary catechetics. He points out that exegesis teaches us that the New Testament is expressed in categories of representation, expressive myths,
and forms of religiosity that are no longer ours. The New Testament
remains the model of all reinterpretation for our own age, and the
Christian mystery as found therein is transcendent to any and every
verbal or notional representation. The only way this mystery can be
grasped is through the opposite pairs of ideas, sentiments, comport-
ments, and ritual expressions. Today's community must find for itself
the same tensions which guarantee the transcendence of the mystery
of faith. Thus, the community *lives* the mystery of the faith in its
totality, but it is unable to *think* it in its totality by using just one
expression of it.[30] Now, Guerin continues, the EP should express
the understanding a given community has of the Paschal mystery the
rite re-presents. The rite, not the expression, is primary. It is thus
normal and even obligatory to retell in modern terms the awareness
the community has of this rite-bearing salvation event.[31] Like the
New Testament for catechetics, the older EPs serve as models for
every re-expression insofar as they furnish a dynamic structure of
paired ideas which should be found in every liturgical family of EPs.[32]
This stable but not rigid structure has a balanced dynamism: to
praise God for Himself and to thank Him for His presence in
history shows God's transcendence and immanence; to remember
Jesus Christ and to offer and to offer oneself shows *Jesus'* giving and
our giving; to invoke the Spirit on the gifts and on the community
shows the consecration of the elements used at the Mass and the consecration of the world.[33] Because Guerin finds this balanced dynamism in the ensemble of Maertens' Prayers, he believes that they
are "radically traditional," while on other grounds already stated,
they are integrally modern.

Now let us look at the Introduction to the second part of the book,
for which René Berthier, Jean Puyo, and Paul-Gilles Trebossen are
responsible. This second part, as we have seen, is concerned with
the interior worlds of the "individual-sacred" as opposed to the
"collective-sacred." Our interest in this second part is not so much
for any connection it may have with the first part (for they have
been separated precisely because the editors believe them two parts
of the prayer needs of man), but with the light these few pages

30 *Ibid.*, pp. 186-187.
31 *Ibid.*, p. 187.
32 *Ibid.*
33 *Ibid.*, pp. 187-188.

shed on the attempts of Oosterhuis. What we find separated in the *Livre de la prière,* we find united in the EPs of Oosterhuis.

After justifying the publishing of what are supposed to be "private" prayers, the authors pose the rhetorical question: "Would our prayers be considered too political if they complain, like the psalms, against the injustice at work in our world?" [34] What these editors see as almost a necessary *tone* in their private prayers Oosterhuis puts into his public prayer. The editors acknowledge that their prayers sometimes run the risk of being too concerned with personal insufficiencies and anguish to the detriment of a disinterested praise, but this is precisely the problem contemporary man faces. It is up to each man to transfigure the reality he experiences into the joy of the Gospel, into the conversion of grace.[35] What these editors see as almost a necessary *content* in their private prayers Oosterhuis puts into his public prayer. Finally, the editors believe that they have avoided the trap of *too much* psychologizing, closed pietism, and self-analysis. Some of it is inevitable since today's man was born at the same time as psychology.[36] It is difficult to evaluate what is *too much,* but what we wish to note here is the wariness on the part of these editors of "private" prayers with regard to the self-concept of the "I." *Livre de la prière* has divided into two parts public prayer (collective sacred) and private prayer (individual sacred). The tone, content, and self-concept that it wishes to leave to the second part—therefore outside of the EP—we have seen to be included in the EPs of Oosterhuis.

We shall now attempt to summarize the intentions of the authors with regard to their EPs, after which we shall examine the EPs in themselves. The preceding pages of this chapter have shown us what we may expect in the EPs we are about to study: a thematic approach in which an importance will be given to the assembly's experience of life, God's ongoing revelation in the world, and man's responsibility. These ideas will be put into a language of today (without forgetting biblical and traditional language) that interprets before God modern man's religious sensibility.

As in the previous chapters, we now turn our attention to the structure of the Prayers, the manner in which the praying community addresses God, refers to Jesus Christ, and characterizes itself; what the praying community finds significant to say about Jesus Christ; how the praying community refers to the action it is accom-

[34] *Ibid.,* p. 192.
[35] *Ibid.,* p. 193.
[36] *Ibid.*

ADVENT	LENT	LENT	HOLY WEEK SUNDAYS	SUNDAYS	SUNDAYS	SUNDAYS	SUNDAYS	SUNDAYS	SUNDAYS
Journeying	Temptation Power Desert	Life Death	Night Death/life Recognition, joy	Baptism Liberty Beloved Son Unity	Poverty Wisdom Foolhardiness Utopia Holiness	Love	Bread Poverty	Seed Delay Slowness Patience	Love
Tnksgvg on the theme of journeying	Tnksgvg for JC who fulfills the theme	Tnksgvg for life for JC	Tnksgvg on the theme	Tnksgvg for JC who was baptized	Tnksgvg on the theme	Tnksgvg on the theme	Tnksgvg on the theme	Tnksgvg on the theme	Tnksgvg on the theme
Acclamations	Sanctus	Sanctus	Sanctus		Sanctus Tnksgvg	Sanctus	Acclamations	Sanctus Tnksgvg	Acclamation "Apology"
Anamnesis Acclamation	"Apology"	Anamnesis	Anamnesis Acclamation	Anamnesis	Anamnesis	Anamnesis	Anamnesis	Anamnesis	Anamnesis Acclamation
Offering Memento Epiclesis	Offering "exorcism" with offering	Offering-Petitions Mementos with Acclamations	Epicleses with Petitions	Offering-Petitions	Epiclesis with Petitions	Epiclesis with Petitions of union	Epicleses with Petitions	Offering	Epiclesis Accl Offering Petitions
Offering-Petition								Petition	
Doxology	Doxology	Doxology	Closing address to JC	Doxology	Doxology	Doxology	Our Father	Doxology	Accl

plishing and the elements it is using; and finally what role the praying community gives to the Holy Spirit.

The Structure of the Maertens Prayers

The group of Prayers we have selected to study are those gathered under the genre of *Eucharistie*.[37] When we study the structure of this group, we still see the linking together of elements as in the Roman EPs. From this viewpoint, we can say that all of them begin with a Thanksgiving and most of them have an Anamnesis, Offering, Epiclesis, Intercessions, and a Doxology. Although some of the Prayers have a very modified Institution Narrative, this is generally omitted, not because the authors do not find one necessary, but because its omission leaves the experimental character of these Prayers more evident.[38] The chart on page 111 presents in schematic form the structure of the elements. It is obvious that not all elements are found to be necessary, but there is no element that is consistently omitted. Since the genre *Eucharistie* is by definition a Thanksgiving Prayer, all of the Prayers begin with a Thanksgiving. This Thanksgiving is elaborated in terms of a theme, generally in function of a period in the liturgical year. Naturally, more freedom is given in the selection of themes for those Prayers composed for Sundays throughout the year. Let us consider the themes of these Prayers more closely.

The Prayer for Advent develops the theme of journeying. The choice is a happy one for it allows the author to bring in such ideas as pilgrims, wayfarers, viaticum, exploration, etc. In short, it has innumerable applications, not only to the life of Christ as related in the Scriptures, but also to our own lives today. The choice of journeying as a theme is vast enough to permit many developments of it. Like a good symbol, it is broad enough to permit everyone to find something in it for himself. One may debate the development but hardly the choice of themes. Here is a chart of them:

[37] The Prayers we are considering begin on the following pages of *Livre de la prière:* 1, p. 24; 2, p. 43; 3, p. 62; 4, p. 72; 5, p. 95; 6, p. 102; 7, p. 115; 8, p. 121; 9, p. 127; and 10, p. 137.

[38] A note after the imprimatur of the book says that the imprimatur does not concern the licitness of the prayers published in the book. This hints at why, for practical reasons, there are no Institution Narratives properly so-called in the Prayers under *Eucharistie.* That is why, when we present our chart on the structure of the Prayers, we omit the Institution Narrative element, preferring to put anything resembling this latter under the heading of Anamnesis.

	Prayer 1				
Advent:	journeying				
		2	3		
Lent:		temptation	life		
		power	death		
		desert			
			4		
Holy Week:			night		
			death		
			life		
			recognition		
			joy		
	5	6	7 & 10	8	9
Sundays:	baptism	poverty	love	bread	seed
	liberty	wisdom		poverty	delay
	well-beloved	foolhardiness			slowness
	son	holiness			patience
	unity	utopia			

Since the thematic development is closely followed, the elements are influenced by it in their content. Let us take the Epiclesis as an example. Prayers 1, 4, 6, 7, 8, and 10 have Epicleses. Here is the way each of them unites Epiclesis and theme:

> . . . may your Spirit inspire their [teamsters, firemen, etc.] work because it is for the service of others. (1)

> Spread your joy and your Spirit on new Christians who give a new meaning to their life in asking for baptism. (4)

> Send upon us your Spirit of holiness. May he teach us to read in the hunger of the poor and the sharing of bread, in their desire for instruction . . . so many ambiguous signs of the utopia of holiness. (6)

> May your Spirit gather us around this table with all those who want to be witnesses of love in our world. (7)

> Send, Lord, your Spirit on this bread in order that it render our hearts poor and available, ready and attentive to all the needs of all the hungry. (8)

> We recognize your Spirit at work in the love that men have in their efforts for more social justice . . .
> Lord, send your Spirit who renews the face of the earth. (10)

A simple glance at the Epiclesis and the corresponding theme reveals that an unspecified Epiclesis would simply not do. The theme determines the wording of the Epiclesis. Furthermore, these Epicleses show that nothing that is of the life of man need be left out. The community is open and open-ended insofar as it desires to include all men and be of service to all men.

We could take any other element of the EP; the result would be the same. Every element is seen in function of the theme, with the possible exception of the Doxology, although even this element may be adapted, as in Prayer 1:

> And may all men of good will at the end of their search for happiness live and reign with you with the Son and the Holy Spirit for ever and ever.

Here, of course, one may object that we no longer have a true Doxology since the glory of God is not proclaimed, but surely it is implied.

However, we cannot stop at the study of the assembling of elements as if this were the only structure of these Prayers. The underlying structure is actually something much larger than this, of which we must now take note.

Unlike the Roman EPs which link elements together in a sort of consecutive manner, the Maertens EPs are composed in terms of much larger controlling ideas used chiefly as organizing devices within which the various elements are placed. Generally the assembly's response follows the same pattern. In Prayers 1, 2, 6, and 8, we have a two-part structure, which may be shown graphically:

1	2	6	8
benediction	what God has done	thanksgiving	benediction
petition	what we try to do	petition	petition

In Prayers 3, 7, and 9, we have a tripartite structure:

3	7	9
thanksgiving	thanksgiving	benediction
anamesis-offering	what Jesus said and did	the Son as seed
petition	petition	offering-petition

It will be noted immediately that the Prayers give a large role to Petitions, but these often include the Epiclesis and the Offering. The Prayers also make frequent use of repetitive introductory formulae: "Blessed be you," "Be blessed," "Accept," "We entrust to you," "May we be attentive," and "Send, Lord, your Spirit." These formulae are varied even within themselves and the effect given is one of a litany. In itself, repetition is neither a good nor a bad thing. It can help attention or lead to boredom. These Prayers do not seem to suffer from the latter since the content after the introductory formula is varied enough to remain fresh.

The Way in Which the Praying Community
Addresses God, Refers to Jesus Christ,
and Refers to Itself

The address to God is limited to several preferred titles, of which the most frequent is the simple "Father," found in eight of the ten Prayers (23 times in all). Three variations of this title are used: "Father of Jesus Christ," found singly in five different Prayers; "Father of the living" (once); and "God, Father" (twice). In Prayer 8, the address "Lord," referring to God, is used ten times. This address is preferred by the Assembly in its acclamations and/or responsorial verses. Where there is a Sanctus, we find, obviously, "Lord. God of the universe." The only other title used is "God of men" (once and, no doubt, an imitation of Oosterhuis). This simplicity in the number and choice of titles is reminiscent of the Roman EPs. There is no hesitation in what to name God. He is named as Scripture and tradition have taught the community to name Him.

There is an equal simplicity in the manner of referring to Jesus Christ. We shall list all the titles:

Jesus (4)
Jesus your Son (1)
Jesus Christ (7)
Jesus Christ your Son (4)
Jesus Christ our Lord (1)
Jesus Christ your Son our Lord (1)
Your Son (6)
Your resurrected Son (1)
Your well-beloved Son (1)
Son (1)
Christ (1)

Word (1)
Lord Jesus (1)
Lord (3)

N.B. The figure at the end of each title refers, not to the number of times the title is used, but to the number of Prayers in which the title is found.

Only Prayer 10 does not use the title Jesus in one of its forms, and only Prayer 2 omits using the expression Your Son. We have seen that the Roman EPs and the American EPs (with one exception) avoided using the simple name Jesus without qualifiers whereas the Oosterhuis EPs used it frequently along with other circumlocutions for the name, such as "that man from Nazareth" or "this unforgettable man." Let us take a look at the four uses of the simple name Jesus in these Prayers:

. . . this fraternal meal that Jesus blessed in sign of his victory over temptation and over himself (2)

As the bread born of grain rotting must die to make us live. As the wine born of the crushed grape spreads to make us sing, Jesus lived among us and turned toward God, knocked down by death and reborn from it. (3)

Jesus took bread and wine and offered them to us as a sign of his love. (5)

Jesus died, faithful to his mission and full of goodness for men. (7, where it is an acclamation of the assembly)

Each time the simple title Jesus is used in the body of the Prayer, it is in connection with the bread and wine. In the one time it is used in the acclamation, it is used in a statement about his death in the service of men. There seems to be a clear desire to lay stress on Jesus as human. In Prayer 2, the meal is a sign of Jesus' victory over Himself; in 5, He offers us a sign of His love; in 3, like the rotting grain and grape crushed, Jesus was knocked down by death. Each time the name of Jesus is used here, it seems perfectly appropriate in its context.

The community prefers to characterize itself, not by the method of using nouns in apposition to its "we," but by telling what it does, desires, has, or seeks to change. There is an emphasis in these

Prayers on the community's understanding of itself as universal, open to all. It sees all men as its brothers (1), and it recognizes that it has a mission to all men (2). The assembly is made up of men who want to share what they have with others (5), to build up the world (5), liberate men (5), be peace-makers (7), and be attentive to the signs of the times (5). The members of this assembly feel called to be witnesses of love in the world (7). Generally, this characterization comes after or accompanies another role that the community fulfills, namely, blessers of God (8).

However, they are also aware that they have a mortal wound (3), that in them there is a constant struggle between death and life (3): they fall (2), they are forgetful (2), they court the powerful (2), and they repent of these things (2). If they do not do these things personally, they assume a responsibility for them so long as the visible Church is marked by imperfections.

This is a community, then, that has a concern for other men, that cares about the world. In its limited gathering, it goes out to all men. Of course, this is not to say that the communities in the other Prayers we have studied cannot say the same things about themselves. We must recall that we are limiting ourselves to what the praying communities say about themselves in their EPs. The Roman EPs, for example, do not bring these things into their EPs as explicitly as we find them mentioned here. The Roman Prayers always concentrate more on what God has done and what Jesus Christ has done. So it is obvious that, if we confine ourselves to the EP of a given community, we find out more about their aspirations with regard to their fellow men than we do in other communities; less obvious is the need or the desirability of doing this in the EP.

Finally, we may mention that the tone of these Prayers is quite different from that of the Oosterhuis EPs. The emphasis in the former is more positive, less given to concentrating on the unpleasant. Whether or not it is overly optimistic is another thing, but whatever optimism it professes is a result of Christ's victory over death. Of this, its faith is sure.

What the Praying Community
Finds Significant To Say
about Jesus Christ

Of all the things that the praying community can say about Jesus, what does it actually choose to articulate? First of all, in one way or

another, it insists from Prayer to Prayer on Jesus' humanity. The
picture we have of Jesus is largely dependent on the theme of each
Prayer, but it is a consistent picture. What kind of man was Jesus
according to these Prayers? He was completely available to other
men (1). He shared His viaticum (1), His hope (5), His holiness
with them (6), His brothers (1). The most complete man (7), the
image of God (2), He rejected the temptation to exalt Himself (2).
Companion of sinners (8), lover of the poor, the least of men (8),
He is a model who showed us how to live and die and revealed
kindness, fidelity, courage, obedience, and love (7). Full of love,
He wanted to unite all peoples, served His brothers, and tried to
overcome death (5).

What did God do for Jesus? He glorified and gave Him divine life
in fulness (2). In resurrecting Him, God gave a meaning to our life
and allowed Jesus to bring His task to fruition (4). He is the First-
born of those who wish to love. Now His presence shines out in all
the universe (4). He is present in the history of men (4), whom
He assembles around a table (7) and takes His place among them
(4). He is the mediator, guaranteeing that death will never again
have the last word, that liberty will be strangled no more, that God's
will is accomplished (5).

What the community articulates about Jesus is that He died and
rose, that He left behind a memorial of this. All else is commentary
on this idea. There is a clear attempt to avoid language that summarizes this faith too rapidly; for example, the implications of the
expression "glorious ascension" are spelled out in terms of their
meaning for Jesus and, what is more, for man.

The two scriptural passages that serve as background to most of
what the community has to say about Jesus come from Philippians
and Colossians, the two famous Christological hymns. It can do no
harm to cite them here.

His nature is, from the first,
divine, and yet he did not see,
in the rank of the Godhead, a
prize to be coveted; he dis-
possessed himself, and took the
nature of a slave, fashioned in
the likeness of men, and presenting himself to us in human form;
and then he lowered his own
dignity, accepted an obedience

He is the true likeness of the God
we cannot see; his is that first
birth which precedes every act
of creation. Yes, in him all created things took their being,
heavenly and earthly, visible and
invisible; what are thrones and
dominions, what are princedoms
and powers? They are all created through him and in him; he

which brought him to death, death on a cross. That is why God has raised him to such a height, given him that name that is greater than any other name; so that everything in heaven and on earth and under the earth must bend the knee before the name of Jesus, and every tongue must confess Jesus Christ as the Lord, dwelling in the glory of God the Father.   (Phil. 2, 6-11) takes precedency of all, and in him all subsist. He too is that head whose body is the Church; it begins with him, since his was the first birth out of death; thus in every way the primacy was to become his. It was God's good pleasure to let all completeness dwell in him, and through him to win back all things, whether on earth or in heaven, into union with himself, making peace with them through his blood, shed on the cross.   (Col. 1, 15-20) [39]

To be sure, it is the Philippians passage that receives more emphasis, especially because of the *kenosis* idea, which so easily translates itelf into Jesus the man for others. Even though John's message of love for one another is at the heart of all these Prayers, the starting point, insofar as the praying community is concerned, is not so much that God sent His son into the world, in the sense that divinity became humanity, but rather that Jesus was exalted, in the sense that His humanity was rewarded. Both Roman EP II and IV speak of God *sending* His Word, His Only-begotten into the world, but the Maertens EPs never use the word "send." There are at least three Prayers in which this word could have been used, but in all three cases another form of expression was chosen.

> We thank you for Jesus Christ, our Lord, the first of men in whom your resemblance remained faithful and perfect. (2)

> Blessed are you, Father, for your son Jesus Christ. He came to the Jordan to put himself among the remainder of the poor and to share with them the hope of your Kingdom. (5)

> God of men, we praise you for the most complete man, Jesus Christ, your Son. (7)

[39] Both of these passages follow the Knox translation, New York, 1954. Any translation of these passages will present difficulties. One has only to recall the reaction in France in 1971 when the Palm Sunday reading was the Philippians passage.

At no time is there any mention of the idea of sending as of something from the outside to the inside. What these Prayers seem to wish to do is to avoid any reference that may create the impression that Jesus was not fully man. There is, of course, no question of denying the divinity of Jesus; rather it is more a question of another emphasis and of creating a certain attitude in a far from perfect community. Because men are so aware of the struggle in which they are engaged, of the constant assaults on the meaningfulness of life, of the vast number of down-trodden in the non-technologized societies (and the scandalously great number of down-trodden within the technologized societies), these Prayers wish to start from the idea of a Jesus struggling to overcome death in all its forms—in sickness, hunger, and despair—in order that the assembly truly accept a flesh and blood Jesus. It must be clear that the emphasis on the humanity of Jesus is biblical as well as a safeguard against ever latent forms of docetism. arianism, apollinarianism in our spontaneous attitudes toward Jesus. The delicate balance to be maintained between Jesus' humanity and divinity—the very formulation is itself an obstacle—is a constant theological necessity.

What the Praying Community Says about
the Action It Is Accomplishing
and the Elements (Bread and Wine) It Uses

As in all the EPs we have studied, the community thanks, praises, remembers, offers, and petitions. We have seen that quite often the major portion of each Prayer is given to benediction (that is, thanking and praising) and petition, that in four of the Prayers a specific mention of offering is omitted. Since the community believes it does what Jesus did, we may apply to its action what it says Jesus performed. The community characterizes what Jesus did as sharing His viaticum (1), giving a meal (6), making Himself bread (8). He Himself has called together the present assembly (7) and multiples the bread for them (9). To the meal He gave a new meaning, that of love and sharing, of death accepted and destroyed (6). The bread He shared was the sign of His infinite love (7) and of His victory over temptation and Himself (2). The community is conscious of repeating His gestures (1).

Before we discuss what the community specifically mentions as its offering, we would like to recall the hermeneutical principle stated in Chapter Two: if something applicable to all the Prayers, because it concerns the nature of the Eucharistic action, is mentioned in one of the Prayers, then it may be pre-supposed in those Prayers where it is not mentioned specifically. Thus, when the community says in Prayer 9, "Accept with the sacrifice of your Son, the first fruits of our work . . . ," we may presuppose the framework from which it is operating in each of the Prayers: the present Eucharistic celebration, the memorial of the Last Supper, receives its meaning from the Cross. Nevertheless, for this principle to function correctly with regard to the EP, considered as a text accompanying an action, cares must be taken. If a given element is considered necessary or pastorally useful to the EP, then this element should be omitted rarely, if at all. However, when the inclusion of such an element is the exception, then the principle loses practically all of its meaning with regard to that element or, at the very least, the given element is not considered necessary by these Prayers. Such appears to be the case with regard to the offering found in the Maertens Prayers. We shall now see what the community offers.

Generally, the community offers itself, even if it expresses this offering in different ways and tries to go beyond itself since its vision of the Church is a large one. At the same time, one has the impression that, by studying the offering and the parts related to it, one can establish the psychic grill of a certain kind of twentieth-century man. However, our study is not a psychological one so we shall limit ourselves to the texts.

Eucharistie 1 has three offerings. The first two are found immediately after the Institution Narrative:

> And now, Father, accept the attempts to divest ourselves in the example of Christ so that we may walk more lightly along a more fraternal route. Accept also that our ways may be winding and our streets dead-ends.

The third offering is made somewhat later:

> Accept the hesitations and conversions of your Church . . .

Admittedly the word "accept" presents a problem. Is it really part of the binome "we offer/accept our offering"? The context shows that we are at the borderline of petiton here, in the sense of the "Memento" found in the Eastern anaphoras. The imperatives used in the second part of Prayer 1 are the following: accept (*accueille*), accept (*accepte*), look on (*regarde*), see how (*vois comment*), see (*vois*), accept (*accueille*). These verbs show that there is a certain lack of precision in the vocabulary. Is the Father being asked to accept an offering, to look favorably on man's efforts, to be mindful of those in need, or all of these? There is the possibility that the ambiguity has been desired by the author. But, whether desired or not, there is no offering here in the strict sense. Nevertheless, since other Prayers (5 and 9) show that such words as *accepte* and *accueille* are words used in place of "we offer," we shall so consider them here. The three "offerings" in effect ask God to accept man's fallibility. In the first offering God is asked to accept "the attempts to direct ourselves in the example of Christ." Whether these attempts are successful or not is not indicated. No doubt sometimes they are and sometimes they aren't for the third offering says, "Accept the hesitations and conversions of your Church," whereas the second puts this more imaginatively: "Accept also that our ways may be winding and our streets dead-ends." The theme is, after all, "Route." Prayer 2 reveals the same kind of offering:

> In his name, Lord, we offer you today their [the Church and its members] will of conversion and their desire of fidelity.

This Prayer, which takes its starting point from the temptation of Christ in the desert, describes the Church in these terms:

> But your Church and its members find themselves still in the desert of trial and temptation. Sometimes they fall, tempted to link their influence to the richness of their means. They forget their earthly condition in setting up as an absolute their disciplines and their truths. They allow themselves to slip toward the self-satisfied and the powerful, abandoning the weak and the oppressed.

At this point, the offering cited above follows. The Prayer continues:

> We wish your people to be purified of a spirit of clannishness and of power, of a taste for comfort and security. Deign, Father, to accept our attitude . . .

The offering, with its accompanying descriptions and petitions, takes up practically the whole second part of the Prayer. In contrast to the other Prayers we have studied, this is obviously a preponderant place given over to the "we." There are two things to be noted. The first is that the old "apology," as well as the *Oratio fidelium,* seems to have found its way in here. Secondly, there is a movement from first person pronoun to the third person pronoun; and, while the former is contained in the latter, one wonders why the first person plural was not adopted throughout. The shift from one pronoun to another unfortunately hints at some kind of lack of identification on the part of the speaker with the Church whose faults he is describing.

This is not true of Prayer 3, which offers to the Father, "our human life, given over to death and nevertheless unique, temporary but still precious." This offering, in the context of an EP constructed around the theme of Resurrection, successfully weaves in and out scriptural allusions, the mystery of salvation, and references to the members of the assembly.

Prayers 4, 6, 7 and 8 have no specifically expressed offerings beyond the offering of praise and the constant petitions that the assembly follow the example of Christ. The Offering of Prayer 5, "Accept, Father, our good will as you accepted the offering of your Son on the cross," is well integrated into its context, where the community accepts the mission of service and reconciliation that the Eucharist confers on Christians. The petitions that follow elaborate on the kind of good will this should be. Yet, there is something wrong with the wording of this offering. First of all, instead of referring to the sacramental sacrifice, it refers to the unique sacrifice of the Cross as a past event, the present event being the community's self-offering. Secondly, the manner of expressing the request to "accept our good will as you accepted the offering of your Son on the cross" has the effect of lessening the Son's offering since two things are put in comparison which are not comparable. In Prayer 9, this is better expressed:

> Accept, Father, with the sacrifice of your Son, the first fruits of our work, our joy of collaborating in his reign over all the world, our desire of seeing happiness spread to all men.

Here the sacrifice of the Son is put first but in such a way that the Church offers itself along with the offering of the Son. Furthermore, the sacramental offering of this sacrifice is put in the context of the commemorative meal both before and after the offering.

Finally, Prayer 10, built around the theme of love shown by the Father, the Son, and the Holy Spirit, has the following offering:

We offer you Father, with the love of your Son, the heartfelt unity of our assembly, its fidelity to the Church, spread across the world, its love of men today.

This offering is equivalent to that in Prayer 9 for the love of the Son, a reflection of the love of the Father, is seen in His giving Himself "even unto death." This love He showed "the evening when he assembled his friends for the last time and gave himself completely to them."

Taken as a whole, then, these Prayers do not see the need to express explicitly an offering. When they do express an explicit offering, the emphasis is generally on their own self-offering. When not expressed explicitly, the offering can often be inferred from the kind of petitions addressed to the Father.

When we asked the question, "What does the community find significant to say about the action it is performing?", we were thinking in terms of the Eucharistic action of offering. That is why our discussion centered around that particular point. We have seen that for these Prayers that is not the essential one. In this sense, the Roman and American EPs are more concerned with being texts accompanying an action. The Maertens Prayers attempt to illuminate less an action than the Gospel in the light of experience and experience in the light of the Gospel, while at the same time speaking in behalf of all creation. We have already stressed this effort at human solidarity in another part of this chapter. These Prayers, considered in themselves and not as EPs, are remarkable for their effort to show what it means to be a responsible, mature Christian today. They are sufficiently nuanced not to be naively optimistic and sufficiently attached to the Pascal Mystery not to be unduly pessimistic.

The Place Given to the
Role of the Holy Spirit

Since most of these Prayers have a Doxology, the Spirit is generally mentioned there from Prayer to Prayer. However, in our study of the structure, we saw that many Prayers do not have an Epiclesis properly so-called. Also, when there is an Epiclesis, the invocation is rarely on the gifts. Yet the Spirit is mentioned rather often, and this presents certain problems.

In Prayer 1, the Spirit is invoked, not on those assembled, but on those the praying community is interceding for: "May your Spirit inspire their work because it is for the service of others." This leads us to ask if the Spirit should be invoked on those not present when it has not already been invoked on those who are present. The question shows that once more we are confronted with the meaning to be given to the Epiclesis as part of the EP. If an Epiclesis is by definition the invocation of the Holy Spirit on the gifts or on the assembly (as the tradition of the anaphoras would seem to have it), can an invocation of the Holy Spirit on all forms of absent truck drivers be considered an Epiclesis? Of course, from the simple viewpoint of the EP as literary genre, it is evident that any literary creation has the right to test the limits of its genre. However, here we are concerned more with an action than a text.

There is no Epiclesis in Prayer 2, but there is what may be called an exorcism (not in the strict sense) in the desire to purify [us] "of our spirit of clannishness and of power, of our taste for comfort and security."

It is Prayer 4 that gives the largest place to the Spirit. In the Thanksgiving, we are told, "Your love and Your Spirit equipped us with boldness and courage." Then, addressing Jesus Christ, the Prayer continues: Your heart, opened by the lance, flows with blood and water, with the Spirit, with life and with joy. Then, in three successive Petitions, Jesus is asked to

> Spread on the Church your life and your Spirit . . . Communicate your life and your Spirit to our departed . . . Spread your joy and your Spirit on new Christians . . .

Perhaps the intention of the author is understood, but there does seem to be a weakening of the teaching about the Holy Spirit by juxtaposing the Spirit with the words life and joy. It is not our intention to explain how each of these may be consonant with one another. What we do wish to point out is that credal and liturgical formulae are usually very carefully worded. However, here, where Jesus is asked to spread His joy and His Spirit on new Christians, the impression given is that joy and Spirit are two things of the same order. Yet joy is a fruit of the Spirit that usually comes from living in obedience to the Spirit. Thus, it is possible to give more space to the Spirit but to lessen His role. It is characteristic of theological language, when used by the expert, to be boring but precise; when used by the non-expert, it can seem more interesting but often its meaning becomes blurred.

In Prayer 5, the community says, "We repeat this gesture in the grace of his Spirit and the praise of his Name." The first half of the prepositional phrase is somewhat reminiscent of Hebrews 10,29, where we have "the Spirit of grace." However, there is a difference between "the grace of his Spirit" and the "Spirit of grace." The latter, according to Mateos, should be understood in the sense that the Holy Spirit is the gauge and the richness of the divine favor (charis).[40] The former refers to something that comes from the Spirit. The latter, used in the liturgy of St. John Chrysostom, is developed therein; the former has no development. Furthermore, we may ask what is the meaning of "in" (*dans* in the French original) since it is governing both the grace of His Spirit and the praise of His Name. Once again juxtaposition seems to make for ambiguity: it sounds nice, but what is it saying?

Prayer 6 invokes the Spirit several times, each time with a Petition attached, under the title of "Spirit of holiness." Prayer 7 asks that the Spirit gather the community around the table with all those who wish to be witnesses of love in this world. Once again we note the universalizing tendency of the community: rather than invoke the Spirit only on those present, they ask for a joining together with certain men not present.

In Prayer 8, the community asks the Lord to send the Spirit five times, each time accompanied with a Petition. The first time we have an invocation on the bread, but not that it be changed into the body and blood of Christ, but that "our hearts be made poor and available, ready and attentive to all needs and hungers." The Prayer continues:

> Send, Lord, your Spirit on men whose names are well-known in this world and whose influence on events is decisive, in order that they mobilize against suffering and misery all the resources of intelligence and love.

> Send, Lord, your Spirit on our countryside, on agricultural workers, on those who make bread and all foods.

We have already mentioned the problem that these Prayers pose in invoking the Spirit on those not present; here, however, the problem is of a somewhat different nature. It is not so much that these Pe-

[40] J. Mateos, "L'action du Saint-Esprit dans la liturgie dite de S. Jean Chrysostom," *Proche-Orient Chrétien,* Tome IX, Fasc. 111 (July-September, 1959), p. 196.

titions might just as well be in the "Universal Prayer" at the end of
the Liturgy of the Word, but that the use of such a formula as "Send,
Lord, your Spirit" as an introductory one for Petitions has the effect
of lessening the Epiclesis as a special Prayer either over the gifts or
the assembly.

Finally, in Prayer 10, whose theme is love, the Thanksgiving
begins with the words:

> You have given us your Spirit
> you have placed love in the heart of men
> so that the husband loves his wife
> and parents love their children.

It is possible that a line or some punctuation has been dropped after
"your Spirit," but we may presume that it appears as the authors
intended. The impression given is that the Spirit is placed in the
heart of men. This interpretation is supported by a later Acclamation: "For your Spirit who dwells in our hearts, Glory to you, Lord."
Does, then, the Spirit equal the love a man has for a woman just as,
for example, the Spirit is the love the Father has for the Son and the
Son has for the Father in Trinitarian theology? The Prayer continues:

> We recognize your Spirit at work in the love men have for one
> another, in their efforts for more social justice, in their attempts
> for peace between nations, in the great expectation of humanity
> which leads men to change the face of the earth in order to
> make it live according to the rhythm of your life. Lord, send
> your Spirit who renews the face of the earth.

This seems to be a better way to speak of the role of the Spirit than
the way used at the beginning of the Prayer. We may note also that
the Prayer's invocation is in line with the tendency of all the Prayers to place the emphasis on man's responsibility. The Spirit renews
the face of the earth through men who change the face of the earth.
Man's responsibility for the secular project is the Holy Spirit at work.

6
CONTEMPORARY EUCHARISTIC PRAYERS AND THE PROBLEMS THEY POSE

Now that we have analyzed our four groups of Prayers individually, we shall discuss the problems they present to us in a broader context. First of all, we shall begin with a study of the Reformation background, which will place in perspective and help identify some of the problems of current experimentation with the EP. Then, we shall reexamine all the EPs studied so that by comparison and contrast we may highlight their differences. This will give us a better understanding of the present dynamics of experimentation. Next we shall see what recent speculation on the EP and "God-talk" have to contribute to our study. Finally, we shall discuss the unique place occupied by the Roman EPs in relation to current ecumenical considerations.

I

BACKGROUND: THE LAST MAJOR PERIOD OF EXPERIMENTATION
WITH THE EUCHRISTIC PRAYER: THE REFORMATION

The Reformation was the last period of history when widespread major experimentation with the Eucharistic Prayer took place. Luther, Zwingli, Calvin, and Cranmer—to mention only the major Reformers—all made substantial changes in the Roman canon or abandoned it entirely in order to bring the Eucharistic action in line with their own understanding of the memorial of the Lord.[1]

Two precepts governing the changes made by the Reformers were to avoid superstition and to recover evangelical practice. Hence the

[1] For what follows we have used the texts collected in Bard Thompson, editor, *Liturgies of the Western Church,* Cleveland, 1961.

Lord's Supper (to say Eucharistic Prayer would be to misrepresent what took place) was organized in such a way that emphasis was placed on the distribution of both the bread and the wine, the kind of presence of Christ in the elements, and the sentiments believers should have at the reception of communion. The idea that the Mass or Worship Service is a sacrifice was eliminated; the Thanksgiving for creation and redemption was diminished or replaced by a Thanksgiving for the bread and wine during or after the reception of communion; and exhortations to be worthy [2] as well as explanations of the one sacrifice of the Cross were introduced.

In attempting to correct abuses and to articulate their own understanding of the meaning of the Eucharistic liturgy, the Reformers broke the unity of the Eucharistic Prayer. Their need to explain what was being done in order that the people not think something magical was taking place led them to neglect the address to God by a collective "we." In its place was often substituted an address, generally didactic, to the congregation. The overriding concern with Scripture and scriptural warrant led the Reformers to concentrate less on praising God and more on telling the people what they should be doing and what kind of reverence and dispositions they should have. This overflow of the exhortatory and moralizing word was also, no doubt, due to the fact that all those extra actions or things that the Catholic Church employed—such as incense, ringing of bells, the elevation of the species, vestments, etc.—and which created a mood and attitude, were often abandoned. It thus became the responsibility of the spoken word to create the mood (just as Shakespeare had to do to make up for the bareness of the Elizabethan stage). Furthermore, if Catholic ecclesiastical practice and popular teaching with regard to the Mass at that time had not given rise to abuses—exaggerated fruits of the Mass, Prefaces with legendary content, votive Masses with various monetary values—ignorance and superstition would not have had to be attacked within the celebration of the Lord's Supper. [3]

Strangely enough, the Institution Narrative, which was given such great emphasis in the Protestant liturgies as the warrant for the Reformers' actions, loses some of its force due to an exaggerated concentration on it *as a text* rather than part of the oral narrative

---

[2] The Pauline text in 1 Cor. 11:27-29 was decisive for this orientation.

[3] In the "Decretum de Observandis et Evitandis in Celebratione Missae," the Council of Trent listed avarice, irreverence, and superstition among the most frequent abuses. See H. J. Schroeder, *Canons and Decrees of the Council of Trent,* St. Louis, 1950, pp. 423-424. English text, pp. 150-152.

tradition, handed on in the midst of a much larger Prayer, the Roman canon. This is not to say that the Catholic practice, which Calvin regarded as magical mumbling,[4] was without fault, if only because it could give rise to aberrant attitudes, especially on the part of the faithful. However, its presence in the heart of the canon, even granted certain effects which tended to isolate it, preserved its oral force in comparison with the absolutizing and isolating of the text proposed by Calvin, for example, when he has the minister say: "Let us hear how Jesus Christ instituted His holy Supper for us, as Saint Paul related it in the eleventh chapter of First Corinthians." [5] Furthermore, this isolation, as Bouyer has pointed out, with regard to Luther's *Formula Missae* (1523), merely stretched the medieval Latin idea that only the words of institution, isolated from their traditional context, were essential for the Eucharistic consecration.[6] Luther's correct emphasis, that the sacrifice of the Cross was not repeatable, prejudiced him to omit any understanding of the Mass as somehow participating in the one sacrifice. His solution to eliminate any reference to sacrifice in either his *Formula Missae* or his *Deutsche Messe* (1525) leads him to omit any offering at all, even a subjective self-offering made by the believer in his grateful commitment to God's service, elicited by his renewed sense of forgiveness.[7] Although this is the classic Lutheran view as stated by Melanchthon in the Apology of Augsburg,[8] it does not find a clear statement in Luther's liturgies, perhaps because it is supposed as the proper response to God's gift in communion. Luther himself was willing to speak about the Mass in terms of sacrifice when in 1520 he wrote:

. . . we do not offer Christ as a sacrifice, but . . . Christ offers us. And in this way it is permissible, yes, profitable, to call the mass a sacrifice; not on its own account, but because we offer ourselves as a sacrifice along with Christ. That is, we lay ourselves on Christ by a firm faith in his testament and do not otherwise appear before God with our prayer, praise, and sacrifice except through Christ and his mediation.[9]

4 Thompson, *op. cit.,* p. 192.
5 *Ibid.,* p. 205.
6 Bouyer, *Eucharist,* p. 386.
7 *Ibid.,* p. 387.
8 In T. G. Tappert, editor, *The Book of Concord,* Philadelphia, 1959, p. 252.
9 Martin Luther, "A Treatise on the New Testament, that is, the Holy Mass (1520)," translated by Jeremiah J. Schendel in E. Theodore Bachmann, editor, *Luther's Works,* Vol. 35 Word and Sacrament I, Philadelphia, 1960, p. 99.

Further on in the same text, he says:

> . . . I also offer Christ, in that I desire and believe that he accepts me and my prayer and praise and presents it to God in his own person.

None of this is expressed in Luther's liturgies so that it can even be said that if any sacrifice received importance it is that of Christ, by the use of the *Agnus Dei,* the Institution Narrative, and the emphasis given the body *and* the blood.[11] The poverty of the *Deutsche Messe* as a Thanksgiving prayer is a result of a misunderstanding of the commemorative aspect of the Mass. Noting that a cleavage between the Memorial-aspect of the Eucharist and the Communion-aspect had taken place in the Middle Ages, Yngve Brilioth has said that, in trying to restore a unity to them, the Lutheran liturgy found no adequate theological expression for the Memorial-aspect. Thus, the Communion-aspect was treated as primary, and communion was seen as the act whereby the memory of Christ's death is made and the sacrifice of praise offered.[12] The misunderstanding or de-emphasizing of the Memorial-aspect, which resulted in the "sacrifice of praise" being limited to the commemoration the individual makes at communion, is forced on Luther's liturgy by his applying the scalpel to any mention of sacrifice.

For Zwingli, commemoration of Calvary is the real meaning of the Eucharist, but he does not understand the Memorial-aspect in all its force and, in fact, can only understand the Eucharist in a symbolistic fashion. As a result, even more than Luther did, he neglects the Memorial-aspect. He regards the Thanksgiving as an act of fellowship, an act of confession of glad anticipation of a share in salvation. The whole conception is a subjectivist one.[13]

Zwingli's second liturgical creation *Action oder Bruch* (1525) has been pronounced a liturgical masterpiece on the condition that liturgy's purpose is to provide an expression in ritual of a thought-out dogmatic conception. Brilioth writes, "Every detail helps to express the character of the action, as a social meal in remembrance of the

[10] *Ibid.,* p. 100.

[11] Kent S. Knutson, "Contemporary Lutheran Theology and the Eucharistic Sacrifice," in *Lutherans and Catholics in Dialogue III: The Eucharist as Sacrifice,* New York, 1968, p. 168.

[12] Yngve Brilioth, *Eucharistic Faith and Practice, Evangelical and Catholic,* revised and shortened, A. G. Hebert, translator, London, 1956, pp. 130-131.

[13] *Ibid.,* pp. 156-157.

great fact, upon which the unity of the congregation is based." [14] Unlike the Lutheran rite, Zwingli's rite provided opportunity for the expression of the individual's self-oblation as we see in the prayer said just before the server reads "The Way Christ Instituted This Supper":

O Lord, God Almighty, who by thy Spirit has brought us together into thy one body, in the unity of faith, *and hast commanded that body to give thee praise and thanks for the goodness and free gift in delivering thine only begotten Son, our Lord Jesus Christ, to death for our sins:* grant we may do the same so faithfully that we may not, by any pretense or deceit, provoke thee who are the truth which cannot be deceived. *Grant also that we may live as purely as becometh thy body, thy family and thy children,* so that even the unbelieving may learn to recognize thy name and glory.[15]

Thus Zwingli's rite states what is a theological principle underlying the Lutheran rite but is never expressed in the *Formula Missae* or the *Deutsche Messe*.

In summary, then, Luther's liturgy did not include one of its essential teachings; Zwingli's liturgy was an excellent vehicle for his own teaching but that teaching had a deficient notion of Memorial. We shall next see that Calvin's liturgy is a defective expression of the deep and spiritual thoughts contained in his Eucharistic teaching.[16] In fact, Bard Thompson recommends that, to understand clearly the significance of what Calvin is doing, the *Short Treatise on the Lord's Supper* (1541) be read along with the liturgy.[17]

In Calvin's liturgy, after the minister reads the words of institution, he repeats Paul's warning against unworthy participation. This led to an excommunication of those who are unworthy and an admonition to the faithful who wish to receive. Then follows an explanation of what it means to partake of the body and blood of Christ. After the bread and wine are distributed (during which the congregation sings Psalm 138), a Thanksgiving is said. It includes an offering of eternal praise and thanks, a wish that the community grow in faith, and the desire that they lead their lives to the exalta-

14 *Ibid.*, p. 162.
15 Thompson, *op. cit.*, p. 154. Emphasis added.
16 Brilioth, *op. cit.*, p. 178.
17 Thompson, *op. cit.*, p. 193.

tion of God's glory and the edification of their neighbor. This prayer
gives an indication then of the only kind of offering made in the
Supper, a self-offering.[18] It is clear also that Calvin's liturgy does
not understand the presence of Christ in the Eucharist in the same
way as do Luther and the Roman Church:

> Let us lift our spirits and hearts on high where Jesus Christ is
> in the glory of His Father, whence we expect Him at our re-
> demption. Let us not be fascinated by these earthly and cor-
> ruptible elements which we see with our eyes and touch with
> our hands, seeking Him there as though He were enclosed in the
> bread or wine.[19]

Brilioth regards the long exhortation after the reading of Paul's
warning as a liturgical monstrosity, failing to give a worthy expression of the strong positive elements of the Reformed view, namely,
Eucharistic praise, communion-fellowship, commemoration, and the
offering of personal devotion. In Calvin's liturgy:

> The first of these is almost confined to the 138th Psalm; the
> second, apart from the act of communion itself, is expressed
> only in the exhortation to charity; commemoration is all but
> absent, and the ancient traditional forms of the liturgy, rich in
> links with the past, are more completely abolished than even
> by Zwingli; and the sacrifice of personal-oblation is only very
> shortly mentioned.[20]

Then, commenting on the essential incompatibility of the theological
ideas of Calvin with the mystery of the Sacrament, Brilioth continues: "the emphasis on God's transcendence above the whole material creation robs the element of Mystery itself of its deepest
meaning; for, after all, the *raison d'etre* of the bread and wine is
not to direct our thoughts to the Lord who is far away in heaven,
localiter circumscriptus, but to testify that he has condescended to
redeem and take to himself the earthly and the material." [21]

Let us now take a brief look at Cranmer's rite, the last of the Reformation rites that we shall consider. Whatever may be thought of
the other liturgies of the Reformation, they expressed clearly what

[18] *Ibid.,* pp. 207-208.
[19] *Ibid.,* p. 207.
[20] Brilioth, *op. cit.,* p. 178.
[21] *Ibid.*

they meant to say, if they did not always say what they wanted to say. Although Bouyer in his *Eucharist* acknowledges that he is following Dix, he takes a different viewpoint from him. Bouyer claims that Cranmer's use of words is essentially misleading.[22] Dix, however, defends Cranmer from the charge of dissembling,[23] but admits that he has radically misconceived the Eucharistic action and consequently changed the shape of the liturgy by which that action is performed.[24] Unlike the other three Reformers mentioned, Cranmer remains rather close to the wording of the Roman canon, but his changes are significant ones. Dix gives a good example of the kind of word manipulation in which Cranmer engaged by setting the 1549 *Book of Common Prayer* Thanksgiving alongside that of 1552. We need not repeat Dix's demonstration, but what does concern us is his judgment that [the change] is all very delicately expressive of Cranmer's personal teaching; but we fail to appreciate its craftsmanship "unless we remember continually that in his idea 'to eat the Body and drink the Blood of Christ' spiritually is nothing else but 'to believe in our hearts that His Flesh was rent and torn for us upon the cross and His Blood shed for our redemption'." [25] We have here a case of "this is what this text means if you remember this extra-textual source." For Bouyer, it is sleight-of-hand that dominated Cranmer's first effort and his bad faith is seen in his retention of the framework of the Roman canon.[26] Whether or not we agree with this judgment, it must be said that Cranmer's liturgy is an example of a text that can easily be misread in the sense that the author's meaning may be interpreted in a contrary sense by an uninformed reader.

Whatever else may be said of the Reformation liturgies, they were all dominated by the critical spirit, that is, they had no intention of saying what they did not want to say. The later history of these liturgies shows that any inherent weaknesses they might pos-

[22] Bouyer, *op. cit.*, pp. 415, 417. The same judgment has been made by C. G. Cuming, *A History of Anglican Liturgy*, London, 1969, who finds that the 1549 service is deliberately ambiguous, pp. 80-81, and quotes contemporaries of Cranmer to that effect even though he admits that Dix's thesis, that this service was intended to express a Zwinglian theology, has not been demolished by the counter-attacks it has undergone, p. 250. J. M. R. Tillard, "Catholiques Romains et Anglicans," *NRT* 93 (1971), pp. 619-620, 632, also finds Cranmer's liturgy deliberately ambiguous.

[23] Gregory Dix, *The Shape of the Liturgy*, London, 1960, p. 672.

[24] *Ibid.*, p. 670.

[25] *Ibid.*, p. 667.

[26] Bouyer, *op. cit.*, pp. 415ff.

sess would be a cause of concern to believers who would try to restore what may have been omitted due to a faulty understanding or hasty reaction on the part of the first Reformers.

The Reformers' attempts at a Eucharistic Service were their practical answer to what they found objectionable in the Roman canon: its doctrinal teachings, the abuses these teachings gave rise to, its being recited in a low voice in Latin, and its not being evangelical. The Council of Trent responded to the objections to the canon (considered in itself as a literary text) first of all on the practical level by not altering it and secondly on the polemical level with Chapter 4 of Session XXII:

> And since it is becoming that holy things be administered in a holy manner, and of all things this sacrifice is the most holy, the Catholic Church, to the end that it might be worthily and reverently offered and received, instituted many centuries ago the holy canon, which is so free from error that it contains nothing that does not in the highest degree savor of a certain holiness and piety and raise up to God the minds of those who offer. For it consists partly of the very words of the Lord, partly of the traditions of the Apostles, and also of pious regulations of holy pontiffs.[27]

Thus, the theologians and Fathers of Trent see the canon as the instrument best adapted for conveying the offering of the sacrifice and the reception of the sacrament in communion. Its human institution is acknowledged, and its integrity is defended. Those who would get rid of the canon are condemned:

> If anyone says that the canon of the mass contains errors and is therefore to be abrogated, let him be anathema.[28]

However, it is not the canon as such which is at the center of the discussion. The entire Eucharistic doctrine is to be defended from the attacks of the Reformers, especially the teaching on the real presence and on the sacrifice of the Mass, against which Reformation opposition was particularly directed. This is why the Chapter on

[27] English translation from H. J. Schroeder, editor, *Canons and Decrees of the Council of Trent*, St. Louis, 1950, pp. 146-147. Latin text in *DS* 942/1745.

[28] *DS* 953/1756. In what follows we have closely followed Joseph M. Powers, *Eucharistic Theology*, New York, 1967, pp. 31-43. Powers has put his study in the context of the Dutch controversy over the best way of talking about the real presence.

the canon is contained within the Decree concerning the Sacrifice of the Mass (Session XXII), 1562, which comes eleven years after the Decree concerning the Most Holy Sacrament of the Eucharist (Session XIII), 1551. In this latter decree, Trent affirms that after the consecration of bread and wine, our Lord Jesus Christ, true God and true Man, is truly, really, and substantially contained in the nourishing sacrament of the Holy Eucharist under the appearance of those sensible things.[29] This teaching is more clearly elaborated in the first canon:

> If anyone shall say that in the sacrament of the most Holy Eucharist there are not contained truly, really, and substantially the body and blood together with the soul and divinity of our Lord Jesus Christ—and therefore the whole Christ, but shall say that He is only there as in a sign, or by way of figure, or in efficacy: let him be an anathema.[30]

The statement is clearly directed against Zwingli, who maintained that Christ is only symbolically or figuratively present in the Eucharist and that the accounts of the institution of the Eucharist are to be interpreted symbolically and figuratively. It takes Calvin's position into account when it adds the adverb "substantially," rejecting Calvin's contention that the accounts of institution should be interpreted to mean that only the salvific power of Christ is present, not His true humanity and divinity.

Furthermore, this real presence, which has no human parallel, is a sacramental presence: "Our Savior, according to His natural mode of existence, sits always at the right hand of the Father, and is at the same time in His own substance sacramentally present to us in many places." [31] The sacramental presence, then, is different from a symbolic or figurative presence. Christ is really present and He is present in His true humanity and divinity. His body and blood is a sacrament, a sign of a still further meaning and power which His body and blood have for us: "Liberation from daily sins, preservation from mortal sin, the pledge of future glory and the symbol of the one body of Christ in which all are joined to the one Head in the bonds of one faith, hope and love." [32] To Luther's contention that Christ is only really present in the act of consecration and commu-

[29] *DS* 874/1636.
[30] *DS* 883/1651.
[31] *DS* 874/1636.
[32] *DS* 875/1638.

nion, the Council answers by affirming the abiding presence of Christ in the Eucharist.[33]

The principal affirmations of this decree can be reduced to two: the biblical faith of the Church in the real sacramental presence of Christ in the Eucharist, and the change of the bread and wine into the body and blood of Christ which this real presence demands.

Eleven years after the Decree on the Eucharist, the Council examined the questions pertaining to communion and the sacrifice of the Mass. The first chapter of the *Decree on the Most Holy Sacrifice of the Mass* presents an integrated view of the real presence, communion, and the sacrifice. The description of the Last Supper places the sacrificial character of the Eucharist in the fact that Jesus offered his body and blood under the appearances of bread and wine to the Father and gave his body and blood to his disciples to eat and drink under the same appearances. His command, "Do this in commemoration of me," is the gift of the new Passover and, at the same time, the constitution of a new priesthood and of a visible sacrifice that re-presents the blood sacrifice accomplished on the Cross once for all. The celebration of the old Passover leads to the gift of a new Passover which is the commemoration of Jesus' return to the Father when He redeemed man and brought man into His kingdom by shedding His blood. Here is an integrated statement of the fact that it is in nourishing oneself with the bread and wine become the body and blood of Christ that His sacrifice is renewed and commemorated sacramentally and the fruits of that sacrifice are granted to the believer.[34]

This reaction of Trent resulted in virtually freezing its Eucharistic teaching in face of the attacks of the Reformers. Although the Catholic Church did initiate extensive reforms to overcome clear abuses of its teaching and practice, it did not change its Eucharistic Prayer, which so many Christians found objectionable. In this regard, Jungmann points out that during the Reformation controversies, discussion centered on whether or not the Mass *is* a sacrifice; as a result the idea of the sacrifice of the Church played only a minor role. He continues that there is nothing plainer than the thought that in the Mass the Church, the people of Christ, the congregation here assembled, offers up the sacrifice to Almighty God. That the Mass is also the sacrifice of Christ is, in the Roman Mass *ordo*, only assumed, but never directly expressed. He continues:

[33] *DS* 886/1654 Canon 4.
[34] *DS* 938/1740-1741.

There is actually a definite contrast between this language of the liturgy and the language we are used to nowadays in sermons, catechisms, and other religious writings. We prefer to insist on the fact that on our altars Christ renews His Passion and death in an unbloody manner. We talk about the renewal of the sacrifice of the cross, about an oblation in which Christ gives himself to His heavenly Father. But it is only in very general terms that we mention the sacrifice of the Church, and for this reason even our theological text-books in discussing the ensuing problem as to precisely where Christ consummates His sacrifice, refer without much reflection to His presence in the sacred Host.[35]

This historical overview shows clearly that in essentials the Roman practice was to express its Eucharistic doctrine in its teaching, not in its EP. However, since the canon is more a prayer than a credal statement, its language is different from that of the statements and canons of the Council of Trent. It needs explanation to avoid misrepresentation. This is obvious with regard to what is meant by calling the Mass a sacrifice.

Before proceeding, we would like to consider the way the Orthodox Church formulates its Eucharistic belief in the course of its anaphora. With regard to the presence of Christ in the Eucharist, the Liturgy of Saint John Chrysostom has the following Epiclesis:

> Send down Thy Holy Spirit upon us and upon these gifts here set forth: And make this bread the Precious Body of Thy Christ, And that which is in this cup, the Precious Blood of Thy Christ, Changing them by Thy Holy Spirit. Amen, Amen, Amen. (The priest and the deacon immediately prostrate themselves before the Holy Gifts, which have now been consecrated.)[36]

Both word and accompanying action make it abundantly clear that the intention is that the bread and wine become the body and blood of Christ. The Orthodox also recognize that the Eucharist is a sacrifice. Immediately at the end of the Anamnesis are the words, "Thine of Thine own we offer to Thee, from all and for all." The common interpretation is that the sacrifice is offered to God and the

[35] Joseph Jungmann, *The Mass of the Roman Rite* (Missarum Solemnia), Francis A. Brunner, translator, New York, Vol. I, 1950, p. 180.
[36] In Timothy Ware, *The Orthodox Church*, Harmondsworth, England, 1964, p. 289.

sacrifice offered is Christ himself. Earlier, at the prayer before the Great Entrance, the priest, addressing Christ, says, "Thou thyself art He who offers and He who is offered." Christ is both priest and victim.[37]

to any particular explanation of the Eucharistic sacrifice, Nicholas Cabasilas (d. 1371) sums up the traditional Orthodox position as follows:

> First, the sacrifice is not a mere figure or symbol but a true sacrifice; secondly, it is not the bread that is sacrificed, but the very Body of Christ; thirdly, the Lamb of God was sacrificed once only, for all time. . . . The sacrifice at the Eucharist consists, not in the real and bloody immolation of the Lamb, but in the transformation of the bread into the sacrificed Lamb.[38]

Although the Orthodox Church has never formally committed itself The late Paul Evdokimov, commenting on the Memorial-aspect of the anaphora, has written that through the liturgy's divine power we are projected to the point where eternity cuts across time, and at this point we become true *contemporaries* with the events which they commemorate.[39]

Thus it is clear, but perhaps it needs saying, that for all liturgies there is a need for commentary since no liturgy is self-explanatory. In fact, the riches of the Eucharistic rite cannot be fully explained even in lengthy commentaries. Nevertheless, it would seem that the EP of a Church should do three things: express its Eucharistic faith; express the essential parts of its Eucharistic faith fully; and express its faith unambiguously.

As to the first point, all EPs do this. However, not all EPs fulfill the second point. It was precisely here that the Lord's Supper of Calvin and Luther suffered. Calvin stripped his Lord's Supper so bare that his service had little of his Eucharistic theology whereas Luther neglected to express the self-offering of the people in his liturgy. The third point is the most difficult of all for it is the nature of mystery to be impenetrable. Ironically enough, Cranmer may be said to be an example of someone who expressed his faith unambiguously even though he is most often thought of as one who expressed himself ambiguously. Dix's analysis of Cranmer's EP showed the weight to be given to each word and, with the help of the *Defence,* showed

[37] *Ibid.*
[38] *Ibid.,* p. 293.
[39] *Ibid.,* p. 294.

how the EP "clearly" expressed Cranmer's teaching. However, given the historical background against which Cranmer was writing, it would take a very careful reader to realize fully what Cranmer was actually saying. The Roman canon, which Trent kept intact in face of the Reformers' assaults, preserved ancient expressions that lacked later theological precision, thus ambiguously allowing for the impression of a new sacrifice. It is against this impression that the Reformers' followers continued to react. Although it would not have solved all problems, it would seem that some expression could have been inserted into the Roman canon to dispel any notion of a repeatable sacrifice.

If we turn now to the twentieth century and to our contemporary EPs within the Roman Catholic Church, we shall see that the problem faced is somewhat different. There is first of all the enormous plurality of official and unofficial EPs. Why such a plurality if they all express the same thing? Secondly, the authors of all the EPs we have studied and the groups for which they have written are all members of the Roman Catholic Church and profess the same faith. This leads us to ask if it is necessary to articulate the Eucharistic faith each time in such a way that differences with other Churches may clearly be seen. These are some of the problems raised by our study, but they are not the only ones. It is time now to summarize the findings from our analysis of the EPs from the four different groups. The background of the Reformation will help us to see the problems raised in perspective.

II
FOREGROUND: THE PRESENT EXPERIMENTATION IN THE ROMAN CATHOLIC CHURCH: THE ERA OF VATICAN II

The Structure of the
Contemporary Eucharistic Prayers

Since the new Roman EPs have been created with a great respect for tradition, they may serve as representatives of the traditional EP or, at least, as what some liturgical scholars regard as EPs reflecting tradition. This is not to say that the Roman EPs do not have certain structural problems, e.g., the introduction of a split-Epiclesis, before and after the Institution Narrative, is less traditional than a unified Epiclesis after the Institution Narrative.

On the highest official level, the Church approved as its own EPs prayers with elements assembled in the following order: Thanksgiving-Sanctus, *Vere Sanctus,* Epiclesis on the gifts, Institution Narrative, Acclamation, Anamnesis with Offering, Epiclesis on the Assembly, Intercessions, and Doxology. Although each of the three new Roman EPs took a different model as its starting point, they all assemble the elements in the above way but with a varied vocabulary and development. The best example of development is perhaps the *Vere Sanctus,* which is minimal in II and extensive in IV.

We shall now see the variations encountered in our study of the other three groups. The American EPs, the efforts of widespread authors acting independently of one another, generally included the above elements if not in quite the same way. It was rare to find an Epiclesis before and after the Institution Narrative, and it was not infrequent to find Intercessions scattered throughout the EP. One Prayer (625) went so far as to have a triple address to Father, Son, and Holy Spirit; it also had the distribution of communion after the Institution Narrative and Acclamation. Two other problems encountered were the kind of offering made and the influence of a theme on the structure. We shall consider these in the next few pages.

Insofar as the lack of a double Epiclesis is concerned, it may be said very simply that the Roman way was one of many options. The explicit introduction of an Epiclesis and its split can be explained better in terms of the historical Orthodox-Roman Catholic controversy over the moment of consecration than in theological terms, even if theology and, in some cases, historical precedent may be invoked to justify the split. If the opinion that it is the whole EP that is consecratory were accepted, there would be no problem arising from the different practice of the American EPs vis-à-vis the Roman ones. At any rate, the fact that the EPs composed by these small, local groups do not have a double Epiclesis shows that they do not consider it an important structural problem. That most of them do have an explicit Epiclesis is significant for this is in contrast to the Roman canon. It is probable that this is traceable to the influence of the *Apostolic Tradition* of Hippolytus and the Eastern anaphoras. In general, the Epiclesis is on the community and not on the gifts, hence the emphasis is on the transformation of the community. That there is a transformation of the bread and wine is evident from the way the community expresses itself after the Institution Narrative. It is not certain that the lack of the Epiclesis on the gifts betrays a reluctance on the part of the community to so express itself or, on the other hand, shows its implicit fidelity to the teaching that it is the Institution Narrative that brings about the change. The Holy Spirit, considered the source of unity and love, is naturally invoked in these EPs because there is also a heightened awareness of community among the small group. It is also most often the case that the union which the presence of the Spirit is asked to bring about is linked to the reception of the bread and wine.

The major structural problem presented by some of these EPs is that the Intercessions are not sufficiently controlled. This is their basic weakness for it destroys the unity of a Thanksgiving Prayer that is said over offerings. It is to shift the emphasis from God's graciousness and gifts to the assembly's needs. It is well-intentioned but poorly-inspired.

The triple address found in Prayer 625 is also a noble effort, but one that must be rejected not only on traditional grounds but also as breaking the unity of the Prayer. In its effort to give "equal time" to all three persons of the Trinity, some of the more profound theological notions of the liturgy are put aside. As Dom Verheul has said, the "we" of the Church is the "we" of the Church community constituted by the Spirit. Therefore the Holy Spirit is He who prays in and with the Church to the Father; and for this very reason, although not theologically excluded, He is less of an object of worship.[40]

With the distribution of Holy Communion after the Institution Narrative, we have a return to Reformation practice, one which clearly challenges the structure of the EP and, in fact, destroys its unity. In an effort to link word to practice, the author is privileging one moment of the Memorial-meal aspect, viz., the distribution of the bread and wine become the body and blood of Christ. However, it is generally accepted that the Institution Narrative itself has been incorprated into a much larger prayer which corresponds to the blessing pronounced by Christ at the Last Supper. The Reformers were unaware that this blessing constituted an EP.

The only other structural problem raised by the American EPs is that related to the themes found in them. First of all, the popularity of the theme approach should be noted. It helps to bring about a unity between the Liturgy of the Word and the Liturgy of the Eucharist. Furthermore, the themes are often worked out in such a way that they shape the wording but not the structure of the elements that make up the EP. The danger in a theme-structured EP

[40] Ambrose Verheul, *Introduction to the Liturgy: Towards a Theology of Worship,* Margaret Clarke, translator, The Liturgical Press, 1968, p. 60.

is that the theme becomes an end in itself or that it distorts one of the elements. However, this is not a problem in the American EPs.

A real challenge to the structure of the EP is presented by the Oosterhuis EPs. We saw how Oosterhuis moved from an assembling-of-elements approach to an address by several voices and to an interior monologue or soliloquy, in which there is no Thanksgiving preface, no Epiclesis, and no Offering properly so-called. It may be possible to read such elements into the latter Prayers, but it must be admitted that not everyone would agree that they are present.

What we are confronted with here is, on the one hand, the straightforward Thanksgiving as found in the Jewish Beraka, the most ancient Christian liturgies, the new Roman EPs as well as the majority of other contemporary EPs and, on the other hand, the sort of philosophical discourse that attempts to puzzle out God's seeming lack of omnipotence with regard to this world, especially as a result of the existence of evil. The Oosterhuis EP 10 is an excellent example of this latter kind of Prayer. God is seen as everywhere/nowhere, living/dying, refugee/stranger. So it is that God is the one in whom opposites are reconciled. In face of this, the only thing that man can do (offer?) is "I will let you exist and simply be what you are . . ." and "I should like to do something, understand you, sit down on your doorstep, endure the silence that you are, that we are." We have here moved so far from the original understanding of the EP, radically beyond anything the Reformers did, that to accept this prayer as an EP we are forced to consider that the very fact the speaker addresses a You beyond him is a sort of Thanksgiving. However, gone is the sense of Jesus Christ as truly present, gone is the offering of the bread and wine become the body and blood of Christ, and gone is any awareness of the final triumph of Christ.

When the principal Reformers turned their hands to the EP, we saw that they removed the idea of sacrifice but found it necessary to prepare their congregations for the worthy reception of the bread and wine which commemorated what Christ did at the Last Supper. In their stress on the reception of the bread and wine, we have seen that they forgot the address to the Father and concentrated on exhorting the congregation. The great Thanksgiving made to God for creation and redemption fell by the wayside. What Thanksgiving remained was generally a Thanksgiving for partaking of the elements and for being able to make a self-offering of some kind. However, in all these cases the EPs were felt to be expressing the faith of the religious group with regard to the Eucharist. In this Oosterhuis EP 10, what we have is an expression of the faith of the speaker (this is the only Prayer in which the pronoun I is used) to endure the silence from God. It is true that the EP has traditionally concentrated on what God has said to men and that the silence of God has not been sounded to any great extent, but the silence referred to in this Prayer is seen through the eyes of a speaker motivated by his effort to understand God's seeming unresponsiveness. It is a legitimate prayer, but is it reconcilable with the faith of the Church in the Eucharist? Is not the Eucharist primarily concerned with what good news God has spoken to man? As Oosterhuis himself has put it, God's Word is near. The speaker does acknowledge this when he says, "I have heard of you, some time, because I hear you in people and in myself." In an EP, the ordinary stance of the speaker is to speak of what he has heard from God and about God. The traditional manner of speaking in the liturgy is to formulate ideas clearly and tersely, not to puzzle out what one says. The EP is called on to express the faith of the Church, not the existential state of one or several of its members.

Oosterhuis' Prayer challenges severely the understanding of the liturgy that Romano Guardini presents. Guardini tells us that, since different men have different conceptions of God, the danger is that a man's longing and prayer may no more reach out freely beyond himself, but may degenerate into a dialogue with an enlargement of his own portrait. In contrast to this subjectivism, Guardini sets forth the objectivity of the liturgy:

> In the liturgy the Church displays God as He really is, clearly and unmistakably, in all His greatness, and sets us in His presence as His creatures. She teaches us those aboriginal methods of communion with God which are adapted to His nature and ours —Prayer, Sacrifice, Sacraments. Through sacred actions and readings she awakes in us those great fundamental emotions of adoration, gratitude, penitence and petition.[41]

This statement stresses God's greatness as Creator and man's place as creature, and in this relationship man is the one who worships, seeks help, asks forgiveness, and gives thanks. This objective and essentialist view of the liturgy allows no doubting, no questioning, no complaining by man, the creature, although these have a necessary place in most personal prayer. Oosterhuis' Prayers seem to represent an existentialist and individualistic stance. They allow, within the

[41] Romano Guardini, *The Church and the Catholic and The Spirit of the Liturgy,* Ada Lane, translator, New York, 1935, p. 65.

liturgy, for a view of man as a doubter, a questioner, and a complainer, as well as one who adores God and seeks His help.

Elsewhere Guardini has insisted that the reserve in the liturgy, where no individual intrudes upon another's inner life, makes fellowship in the liturgy possible. The liturgy never allows the soul to feel that it is imprisoned with others, or that its independence and intimacy are threatened with invasion.[42] Here one might be tempted to apply this as criticism to some of the Oosterhuis or Maertens Prayers, but only if their Prayers were imposed on groups other than those for whom they were written. There is no indication that the Oosterhuis Prayers, articulating as they do man's search for meaning, have not increased the fellowship of the Amsterdam student community. It is our intention to study the texts and not the actual lived experience of the group that has elaborated these texts (interesting as that may be), but we would simply like to point out that Guardini's position may actually be more individualistic than that of the Amsterdam student community. Since Guardini's day some segments of the Church have a new understanding of what it means to be community and what it means to be a local Church.[43] Nevertheless, the Amsterdam community poses with its Prayers some problem areas: how does it see itself in relation to the larger communion? Would, in fact, the larger communion recognize itself in the Oosterhuis Prayers? In fact, these Prayers rarely indicate this relationship and it is problematic whether or not the entire communion would accept them as they now stand.

It can happen that the very tone and stance adopted by the Oosterhuis speaker cannot support the traditional structure of the EP. We know that Oosterhuis can write brilliantly within that structure, as his earlier Prayers show. At the same time, Prayer 10 shows the dangers that arise when he steps too far outside that structure. This is not the only problem raised by the Ten Table Prayers. As we have already seen in the American EPs, the lack of an explicit Epiclesis is not so important a problem as the lack of an Offering. The traditional liturgies and/or their accompanying theologies generally look on what they are doing as some kind of offering. The Byzantine Church makes quite clear that it is offering the body and blood of Christ as does the Roman Church in its most recent EPs. The Reformers, we have seen, could not accept a second

---

[42] *Ibid.*, pp. 148-149.

[43] Romano Guardini, "Letter from Romano Guardini," *Herder Correspondence*, August, 1964, pp. 237-239. See especially the closing paragraphs where he hints at what educational trends can contribute to the Liturgy.

offering or sacrifice alongside the one sacrifice of Christ, but they generally introduced some notion of a self-offering. However, recent ecumenical discussion has shown that both the Protestant Churches and the Roman Church agree that the one sacrifice is not repeated and that in some way the offering made present at Calvary is made present again at the Eucharist. Since the world's salvation and redemption depend on this one offering of Christ and since the memorial we make of it allows us to participate in it, we speak of offering a sacrifice at the Mass. What Christ did is proclaimed at the Mass; not to speak of his sacrifice but to say, as Oosterhuis' 10 does, "I should like to do something" takes on Pelagian tones. It is exquisite understatement. No doubt, it is a beautiful Prayer for a man caught in the moment of oppression by evil or doubt, but it is hardly the kind of Prayer that the Church would express at its Eucharist. It reflects the sentiments of the moment but not the sentiments of the Church universal across space and time.

There are two innovations that Oosterhuis makes that affect the structure of the EP. The first is that he introduces the Our Father into the heart of the EP, either by rewording it or by placing it immediately following the Doxology as a kind of overflow from it. Luther's *Deutsche Messe* had introduced a public paraphrase of the Lord's Prayer just after the sermon and before the admonition for those who wanted to partake of the sacrament,[44] but Oosterhuis introduces it into the EP itself. Once it is a kind of Christological Prayer and twice it is rephrased in such a way that it becomes a very personalized presentation of the assembly's petitions. It is a very clever way of giving new life to a prayer that repetition can render an unthinking recitation.

The second innovation, found in Prayers 4, 7 and 8, is the increased role given the assembly and the choir. However, for the sake of precision, it should be noted that, while the choir is a distinct entity, the assembly includes all present, priest and choir. In our study of Prayer 7, we saw that neither choir nor assembly had the role of mere acclaimer of its assent or its faith. The choir played a distinct role by furnishing questions or developing a progressive chain of thought. The whole assembly had a similar role. It was not possible to determine on what basis all the parts of the Prayer were distributed although we did note certain constants. Since the Prayers were meant to be sung, it is possible that the distribution is based on musical desiderata. In fact, the chapel in which the Eucharist is celebrated could also have a determining influence. Over and above

[44] Thompson, *op. cit.*, pp. 132-133.

this, Prayer 7 also challenges the idea that the EP should conform to the Beraka form.

The Maertens EPs also present us with several new structural changes. In the first place, as we have seen in Chapter Five, the double structure of these EPs is made apparent. By double structure, we mean the possibility of discovering a structure based on a certain assembling of elements as in the Roman EPs, but one that would be subordinated to a larger two-part structure: the first part emphasizes benediction and thanksgiving while the second part, more intercessory, expresses the attitude of care and concern for this world. Although the Institution Narrative is not published in these Prayers, it seems that it has an influence on their structure. The self-gift of Christ "for many" appears to be the motivating force that leads to the community's desire to give itself and to bring into its own embrace all humanity. The danger is that the Memorial-aspect tends to lose the center of attention since the Intercessions dominate the structure by the space and time given to them. Unlike the American EPs which tended to spread the Petitions throughout the EP, these Prayers have the tendency to let the Petitions take over the whole second half of the Prayer. This is próbably due to at least two considerations: the influence of the theme and the desire to vary the Intercessions from Prayer to Prayer so that different categories of people can be prayed for. The specification of the theme with regard to actual living people demands more space since both the specific people and the theme must be brought together. Sometimes a litany form is used allowing for a repetitious acclamation.

This leads naturally to the final problem these Prayers present to us, namely, a tendency to allow the theme to so structure the content of one of the elements, such as Epiclesis or Doxology, that as a result we no longer have a traditional liturgical Epiclesis or Doxology. In this way, these Prayers challenge any rigid understanding of set liturgical elements in the EP. At the same time a theme approach always runs the risk of didacticism in the service of a certain ideology or even propaganda. Once it does not ground itself in specific biblical events but rather favors "up-to-date" events, it also tends to use an emotive language particular to its authors. It is debatable whether or not the Maertens Prayers are successful in avoiding either of these two risks.

The above problem is not unrelated to that raised by Baumstark with regard to the feast of the Epiphany as a feast of an idea or a feast of an event.[45] This should caution us to distinguish among

45 Baumstark, *op. cit.,* pp. 174ff.

possible liturgical themes. Some themes, such as memorial and sacrifice, are already in some way in the EP. Others may take up an event of the history of salvation and be incorporated more fully into the EP as is possible with the Roman canon through its variable Prefaces. Finally there are themes that start from a circumstance or idea coming from outside the Eucharist and the history of salvation which may be more or less successfully woven into the EP. This last choice is the one the Maertens Prayers follow with their themes of temptation, growth, and light.

The Way in Which the Praying Community Addresses God, Refers to Jesus Christ, and Refers to Itself

In the Roman, American, and Maertens EPs, there is no difficulty in naming God. He is first and foremost *Father.* The Roman EPs also use *Lord* as do the Maertens EPs, but these latter generally limit that use to the Acclamation. The American EPs have the peculiarity of frequently using qualifying adjectives with the word *Father,* something the other Prayers do not do or do infrequently. This may be explained by Roman terseness, but the same cannot be said of the Maertens EPs, which even when they are not overly long tend to be wordy. Here, however, it would seem to be a deliberate choice to avoid appending adjectival expressions to the divinity that may seem to limit man's responsibility for his world.

The Oosterhuis EPs are a case unto themselves. Unlike the other Prayers, which simply employ the most traditional forms of address to God, the Oosterhuis EPs show concern with the question, "How do you name the unnamable?" Thus, along with the traditional *Lord* and *God,* accompanied often by such expressions as *God of people, God for us* (which is implicit in the word *Father*), Oosterhuis draws on a wide variety of names inspired from the Bible or his experience of the world. He is clearly making an effort to bridge the gap that can occur by a too frequent use of the same forms of address. While this effort to name God in relation to man's experience of Him is praiseworthy, the simple solution taken in the Maertens EPs seems equally successful on the grounds that one does not have to create a problem where it doesn't exist. In other words, if everyone is agreed that God is essentially unnamable, then it is not difficult to address him as Our Lord taught us, *Father.*

The Roman EPs used *Christ* or *Son,* with modifiers, as their preferred way to refer to Jesus Christ. There was in the Prefaces a wider variety, based generally on the salvific role of the Son as Redeemer, Savior, or Lamb. The American EPs preferred the expression *Your Son* to all others although *Jesus Christ our Lord* was another favorite form of reference. The Maertens EPs retained a like simplicity, clearly preferring *Jesus Christ Our Lord,* but occasionally using the simple term *Jesus.*

Once again it is the Oosterhuis EPs that take an entirely different approach. There is a wide variety of ways of referring to Jesus Christ, generally drawn from biblical and poetic sources. There is a clear attempt to make more effective use of the idea-content of such titles as *Redeemer* or *Savior.* In Chapter Four, we saw this effort to make concrete what Jesus' dying meant for us. Another emphasis in the Oosterhuis EPs was that Jesus was a man and we also saw how often the word *man* was used to refer to Him with or without the name *Jesus* accompanying it.

At this point we must comment on this clear difference in the practice of the Oosterhuis EPs and to some degree in Maertens' EPs in contrast with the practice of the Roman and American EPs. The liturgical reflex is to refer to Jesus as *Lord Jesus.* Why is it, then, that we find Jesus being referred to in these liturgies as *Jesus* and why does there seem to be an emphasis on his humanity? The answer may be that those involved with educating the young have found that a unilateral presentation of the divinity of Christ is responsible for a certain failure of Christian education. After summarizing the findings of Pierre Babin, Antoine Vergote arrives at the same conclusions as the French catechist. He says:

> Christ spoke to men first of all on the level at which they could understand him: the level of evangelical wisdom and of the experience of God as Father. Christ is himself the model and teacher of this wisdom. It is in his visible humanity that we see his filial attitude towards God. *There are few Christians, we think, who are conscious of this fact that Christ was really man.* As a result of an insufficient theological formation they tend to interpret the humanity of Christ as a veil covering his divinity. Nevertheless, it is in his very real humanity that Christ is the model of the religious attitude and that he shows himself to be the one who reveals the Father.[46]

[46] Antoine Vergote, *The Religious Man: A Psychological Study of Religious Attitudes,* Marie-Bernard Said, translator, Dayton, Ohio, 1969, pp. 213-214. Emphasis added.

In the *Guide for the Christian Assembly,* the editors (one of whom is Maertens) discuss the same problem only in a slightly different way. Recognizing that the unique mediator of salvation is Jesus of Nazareth, they say that all the other titles of the mediator simply qualify the name of Jesus. This name is fundamental for it designates a man who was placed in the most banal condition of all men here below, the only son of a very modest Nazarean family.[47] The *Guide* makes quite clear the danger that it is reacting against when it continues:

> To recognize Jesus of Nazareth, a real man of humble parentage and ordinary condition, as the sole mediator of salvation was to immediately eliminate the temptation to make him the sort of intermediary between man and God natural paganism dreams of so gladly. We might as well learn to call the mediator by his proper name: Jesus of Nazareth, for this is the particular man who today is the Resurrected One and the Lord! There is a total identity between one and the other. Not to mention the name of Jesus and to speak exclusively of the Lord or of Christ runs the risk of making the Saviour an intermediary being between God and us, signifying that we really lack a true mediator! [48]

No doubt, for the ordinary layman, the distinction drawn in the above passage is a subtle one: Christ is mediator, not an intermediary. He is not someone who is a little more than man and a little less than God, someone who brings both man and God together. He is God and man, and it is on that basis that He is the mediator between God and man. The *Guide* is suggesting that to call Jesus by His proper name is one way of preventing His being thought of as some kind of demi-god.

Hence we are faced with the ironical situation that an unanticipated emphasis on the humanity of Jesus in the EP may very well seem to some people to de-emphasize His divinity. However, a long-standing catechetical problem with regard to Jesus' humanity arises from the fact that His humanity is poorly expressed or little understood, certainly in comparison to the ordinary Catholic's understanding of His divinity. Both the Oosterhuis and Maertens EPs are attempts to redress the imbalance. Maertens' EPs do it more subtly whereas the Oosterhuis EPs do it rather joltingly for those unaccus-

---

[47] Thierry Maertens and Jean Frisque, *Guide for the Christian Assembly,* Vol. I, Bruges, 1965, p. 121.
[48] *Ibid.,* p. 122.

tomed to hear Jesus referred to in such terms in the liturgy. However, that would seem to prove the point that the divinity of Jesus has been over-emphasized to the point of making His humanity disappear, if not in the sea of His divinity, then in the consciousness of the believer.

Once again, if we turn to Guardini, we will find an opposite viewpoint being stated. Guardini addressed himself to the problem that the Jesus of the gospels seems more earthly than the Jesus of the liturgy. Admitting the difference and the problem it can create, he says that Christ's human nature remains intact, "but [his body and soul] are now utterly transformed by the Godhead, rapt into the light of eternity, and remote from space and time. He is the Lord, 'sitting at the right hand of the Father,' the mystic Christ living on in his Church." The liturgy has for its own purpose placed greater stress on the eternal and supertemporal elements of Christ. Thus the liturgy is no mere commemoration of what once existed; it is the enduring life of Jesus Christ in us, and that of the believer in Christ, eternally God and Man.[49]

Guardini's passage was written at a time when there was no thought of any change in the liturgy's formulae or the possibility of writing new EPs for the Roman Church. His task is to explain what is the case with the liturgy as it has expressed itself up until the present time. The approach taken in the *Guide for the Christian Assembly,* while not directed toward creating new EPs, thinks more in pastoral terms, in the sense that it attempts, not so much by explanation but by a different practice, to redress difficulties inherent in a fixed theological-religious vocabulary inherited by our century. If the liturgy has for its own purpose placed greater stress on the eternal and supertemporal elements of Christ, can it now for its own purpose place some stress on the humanity of Jesus? However, we have already entered upon a discussion which we shall necessarily return to when we summarize what the praying community finds significant to say about Christ.

The community in the Roman EPs, as befits the *Romanitas* characteristic of them, is very discreet in referring to itself. This reflects the terse, sober style reflected in the Roman canon.[50] It is rare that it makes a reference to itself or characterizes itself, except in the

---

[49] Guardini, *op. cit.,* pp. 157-158. For a richer understanding of Guardini's Christology, see his *The Lord,* Elinor Castendyk Briefs, trans., Chicago, 1954.

[50] Edmund Bishop, "The Genius of the Roman Rite," *Liturgica Historica,* Oxford, 1968, pp. 1-19. See also Christine Mohrmann, *Liturgical Latin, Its Origins and Character,* Washington, 1957.

Intercessions where we receive some idea of a Christian family in the terms used of the living and the dead. The American EPs had many more designations of the "we" together with an emphasis on the responsibility of the assembly for the world and the people in it. There was also a greater emphasis on the assembly's own spiritual journey as a continuation of salvation history. No doubt this is a reflection of the prevailing catechetical approach of the time when these prayers were composed.

The Oosterhuis EPs place the emphasis somewhat differently. There is a feeling of solidarity with all men and a realization that the assembly must do something to heal the ills of this world. Quite often this awareness is expressed in terms of opposites, such as love/hate, war/peace. The recognition of solidarity in the good and evil that all men commit almost precludes them from characterizing themselves as a holy people. This would mean setting up one more separation in the world. The Roman EPs, with a much longer tradition and a certain age-old wisdom, can without too much difficulty reconcile that the assembly are, at one and the same time, a holy people and sinners.

In the Maertens EPs we have a stress on reaching out to the world. There is a feeling of solidarity with all men as well as a constant urge to work side by side with Christian and non-Christian alike in building up a better world. The "we" of this assembly has a very high cognizance of being constituted as an assembly that must give witness by doing. It is for this reason that the assembly generally characterizes itself, not by means of nouns or adjectives, but by action verbs. This community sees itself as the promise of the eventual brotherhood of all men. It works in the present to bring about the ideal of the future, but it does this conscious of the mediatorship of Jesus Christ. That is why these Prayers cannot be dismissed as horizontal. As Joseph Ratzinger has remarked, the governing principle of Christian worship is a movement of exodus with a two-in-one direction toward God and fellow man. By carrying humanity to God, Jesus Christ incorporates it in His salvation. The reason why the happening on the cross is the bread of life "for the many" is that He who was crucified has smelted the body of humanity into the "yes" of worship. It is completely "anthropocentric," entirely related to man, because it was radical theocentricity, delivery of the "I" and therefore of the creature man to God.[51] Ideally Christian living forms part of this worship and in turn is a verification of the

[51] Joseph Ratzinger, *Introduction to Christianity,* J. R. Forster, translator, New York, 1970, pp. 219-220.

cult. It is supposed in every liturgy, but it is made more explicit in the Maertens Prayers.

There is no doubt that these four "we's" are different and yet the same. The Roman "we" represents a kind of classical reserve while the Oosterhuis "we," in a sense, represents a romantic "we" that has a heightened awareness of its feelings. If the Roman "we" strikes one as a detached "we," then the Maertens "we" strikes one as a "we" engagé. The American "we" is expressive of an optimism within bounds. Like all literary genres, the EP, when opened up to experimentation, will reveal shifting attitudes in the speaker with regard to himself. The way this "we" pictures itself will correspond to prevailing philosophies and theologies. The Roman "we," it may be thought, transcends these, but that simply is not true. The stance of any "we" is always influenced by the models of thought open to it.[52]

There is one basic difference that the "we" of the Oosterhuis EPs presents: there is a closer existential link between the "we" of the service of the word and the "we" of the EP than is found in the Roman or the American EPs. There is a consciousness of a concrete community in the Oosterhuis "we." It is a "we" from the inside, not one from the outside. This results from the fact that the Oosterhuis EPs are created for a particular congregation. The un-official EPs are without fail more particular than official ones. The former have the task of articulating the particular and the universal "we"; the latter need only concern themselves with the universal. However, to become particular is to run the risk of subjectivism. Then the problem is just how the author of a particular group reflects that group or imposes unconsciously his own perception of the group on the group. This leads us to ask, granted that the author's image of the group is true, to what extent does this local group reflect the universal Church. Is it, in fact, in communion with the universal Church?

Michel de Certeau has stressed the need for the Other to fill in the meaning of Christianity. Using the concepts "permission" (the Christ event permits a variety of interpretations) and "limit" (no single interpretation is the whole), he argues for a plurality of Christian appearances and languages which are not unrelated but each one is limited.[53] Karl Rahner also has stressed the possibility of the end

52 Cf. Virgil Fiala, "Les prières d'acceptation de l'offrande et le genre littéraire du canon romain," in Eucharisties d'orient et d'occident, Lex Orandi 46, Paris 1970, pp. 130ff.; and Gottfried Hierzenberger, Der Magische Rest: Ein Beitrag zur Entmagisierung des Christentums, Dusseldorf, 1969.

53 Michel de Certreau, L'étranger ou l'union dans la différence. Foi Vivante 116, Paris, 1969, passim. Also see his "How is Christianity Thinkable Today," Theology Digest 19, 1971, pp. 339-341.

of a single theology and the beginning of a period of theologies, no one of which can be elevated to a comprehensive system, but each one starting from its own premises and experience of reality, giving rise to *different liturgical expressions.*[54] It is precisely here that a problem arises with regard to the composition of literally hundreds of unofficial EPs. The liturgy, considered as a fundamental source of the Church's teaching, cannot permit itself just anything. Moreover, although we have thus far concentrated our efforts on the text of the EP, we should not forget that the liturgy is also made up of bodily expressions that convey tone and attitude toward what is being carried out. Surely a starting point before composing unofficial Prayers should be a consideration of the maxim *lex orandi, lex credendi* since there is an intimate connection between the way the Church prays and what it believes. Any EP or liturgical expression should reflect the faith of the Church and not just personal or subjective sentiments. This is what makes the composition of an EP a serious undertaking and removes it from rule by arbitrary decision. If we use the word rite to refer to a given liturgy and the word liturgy to apply as a generic term for all rites, we may see more clearly what this involves. Up until recently the Latin rite succeeded to a great degree in remaining aloof from the quarrels of different theological schools. This was a result not only of the fixed form of its rite but also its exclusiveness revealed by its considering the Eastern rites as a block over against itself and by its excluding of heretics as well as their heretical rites. Yet it is clear that the conceptions of Christology and sacramental theology have influences on how rites express themselves. The Protestant forms of worship are examples of a diversity of rites based on a diversity of theologies. Even where the faith of the Church is essentially the same, as between Easterns and Latins, the expression of this faith in their Eucharistic rites is quite different. There are two different responsibilities here: the first concerns the responsibility of formulating expressions of the faith. This is the task of the universal Church composed of local Churches as when they meet in Council. The second is the responsibility of a local Church within a larger communion to express this accepted faith in its particular liturgy. Nevertheless, since the faith is one, there ought to be the possibility of one liturgy (at least theoretically). Here, however, the term liturgy and the term faith have meanings that must be clarified. Thus liturgy includes the rites of East and West. We have an individual rite only in reference to an individual Church. The faith—considered here as something that can be formulated—is the responsibility of an individual church.

[54] Karl Rahner, "L'avenir de la théologie," *NRT* 93, 1971, p. 14.

An individual rite, for example the Latin rite, expresses certain things about creation, redemption, and the memorial Christ left behind. Now rites grow out of reflection on the faith, but this reflection is not divorced from historical and cultural determinants. It is for that reason one can speak of a diversity of rites arising from a diversity of theologies, for neither theology nor a given rite is divorced from life. Since the universal (the one faith) has to be clothed in the particular (the many rites), the liturgy never succeeds in being disembodied from the diverse theologies. Yet, what should and can remain constant from rite to rite is the one faith. Nevertheless, it is precisely this one faith that will have a variety of expressions, for theology today is setting itself the task of reformulating the one faith. We see, then, that it is not so easy to distinguish between the faith of the Church (expressed in a rite) and the diverse theologies. If we grant that the first role of the liturgy is not to instruct but to bring to life the mystery of salvation, still, to do that, it makes use of those modes of expression most adapted to the faithful. The unity of faith that can exist despite the many theologies may be expressed in many rites because fundamentally there is only one liturgy, that which Christ gives to the Father and to which the rites of the churches are associated. The Roman EPs, by incorporating the best values of the Eastern anaphoras and by the approbation of the Pope, reflect, not only continuity in space and time with tradition, but also a present liturgical theological synthesis. The Prayers of Oosterhuis and Maertens reflect a challenge to that synthesis because they arise from their own starting points.

At the same time, on the level of authority, there is another aspect to the problem of particularization as it touches the Church, namely, the relationship of the "local" or "particular" Church to the universal Church. Recently, Henri de Lubac has warned that the tendency to loosen the bonds of each Church with the center threatens to compromise the catholic equilibrium of unity in diversity, whose guarantee, instituted by Jesus, is the reference to Peter.[55] It is the tendency toward a plurality of theologies (and hence liturgies) together with the need to keep the "catholic equilibrium" that must be continuously worked out for there is risk and danger involved in the present consciousness of being particular within the Church. Père Refoulé, writing on the Dutch situation, has shown the risks of renewal for local Churches that undertake a reform. Recognizing the

---

[55] Henri de Lubac, *Les églises particulières dans l'église universelle*, Paris, 1971, pp. 100-123. See also his conference in *Documentation Catholique*, 69 (1972), p. 130.

good in these efforts, he nonetheless finds a lack of catholicity in the Amsterdam ecclesiology.[56]

While we do not wish to enter into the debate of contemporary ecclesiology, that it has an influence on the Oosterhuis EPs is evident from an address he gave in which he contrasted the meaning of Church as applied to his student community and as applied to what he calls the official Church:

> We, here in this place, with the task of proclaiming the Gospel in this city, in this so-called secularized milieu that is in such a ferment, we have in recent years experienced this conflict with the official Church more and more from her forms, her words, from that whole churchly climate. Hence, we felt an increasing sense of alienation, a growing realization that we no longer could and no longer wanted to answer to the norms and expectations of the official Church.[57]

As an example of the interference of the official Church with the Dutch Church, Oosterhuis cites the Dutch Catechism incident:

> . . . when the highest authority in the Church, to correct the formulations of the Dutch catechism . . . states: that Jesus, in restitution for our misdeeds, offered himself to the Father as a holy sacrifice in which God was well pleased, that the sacrifice of the cross is continued unbroken in God's Church in the Eucharistic sacrifice, that in the communion the victim offered to God is digested as food—then we, along with many others, can only understand that as a caricature of what we are trying to live and to proclaim in the breaking of the bread, the celebration of the Eucharist.[58]

There are two different problems presented in these passages. The first concerns the caricature of which Oosterhuis himself is guilty in contrasting the simple people with the "official Church." The discussion, represented by such a contrast, is a real one, but, in many respects, a secondary one that obfuscates the understanding of the relationship of the particular Church with the universal Church. The second problem concerns the contrast between dogmatic statements and what Oosterhuis and his community are trying to do in their

[56] François Refoulé, *Au bord du schisme? L'affaire d'Amsterdam et l'Eglise de Holland,* Paris, 1969.

[57] In Lucien Roy and Forrest L. Ingram, eds., *Step Beyond Impasse: A Chronicle of the Dutch Church,* New York, 1969, p. 149.

[58] *Ibid.,* p. 150.

Eucharistic assembly. It must be clear to anyone pastorally oriented that dogmatic statements are in a certain sense lifeless ("a caricature") in comparison with the lived, experienced, and shared faith of a community trying to make word and rite speak. It is not the idea of sacrifice, but the whole sacrificial vocabulary that apparently is unacceptable. In a short sermon on the breaking of bread, Oosterhuis himself says: "It is only when you yourself have become 'someone' that you begin to understand what you have for a long time past experienced personally: that you live by the grace of . . . yes, of what? the sacrifice of others? Perhaps that word is too heavy, too dramatic. That you live by the grace and the work and the faithfulness of others." [59] In other words, the celebration of the Eucharist is not seen as "public cult," what Herman Manders describes as a long-held view of the liturgy. This view regards

> liturgy [as] an official act of the church as a public body, an act regulated by laws and performed by official ministers in the name of the authorities. In this public sense it is an act of the community, but they need not be directly involved in it. The priest performing the act represents them, and that suffices. There is no room here for personal creativity. Texts and rubrics are determined by official commissions. Even when the service is made comprehensible to the participants through translation, it is not the concrete way of living their faith that is being enacted, but the faith of the church as a public body. By "active participation" those present assimilate this faith, so that they share in the official activity of the church as performed by the ordained priest. The total impression is of a religious solemnity, untouchable, handed down from above, and performed as a manifestation of God's mystery and transcendence.[60]

Manders here intermingles three views of cult that should be distinguished. The first is public cult wherein the focus is on the community, not individuals, worshipping. The second consists of official, ordained celebrants as the essential subjects of the cult. The third

[59] Huub Oosterhuis, *Open Your Hearts,* p. 3.
[60] Herman Manders, "Who Performs the Liturgy?" *Theology Digest* 16, 1968, pp. 227-231. A condensation of "Wie voltrekt de liturgie?" *Tijdschrift voor Theologie* 3, 1967, pp. 268-287. For a full and rich discussion of the subject of the Liturgy see Yves Congar, "L' 'Ecclesia' ou Communauté chrétienne, sujet intégral de l'action liturgique," *La Liturgie après Vatican II* (Unam Sanctam 66) J.-P. Jossua and Yves Congar, eds., Paris, 1967, pp. 241-282.

view of cult sees it as a rigid and highly ritualized liturgy. The Eucharistic liturgy, both before and after Vatican II, has been increasingly criticized precisely in regard to certain regulating laws as well as a faulty notion of community, leading to a faulty notion of participation. The Eucharistic celebration always remains an official act carried out by an ordained minister in union with the bishop. However, what the liturgical movement has shown is, first, that the laws regulating this act may be changed and, second, that it is properly the whole community, presiding minister and faithful, that celebrates the Eucharist. The emphasis shifts from a juridical, official way of regarding the Eucharistic celebration to considering it as this community's celebration. Thus, opining that many people still experience the Church's celebration of the Eucharist as the "public cult" described above, Manders presents another view which he characterizes as new but nevertheless very old and traditional. Here the whole people of God are the subject of the liturgical activity. The Church-community works together and bears responsibility together. A pre-formed liturgy no longer answers to the religious sensibilities of such a group. If the element of divine transcendence may actually be more difficult to experience, the people seek God's nearness in the brotherly love and feelings of solidarity that they have with each other.[61] Clearly this is describing what the Amsterdam community is doing and shows to some extent how the "boldness" in the EPs of that group is possible. Of course, the crux of the problem is the jump from the assembled community considered as the Church to its elaboration of its own texts. It is at this point that the question of competency to create new texts, for example, new EPs, involves not only all the problems associated with the creation of any literary work but also those associated with authority. The point is, however, that once the assembled community is regarded as the subject of the liturgy the question of the creation of texts, even EPs, inevitably arises.

Has our study of the "we" in these Prayers shown that they can be reduced to the representation of a personal "sentiment" and/or an outlook on life that imposes on liturgy contemporary sociopolitical issues? In the first case, it would mean that contact with the biblical and liturgical tradition of the Church has been lost. In the second case, it would mean that an option no different from any other option had been adopted and represented, rather than one that embodies man's fundamental relationships with God. However, neither of these two reductions fits the actual situation. With the

[61] *Ibid.*

notable exception of biblical certitude, most of the Oosterhuis EPs are so rooted in biblical language that even their thought-form is inspired by the Bible. They touch just as the Psalms touch; they have the simplicity and directness of language—even though poetic—that the Gospels have. The Maertens EPs literally force the congregation to go out beyond itself precisely at a time when human solidarity on an experiential level is at a higher consciousness than ever before. This means that these Prayers reflect a real change in consciousness. Also, it may be argued that both groups are scripturally oriented because they show that the experience of the reality of our time has meaning for the present assembly in the same way the events recorded in Scripture had meaning for the people undergoing them at that time. The community interprets its understanding of life—its own life and its growing relationship with God—from an awareness that somehow our present age is involved with a gigantic struggle to direct the future of the human species. Such a struggle has its moments of uncertainty and doubt, but it requires a constant effort to interpret present and past. The Roman EPs with their reliance on familiar biblical or credal statements give the impression of tapping the deposit of faith while the American, Oosterhuis, and Maertens Prayers to varying degrees seem less close to reformulating truths because they regard the present moment as important and in need of interpretation. In this way these Prayers reflect present theological rethinking of the concept of revelation. At the same time, some kind of balance in the EPs must be kept between the accumulated experience of the Church as expressed in its teachings and the present experience of Christian communities becoming aware of a God who is revealing.

What the Praying Community
Finds Significant To Say
about Jesus Christ

In the EP, the starting point for what is said about Jesus Christ is always the significant statements about him as summarized in the creed. The Roman EPs give a large place in traditional language to what Jesus Christ did for us. It is a message presented in a sort of kerygmatic shorthand, that is, announced but not developed at any great length since the EP proclaims, rather than discourses upon, what we believe. Faith language in the EP is always the kind of discourse that concentrates on the essentials of its message to be used for purposes of praise rather than didacticism. The Roman EPs contain all the essentials: God sent his only begotten Son, who dwelt among us; He died, rose, and was crowned with glory. He left behind a memorial which the faithful celebrate around the table and in which Christ becomes present in the bread and wine. He will also come again, and we shall all be assembled in His Kingdom. It is through Christ that glory and honor are given to God. So intimately are the essential salvation events of Christ's life connected to the memorial meal that it is difficult to omit them. The American EPs retain them while at the same time trying to give a little more emphasis to Christ's humanity. Thus, what the community finds pertinent to say about Christ is not so much different in content from the Roman EPs, but different in style.

Oosterhuis' efforts are generally concentrated on putting new life into old concepts by choosing words that cry out to be heard, although in his last table prayer he makes only a minimal reference to "that man from Nazareth who was killed." This last prayer, as we have already mentioned several times, tests the limits to which an EP may go. The word accompanying the rite does make reference to Jesus and does make reference to the bread, but there are none of the elements in this prayer that are traditionally found in the EP. There are none of the statements about Christ that the other EPs of Oosterhuis make. Are all these other references to be supposed here? No doubt, but their omission seriously truncates the full entry of the Church into the full mystery of Christ, "killed" but raised from the dead and gloriously enthroned on high. However, this last prayer should not distract us from the accomplishment of Oosterhuis in the majority of his Prayers. In Chapter Four, we saw the deeds of Christ receive their due place, expressed in a language that was fresh and yet biblically significant. What is more, the mediatorship of Christ was made quite clear; Jesus is the one through whom we must pass to get to the Father. Just as of old the Jew called (and still calls today) on the God of Abraham, Isaac, and Jacob, so the Christian calls on the God of Jesus, with the realization that he must do what Jesus did.

The Maertens EPs concentrate on articulating what God did for Jesus and what Jesus did for man. This is an interesting way of stressing the divine/human aspect of Jesus. As we saw in Chapter Five, the emphasis on what God did for Jesus centers around the completion of Jesus' faithfulness unto death. It is not something that God did for Jesus prior to His coming on this earth or some kind of supernatural endowment that accompanied Jesus. Rather,

Jesus, by being faithful to Himself and to God's plan is rewarded with being the first-born among all men, with becoming the most complete man. In other words, He is not presented here as being the most complete man before He does anything, but He becomes the most complete man because he is faithful to the Father's will at each stage of His life. There is a clear concentration on the struggles of Jesus and thus a stress on his humanity. While the divinity of Jesus is never in doubt, it is these things the community wishes to articulate. This option has the advantage of making the assembly aware that full cooperation and identification with a Christ who really and truly struggled is possible. Once the Eucharistic celebration is over, the community must return to the world and continue the struggle, confident that, because Christ overcame, with His help they too can overcome.

One of the differences between the Maertens and Oosterhuis Prayers is that, for the former, man's relationship to God does not present a problem while for the latter there is a problem. The former accept the tradition; the latter have a tendency now and then to emphasize their present experience which, while not an absolute expression of the absence of God, contains nonetheless a sense of His absence. This is why there is an insistence in Oosterhuis on Jesus of Nazareth and why the community realizes an obligation to be Him in this world. Otherwise Jesus is in danger of becoming a past figure. For both of these groups of Prayers, however, there is the same emphasis on Jesus as servant. Without forgetting that God raised up His servant (with rare exceptions in Oosterhuis), they especially stress Jesus' presence to men who treated Him precisely as a man.

Inevitably the question of Jesus' divinity is asked with regard to unofficial EPs. In their study we have consistently distinguished between what the community calls Jesus and what it says about Him. We have already discussed in another section the implications arising from the first distinction. The second shows us that, although these Prayers do not enter into the problem of the divinity of Christ *per se,* yet, since they make mention of Christ, they do reflect some kind of Christological thinking. What complicates the problem is that recent Christological studies have resulted in the Doctrinal Congregation's caution that those who question the full divinity of Christ are far from the true faith.[62] Any Christology that failed to take into account the Church's developed understanding of Jesus as God and man and simply limited itself to a one-sided selection of scriptural references would enter into difficulties. Now the EPs of Oosterhuis

[62] See *L'Osservatore Romano,* weekly English edition, March 30, 1972, p. 6.

and Maertens suggest similar reductions by their way of talking about Christ and the events of His life they select.

The Oosterhuis EPs emphasized the full humanity of Jesus whereas the Maertens EPs, instead of starting from God becoming man, gave more attention to Jesus' faithfulness in this life and how God rewarded Him. Both of these are grappling with the same fundamental problem, one which the Roman EPs tend to take for granted, namely, the humanity of Jesus. Roman EP IV is not really an exception to this when it says, ". . . he was born of the Virgin Mary and became man, in all things like us, except that he was without sin," for it uses the Pauline reference to point out immediately Jesus' difference from us. This approach, not only legitimate but eminently correct, differs from that of some unofficial EPs written for concrete communities having difficulties accepting primarily, not the divinity of Christ, but His humanity, and hence His true role as mediator. The Roman EPs start directly with faith formulae rather than any preoccupation of assimilating them in Prayers today. The Doctrinal Congregation's warning sees in the present theological ferment dangers to the Church's teaching concerning the divinity of Christ. The Oosterhuis and Maertens EPs reflect the ferment, all the more so because they are grappling with the problem of creations that take as their model, not past EPs, but their present effort to make sense out of the ambiguity of human experience. Furthermore, the Maertens and Oosterhuis Prayers, in contrast to the Roman EPs, also reflect now and then each in their own way the elusive exegetical search for the historical Jesus. Finally, these unofficial EPs suggest by their practice that for them the emphasis given in the liturgy to Jesus' divinity as a result of orthodox response has been too long with us. Only the future will tell whether or not they themselves are running the risk of a new kind of arianism or adoptionism.

What the Praying Community Says about
the Action It Is Accomplishing
and the Elements (Bread and Wine) It Uses

In our preliminary survey of the last major period of experimentation with the EP, we saw that the Reformers were most concerned with what the action of using bread and wine meant and what relationship the risen Christ had to the bread and wine. All the changes the Reformers made in the Lord's Supper were not only in reaction to certain popular Eucharistic ideas and practice of the day, but also to the Roman canon, with its dominating idea of offering. The writers of our contemporary EPs show a similar concern to state their understanding of the Eucharistic action. In doing so, some clearly react to the sacrificial emphasis of the Roman canon.

The Roman EPs, following in their own tradition and that of the Eastern anaphoras, make quite clear that the bread and wine become the Body and Blood of Christ (II, III, and IV); that Christ is present in the offering made by the Church as its sacrifice to God (III and IV); that the assembled community enters into the sacrifice of Christ through receiving the Body and Blood of Christ in communion (IV); that the sacrifice which the Church presents is acceptable because it is none other than the sacrifice of Christ (III and IV); and furthermore that this sacrifice is salutary and propitiatory for the whole world and is offered for the living and the dead (III and IV). All this and more is what the Church is conscious of doing at its Eucharistic celebration.[63] How it does it, as well as all theological speculations about this "how," would fill several books. Karl Rahner, for example, sees the Church included in the sacrifice because it concretely and individually gives reality to the objective meaning of its ritual action, that is, offers the Body and Blood of Christ to the Father in faith and love, thereby praising God in a perfect way.[64] This interpretation is quite in line with the new Roman EPs, in which the Church offers the Body and Blood of Christ and prays that God will "gather all those who share this bread and wine into the one Body of Christ, a living sacrifice of praise" (EP IV).

In addition to offering, the community also recalls, thanks, and petitions. The offering itself is made in an attitude of thanksgiving and is rendered present through the recalling. Likewise the whole Eucharistic Prayer begins with a Thanksgiving that is essentially anamnetic in character. The epicletic characteristic of the EP is implicitly present throughout the whole Prayer as well as at the Intercessions.

The American EPs also thank, remember, offer and petition, but these Prayers tend to avoid the word sacrifice in favor of the word

[63] For a Protestant reaction to this sacrificial language in the new Roman EPs, see K.-H. Bieritz, "*Oblatio ecclesiae:* Bemerkungen zu den neuen eucharistischen Hochgebeten der römischen Liturgie," *Theologische Literaturzeitung* 94 (1969), cols. 241-252. Bieritz isolates the above references and finds that while they contain difficulties for Protestants they can lead to fruitful discussion of the "Church's offering." See Edward J. Kilmartin, "Sacramental Theology: The Eucharist in Recent Literature," *Theological Studies* 32 (1971), pp. 233-277.

[64] Karl Rahner and A. Häussling, *The Celebration of the Eucharist*, W. J. O'Hara trans., New York, 1968, pp. 30 and 92.

offering even though there is no doubt about the bread and wine becoming the Body and Blood of Christ. There is more explicit emphasis on the community's offering itself, while the offering of the bread and wine become the Body and Blood of Christ is more often not expressed. Nevertheless, these Prayers are in the tradition of the Church, expressing themselves in such a way that there is no doubt that they are Prayers of the Roman Church. This is not always the case with the other two groups of EPs that we have studied.

By avoiding such terms as sacrifice and offering with regard to the Body and Blood of Christ as well as by emphasizing the self-offering of the assembly, the Maertens EPs may be creating more problems than they solve. The Roman Church has maintained that somehow the Mass is a sacrifice, and she does not mean that the assembly's self-offering is *that* sacrifice. The Church can and should enter into the one sacrifice (ephapax), made sacramentally present, but explanations of how it does this may vary. Since everyone agrees that Eucharistic faith and practice ought to converge, it would seem that in neglecting to express the idea of sacrifice in the sense of the Roman EPs, the EPs of Maertens and Oosterhuis are not clearly representing in their practice the Eucharistic faith of the Catholic Church. In fact, as we have seen in Chapter Five, the emphasis on the self-offering in Maertens may take away from the sacramental offering of Christ insofar as there is an inadequacy between the two. In a recent work of ecumenical import, Catholic W. Averbeck judges that the Reformation objections to the traditional Roman Catholic teaching stem from a misunderstanding of the role of the humanity of Christ in the redemptive process. Since Christ is both representative of God before men and the representative of men in their encounter with God, Christ acted at the sacrifice of the cross not only for Himself but as the new Adam in the name of the "many" who ought, in their turn, to consent in worship and in their everyday lives, thus sharing in the glory of their representative.[65] This clearly makes room for the self-offering of the Church, but puts the emphasis in the correct place. Thus, the christology of a group will not leave its worship and the expression of its worship untouched.

This may explain why Oosterhuis' EPs have so little reference to the sacrifice of Christ. His community is more concerned with its own existential present than with the idea of using a traditional sacrificial language. The idea of offering Christ or of offering oneself

[65] Wilhelm Averbeck, *Der Opfercharacter des Abendmahls in der neueren evangelischen Theologie,* Paderborn, 1967, pp. 803-804.

as the expression of what the community is doing may be a "caricature" of what the community is actually doing. In point of fact, for the Amsterdam community it is not even certain that the Eucharistic service is more important than the service of the Word.[66] There is no doubt that such thinking is a great source of confusion to many outside the Amsterdam student community, but it seems to us that condemnation of the latter is not in order. What is being enunciated is an entirely different awareness of what it means to be Church; what is being rejected is that the idea of being a Christian somehow comes from outside the community. We are not spokesmen for any group, but what we may say is this: the idea of sacrifice as contained in the Roman EPs is not the idea found in the Oosterhuis EPs nor in the Maertens EPs. What this means is that the latter do not consider the idea of sacrifice as found expressed in the former as necessary today for an EP within the Roman Church. It is for them a problematic or problem of a previous age, the Reformation. Their memorial of Christ and their eating of the bread are fundamentally bound up with their existence as a community. An inherited terminology, such as that found in the Roman EPs, does not express this sufficiently for them. What does this perspective mean when applied to the Oosterhuis EPs?

When Oosterhuis EP 1 refers to the "bread" and "cup" without any qualifying adjectives, it is clearly speaking in a manner different from the Roman EPs (although not from Hippolytus' *Apostolic Tradition*), which after the Institution Narrative speak about the bread and wine so as to indicate that the moment after the Institution Narrative they are different in kind from the moment before the Institution Narrative. That difference is that Christ's sacramental presence is now acknowledged and it is linked to a sacrificial framework. Oosterhuis EP 1 privileges the moment after the Institution Narrative by using the Pauline expression of proclaiming the death of Christ until he comes. In other words, there is no reason for not assigning to these words the full theological significance of the Paschal mystery. At this privileged moment, the expression "sign of our faith" is used. Catholic teaching emphasizes that when the word "sign" is used of the Eucharist it should be interpreted as having the full value of sacramental sign. This sign is presented (or offered) to God. The word sacrifice is not used, but there is nothing contrary to indicate that this Eucharist is not a sacrificial sacrament. The idea that the Eucharist reconciles is brought out at the moment of communion when attention is directed to the sacrificial act of recon-

66 Roy and Ingram, *op. cit.,* pp. 237-238.

ciliation accomplished by Christ: "This is the forgiveness of sins. This is the body broken for you."

In Prayer 2, the sign of faith becomes the sign of love when the bread and wine, by word and action eucharistized, gives communion with the body and blood. Here sacrifice, presence, and communion come together by the use of the biblical "Does not the cup that we bless give communion with the blood of Christ? Does not the bread that we break give communion with the body of Christ? Because the bread is one we all form one body, for we all share in the one bread" (1 Cor. 10:16-17).

While Prayers 3 to 6 had what might be considered minimal references, there is no reason why they should not be given maximum interpretation. Thus, when Prayer 3 refers to the "sign of our faith" may we not attribute to the word "sign" the full force of *mysterion* and *sacramentum?* May not the word "faith" be interpreted not only as the individual's faith but the faith of the Church which is not to be divorced from God's faithfulness to his covenant? Prayer 4, which does not employ the expression "sign of our faith," uses the Pauline "proclamation of the death of Christ until he comes" (1 Cor. 11:26). Furthermore, at the communion, the Eucharist as viaticum, as the bread of life, and as the sign of reconciliation and participation in the sacrifice of Christ is emphasized by using the expression: "Come, for everything is prepared. The body of Christ will preserve you and may the blood of Christ come over us."

Prayer 5 simply shifts attention from the functional aspect (nourishment) of the elements to the elements themselves, but, as is customary in these Prayers, the expression bread and wine is unadorned with adjectives. Yet, they are clearly linked to the Paschal mystery of Christ in the phrase: "Therefore, Lord God, with bread and wine we remember, until he comes, his death and resurrection." The word "remember," while linking together past and future, may be given its full sense of a "memorial which is actualized." In contrast with traditional liturgies, however, there is no expression of an offering at this point. It is possible, too, that some will find Prayer 6's laconic "accept what we are doing here in memory of Him" not explicit enough although it fulfills and responds to "Do this in memory of me."

A clear break with liturgical tradition is found in Prayer 7, where there is no Institution Narrative. This contrasts strongly also with the great insistence of the Reformers on retaining the Institution Narrative while getting rid of most of the Roman canon. Here, perhaps, the poet and musician has taken over too much in the effort to achieve a dramatic effect. The "If" clauses (which we would suggest should be seen not as grammatical conditionals but rather as verbal thrusts forward) gather up in them such ideas as Jesus is the one through whom we arrive at God, that His life was a sacrificial one, that the bread and wine give access to Him, and that we are called to join in His sacrifice. The climax, "the strength to be him" is like an existential cry of the man who dares in this world to follow Christ. If we put aside for a moment the difficulty the ordinary parishioner would have to accept the questioning approach in this Prayer, is this highly poetic expression of faith proper to the EP? The question raises the whole problem of the use of the "second language." We saw that Oosterhuis thinks it is only the "second language" that is rich enough to convey the deep relationship between God and man. The liturgy does make use of language that is poetic, but the particular poetic stamp of Oosterhuis' Prayers owes more to his Dutch predecessors than it does to the Roman liturgical tradition.

Prayer 8 stresses the fragility of our present signs: the faith is "groping," the bread is "this small sign" of promised intercourse with God at the same time that it is Jesus, who is God's name, His Son, and our life. The understanding of the Eucharist herein proposed is in strong contrast to the "O sacrament most holy, O sacrament divine" school. The Eucharist is not so much to be adored as it is sustenance for life. Hence, instead of the explicit references to the body and blood of Christ, the celebrant says "Open your hands and take this bread and peace be with you." The emphasis is on the "opened hand," the attitude of acceptance and receiving, whose fruit is peace in the sense of reconciliation.

Prayer 9 is too laconic and ambiguous, despite the Emmaus reference, from a Catholic point of view. It says that Jesus who became bread and wine (which from the other Prayers we know means that he suffered and died for man) is recognized in the breaking of the bread of this particular Eucharist. It is in Prayer 10 that we have the most striking reference to the Eucharist that we have yet seen in any of the EPs: "This simple piece of bread that does not appease our hunger." Here we are at the other end of the scale of the Eucharist considered as the "bread of angels." In other Prayers of Oosterhuis we saw a more rounded Eucharistic theology, but here all is ambiguous if not inadequate. In comparison with the Roman and American EPs, we are purely and simply in two different realms of discourse. The American EPs, for example, have their own special language, influenced a great deal by the traditional religious language employed by the Church. Thus, we have, "We offer our entire lives for the spreading of the Gospel among men of every class and nation"; "we offer our entire lives"; "this most holy sacrifice"; "the sign of our surrender"; etc. The starting point in these two groups of Prayers is clearly different. The later Oosterhuis Prayers do not begin with the idea of expressing the faith of the universal Church; rather in expressing what the community believes they hope to reach the universal Church.

The Maertens Prayers run a risk in their attempt to overcome a cultic sacrificial language in favor of, for want of a better term, an "offering up" language. The former speaks of holy and living sacrifices, victims of reconciliation, great mysteries, and the Body and Blood of Christ; the latter offers up everyday concrete things (as in Lent, cigarettes, liquor, etc.). Thus, instead of concrete things, the Maertens Prayers offer up their "hesitations" or their "good will." Furthermore, these Prayers run into the same difficulty as the Oosterhuis Prayers, namely, the lack of a specific offering of the sacrifice of Christ. However, it is more noticeable in the Maertens Prayers for they are less connotative than those of Oosterhuis. With respect to this, we may find interesting a consideration of articles 47 and 48 of the Constitution on the Sacred Liturgy.

Article 47 presents the theological basis of the Eucharistic Mystery and speaks of the "Eucharistic sacrifice of His Body and Blood" which was instituted at the Last Supper. Article 48 says that by offering the Immaculate Victim, not only through the hands of the priest, but also with him, the faithful should learn to offer themselves, too.[67] Now the Maertens EPs make primary the self-offering at the expense of what the Council document has made the very basis of the self-offering. Maertens in his criticism of the new EPs suggested that *Gaudium et Spes* could have inspired their authors to make them more contemporaneous.[68] Yet, another council document, *Lumen Gentium*, which treats of the Church in the world, sees the offering of the Lord's Body as primary at the Eucharistic celebration, without thereby ignoring the faithful's self-offering:

> For all their works, prayers, and apostolic endeavors, their ordinary married and family life, their daily labor, their mental and physical relaxation, if carried out in the Spirit, and even the hardships of life, if patiently borne—all of these become spiritual sacrifices acceptable to God through Jesus Christ. Dur-

[67] Walter M. Abbott, General Editor, "Sacrosanctum Concilium," *The Documents of Vatican Two,* Joseph Gallagher, translation editor, New York, 1966, p. 154.
[68] Maertens, "Les nouvelles prières eucharistiques. . . ," p. 198.

ing the celebration of the Eucharist, these sacrifices are most
lovingly offered to the Father along with the Lord's body. Thus,
as worshippers whose every deed is holy, the laity consecrate
the world itself to God.[69]

The Maertens EPs try to inculcate in the make-up of their assembly
this consecration of the world through actions, announced in the EP
but carried out in the world. However, it is the offering of the Lord's
Body that should be primary. What Maertens' EPs show is the difficulty of articulating the everyday sacrifices of the laity in a concrete
way along with the offering of the Lord's Body.

While the Church teaches that Christ is present in different manners
at the Eucharistic celebration, the EPs usually articulate only what
is called the "real presence." The Roman EPs affirm this presence
by Epiclesis–Institution Narrative–Acclamation–Anamnesis block,
and by the reference to the communion to follow, where the faithful
communicate in the Body and Blood of Christ. Not every EP that
we have studied has this block nor does every one make mention
that the faithful communicate in the Body and Blood of Christ. Yet
there is sufficient indication that Christ is present. What is not
clear is *how* Christ is present, in the sense of the manner of His
presence and in the sense of the way this presence comes about. The
latter sense generally involves discussion of transubstantiation and
memorial. It is theology's role, not the EPs' to discourse on this.
The former sense may refer to Christ's presence in the assembly,
in the minister, and in the bread and wine. As we have seen, the
Catholic Church holds a realist interpretation of Christ's presence
in the sacrament of the Eucharist. The point at issue, however, insofar as the contemporary non-Roman EPs are concerned is: may verbal reference to this presence be omitted? It is clear from the
practice of the Church that verbal reference to the presence of
Christ in the Word and in the celebrant may be omitted. May
reference to Christ's presence in the Eucharistic species be omitted?
The answer is that in the EP it is fitting to express this presence at
the very least in its relationship to the reception of the bread and
wine. J. M. R. Tillard makes this same point when he notes that
the Roman EPs, though asking for the transformation of the bread
and wine, do not delay over the presence in itself but rather look to
an ulterior transformation, the one which the Body and Blood of
Christ should bring about in the life of Christians.[70] Furthermore, as

[69] In Abbott, *op. cit.* "Lumen Gentium," p. 60.
[70] J. M. R. Tillard, "Catholiques Romains et Anglicans: L'Eucharistie,"
NRT 93, 1971, p. 629.

Cardinal Bea pointed out at the Council, the mystery itself should be understood through the prayers and rites.[71] Thus, while it may be argued that the rite leads to the conclusion of the presence of Christ in the species, it is more fitting that this be made clear, especially since we know that Christian division has arisen over the understanding of this presence. Even though the EP is not first and foremost a dogmatic statement, it is appropriate that it express the contact the community makes with the risen Lord in the Eucharist.

The Place Given to the Role of the Holy Spirit

The role of the Holy Spirit receives its most succinct and coherent treatment in the official EPs. He is shown at work in the divine economy, and He is invoked always in relation to the gifts offered, first on the bread and wine that they become the Body and Blood of Christ, secondly on the community in view of its reception of these same elements now become the Body and Blood of Christ. The Doxology, which is the return at the end of the Prayer to the initial praise of God, always prays through Christ in the unity of the Spirit.

All the other Prayers, whether American, Dutch, or Belgian, do not present this same coherent use. The American EPs, while they give a place to the Spirit, have the tendency to make the invocation on the community as if it were one Intercession among many. Since this invocation is not always directly linked to the reception of the elements as a rule, it could take place outside of the context of the EP. Thus, when this is the case, there is no clear reason why the Spirit should be invoked within the structure of the EP. The role of the Epiclesis is confused with that of the Intercessions.

The Oosterhuis EPs give a lesser role to the Holy Spirit, even to the extent that there are Prayers where He is not invoked at all. There is never any invocation of the Holy Spirit on the bread and wine. However, we must immediately remark that, within the context of certain of the Oosterhuis Prayers, to introduce the Holy Spirit into their development would break the unity of discourse. From the framework within which the Oosterhuis EP operates, there is no compelling reason why the Holy Spirit should find a place. On the other hand, it could be argued that His introduction into the Prayer would not destroy the unity of the Prayer—indeed could not —so much is He necessary to the action taking place. However, in

[71] Cited in Jungmann's Commentary on Sacrosanctum Concilium," *op. cit.*, p. 52.

answer to this, we have seen that the minimum counted necessary from the practice of these Prayers is that an address be made to God and some mention be made of Jesus and the bread. We may say this much: when the Holy Spirit is invoked, He is given first place among the Petitions, and often His role is characterized in an incisive fashion. Always He is seen as an active agent in this world, someone who moves, who gives power.

It is the Maertens EPs that presented the greatest problem with regard to the place given to the role of the Holy Spirit in the EP. We found that these Prayers gave more space to the Holy Spirit, but at the same time we were led to ask to what advantage. Three problems were presented to us: first, there was the invocation of the Spirit on those not present at the assembly rather than on those present; secondly, there was a decided looseness of language in referring to the Spirit; and thirdly, there was in some Prayers such an extensive invocation of the Spirit that paradoxically His role seemed actually to be lessened.

The Invocation of the Spirit on those not present cannot, of course, be faulted. However, since the Eucharist is a privileged moment, at which the Holy Spirit is felt to be particularly at work in the divine economy, it seems that it is more fitting and theologically sound to invoke Him on those present and in reference to the reception of the Eucharist. The entire coherence of the EP calls for this.

The slackness of language in referring to the Holy Spirit is inexcusable given the importance of the EP to the Christian Assembly. Unless one is for total spontaneity, one does not simply say just anything or in any fashion at the Memorial meal.

Finally, to invoke the Spirit in a kind of litany fashion is laudable in itself but not necessarily within the confines of the EP for, of all the elements of the EP, the Intercessions are the least important or essential. They can be omitted without interfering in any way with the EP. Their presence is always the result of a continuation of a practice that was introduced at a much later date within the EP than other aspects. A certain neglect of the Spirit in Western liturgical practice has perhaps led to this exaggerated kind of introduction into the Maertens EPs. J. M. R. Tillard has said that in the New Testament the lordship of Jesus is linked with the activity of the Spirit in the sense that Jesus comes to men only through the Spirit.[72] This, then, is the orientation that the invocation of the Spirit should have in the Eucharist: the transformation of the assembled believers.

---

[72] J. M. R. Tillard, "L'Eucharistie et le Saint-Esprit," *NRT* 90, 1968, pp. 384-385.

This emphasis or rather this rich theological implication may easily suffer in those EPs that demand variety from one to the other. So the profound theological understanding of the Holy Spirit's role in the worshipping community here and now is sacrificed to an attempt to introduce the Spirit in some other way, such as asking that He inspire leaders in high places. It is debatable whether or not this is more desirable than the complete omission of any reference to the Spirit.

It is obvious that the rich pneumatology of the Eastern Liturgies, such as that presented by Orthodox Boris Bobrinskoy, for example, in his writing on the real presence and Eucharistic communion, is lacking in these unofficial EPs for there is no compelling necessity for an expression of the role of the Spirit at their base.[73]

III
CONTEXT: THE WIDER PROBLEMATIC
OF THE PRESENT EXPERIMENTATION

During the course of our study we have seen that the terminology used with regard to the EP varies. Now it is called canon, now anaphora, table prayer, or Eucharistic Prayer. It is not the first time that the great Thanksgiving Prayer of Christians has had a variety of names applied to it. By "canon" is meant specifically the Roman canon, the prayer used in the Roman Church from the fourth or fifth century A.D. It is only by extension that it is applied to any of the new EPs although it is possible that the time will come when the new Roman EPs may be legitimately called canons in the sense that all other EPs must follow them as norms and/or measures as to what constitutes an EP. By "anaphora" we mean any one of the EPs of the Eastern Churches. The new Roman EPs, at the time they were presented officially to the Church, were thought of as anaphoras, but this term only shows their dependence on the Eastern anaphora as a model. For the Western Church, this term can remain at best only a scholarly one. By "Eucharistic Prayer," the term that we have been using throughout this study, we refer directly to the thanksgiving prayer accompanying the actions of recalling what Christ did at the Last Supper. The very word "Eucharist" focuses on the thanksgiving aspect as well as on the elements which have received the name eucharistia, just as the word anaphora em-

---

[73] Boris Bobrinskoy, "Présence réelle et communion eucharistique," *Revue des sciences philosophiques et théologiques* 53, 1969, pp. 402-420.

phasizes the offering (for the word means that) as well as the gifts that are called offering. Thus, Eucharistic Prayer is not really a category under which "canon" and "anaphora" may be subsumed. The largest category used to refer to the literary genre about which we have been speaking is "table prayer." Whether or not it is the most appropriate term is debatable. At a time when there is a definite movement against a specialized or sacral language, it does have advantages over the other terms. Although its weakness may be that it does not say enough, it does emphasize the meal aspect of the Eucharist. Thus, by its very name it focuses on an aspect not covered by the other terms. This change of terminology reflects the search for the meaning of the Eucharist and the attitude that one wishes to emphasize when Christians come together to celebrate the memorial of the Last Supper.

The Roman canon, therefore, instead of being *the* model for an EP is clearly seen now as only itself *an* EP, however much respected for the tradition it represents, however much reviled by the Reformers who attacked it as an abomination. Nor are the Eastern anaphoras *the* model of an EP for they are bound up with a temporal manner of speaking about God. Furthermore, the attitude or emotion of reverence present at the Eastern Eucharist is one that has been at one and the same time theologically and culturally determined.[74] Since the Roman canon and the Eastern anaphoras are the two principal kinds of models that have come down to us, the question arises, "Can we get at the essentials that must be expressed in an EP and which go beyond cultural conceptions of God and human models of behavior adopted in the presence of God?" Another way of putting this is to ask what are the essential elements to be included in an EP. Answers to this question depend on: an understanding of what *Do this in memory of me* means; what may be presupposed as part of the believing community's faith and their faith-stance; what the understanding of the literary genre of the EP is; and whether or not one wishes to look to the past for models or to create anew simply with the Last Supper in mind.

One of the first authors to probe the understanding of the EP was

---

[74] Joseph Jungmann, *The Place of Christ in Liturgical Prayer*, A. Peeler, trans., New York, 1965 (second revised edition), pp. 245-252. Jungmann takes up Edmund Bishop's suggestion that the fourth century saw a great change in the religious thinking and feelings of the faithful with regard to the Eucharist and this change found its way into the anaphora. Jungmann amplifies the discussion and gives the recent literature. For Bishop, see R. H. Connolly, *The Liturgical Homilies of Narsai*, with an Appendix by Edmund Bishop, Cambridge, 1909, pp. 92-97.

Godfrey Danneels, who has offered several ways of looking at the "anaphora." [75] He calls it the focusing on a given community's re-enactment of the Last Supper, the expression of what is being done, of a lived fact, of the global meaning of the Eucharist, of an existential step taken, of the whole community's disposition to the whole Eucharistic event, of an expression that is intentionally total but partially fulfilled. Thus, when Danneels studies the EPs that have come down to us, he sees them taking into consideration the Last Supper, the present act, the articulation of these two, the global experience, the existential act, and the relationship of one whole to another whole that is necessarily partial in expression. The Institution Narrative, considered as a condensation of the complete signification of the Eucharist, may thus have any one of its aspects elaborated: remembrance, invocation, offering, communicating, reconciliation, or expectation. Expansion of any one of these concepts would lead to varying EPs.

Herman Manders also sought new creations from an analysis of the EP as found in the Roman canon and the anaphoras of the Eastern Churches.[76] His starting point was the memorial character of the EP, which led him to ask who carries out this memorial, in whose presence is it carried out, and what does it commemorate. The answers to these questions he finds in the different Eucharistic practice of the major Churches.

Next, he isolates the structural elements of the EP: thanksgiving, invocation, proclamation, supplication, action, sacrifice, eating, and presence. Any one of these elements can be raised to a structural principle around which the others can form, but not necessarily in an explicit fashion. This too permits a variety of EPs, based on the structural elements that make up any EP.

Neither Danneels nor Manders wishes to do away with any elements that have been regarded as traditional in Eucharistic practice in the Roman or Eastern Churches. Using the Roman canon as an example of an EP with a theme or structural element that serves as a structural principle (the idea of offering), Manders calls for EPs that allow other structural elements to become structural principles. The real problem with working these ideas out is that one must presuppose a great deal when reading some of the EPs that we have studied. Thus, if one starts with the idea that the Institution Narrative is a pass-word

---

[75] Godfrey Danneels, "A la recherche des lois de composition de la prière eucharistique" in Godfrey Danneels and Thierry Maertens, editors, *La Prière Eucharistique,* Vivante Liturgie 79, Paris, 1967, pp. 65-94.

[76] Herman Manders, "Het eucharistisch gebed," *Tijdchrift voor Liturgie* 68, 1967, pp. 27-47.

that summarizes the whole Prayer, then its inclusion in all of the EPs would mean that there is no *essential* difference between any of the EPs. This, however, could not really be the case for it would make the Institution Narrative into some kind of magic formula. Also we know that serious differences of interpretation can arise with regard to the Institution Narrative. Its inclusion in any EP does not really guarantee that the EP necessarily expresses the faith of the Church. It would be better to say that any EP that expresses the faith of the Church should contain the Institution Narrative. This is what Danneels is getting at when he says that it is the job of the EP to articulate the relationship of the present celebration with the Last Supper.

In Chapter Five, we saw that contemporary EPs were sought by wedding a biblical and liturgical language to the language of everyday as well as by making the assembled "we" the interpreter of all humanity to God. Neither of these two ideas has failed to preoccupy the Church. In the first place, the document on the translation of the Roman EPs has made it clear that the Church is concerned with the expression of the EP in the language of the people.[77] It recognizes without using the linguistic terms that the language of the people is both *langue* and *parole*.[78] Originally the entire question of the language of the people tended to be discussed on the level of *langue*, now it has shifted to the level of *parole*. What is happening at this latter level is that the center of attention is moving from *parole* to idiolect.[79] Another way of saying this for the American situation is that EPs should not only be in English, they should be in a comprehensible American English that touches the participant as being authentic or meaningful since they reflect his experience. In the second place, the Church has frequently spoken as the authentic voice of man before God since all men are redeemed in Christ. This is a major consideration in coming together to meet in council or synod. The emphasis in unofficial EPs is precisely on immediate concerns

[77] "Instruction du 'Consilium' sur la traduction des textes liturgiques pour la célébration avec le peuple," *Notitiae* 44, 1969, pp. 3-12; reprinted in *DC* 66, 1969, pp. 367-372.

[78] The distinction we are here using should not be confusing. *Langue* is the language system; *parole* is the speech act of an individual in a specific context. The best introduction for all this in English and for the liturgist is perhaps David Crystal's *Linguistics, Language and Religion*, Faith and Fact Books 131, London, 1965. See especially pp. 59-63.

[79] Idiolect is the habitual patterns utilizable by one individual and derivable from the totality of his speech acts. We apply it here to the Oosterhuis EPs which have a stamp quite different from the Maertens EPs, which are composed in their own idiolect. See Crystal, *op. cit.*, p. 63.

and points of reference to the world today. Quite often these Prayers
have among their major themes relationships that bind men together
beyond religious lines. In other words, these unofficial EPs often try
to see the fundamental human strivings at work in all men as basically religious.

Guerin's thought, which we summarized in Chapter Five, stressed
the variety of approaches taken in different liturgies in the assembly's address to God in its EP. This was seen as an indication that
the same faith was being transmitted through a different religious
sensibility. Guerin's claim is that the time has come to put the faith
into a modern religious sensibility that is significantly different from
the old one. We saw that his articulation of the contours of this
modern religious sensibility had to do with God, Christ, the Church,
and the Christian. What he said was similar to the approach of
Oosterhuis as we outlined it in Chapter Four. Hence, since it is the
Eucharist as rite that is primary, the praying community has an obligation to put into modern language its understanding of the "rite-
bearing salvation event." Guerin's argumentation in favor of the
Maertens EPs is that if one studies the liturgical families of EPs, one
will find certain paired ideas that give a stable but not a rigid
dynamism. He finds this in the Maertens EPs and therefore is able
to declare them radically traditional. Since their language and their
outlook on man is up-to-date, they are integrally modern. The
logic of the argumentation is difficult to refute. What is, however,
a matter of conjecture, and even Guerin admits this, is whether or
not the Maertens EPs in themselves are successes. The most that can
be said is that they are necessary stages toward better EPs. But, in a
sense, this leaves us where we were at the outset. Everyone wants
contemporary EPs, but not everyone is sure that a contemporary EP,
once it is written, is successful or not. The "expert" may declare
such-and-such an EP as totally lacking in theological expression
whereas the layman may confess that he was very much touched
by the same prayer. The crux of the problem seems to reside with
two problems presently confronting modern man: a shift in his attitude toward God and a crisis of religious language. We must now
say something about both of these.

Gregory Baum has tried to translate the Christian creed into ordinary secular language.[80] He describes his theological approach as
"the Blondelian shift," which is both a method of immanence and
a philosophy of action. The shift is from an outsider to an insider

[80] Gregory Baum, *Man Becoming: God in Secular Meaning,* New York,
1970.

God. Baum applies this "shift" to redemption, holiness, the Church, eschatology, the doctrine of God, divine creation, and divine transcendence.

Baum finds inconsistent with his approach the idea of a supreme being, called God, with an omniscient mind and an omnipotent will, who has planned the world of men in all its detail and who rules over history with a power no one can resist.[81] Specifically what Baum is rejecting in its most crude form is the idea of a God who is a super-person that man observes and classifies. Thus he reinterprets God's omniscience as God's summoning of man to greater insight in every human situation, no matter how frightening, no matter how difficult; God's omnipotence would mean that there is no situation, however destructive, in which an inner strength is not offered to man, allowing him to assume greater possession of his humanity.[82] In other words, Baum is trying to retain traditional religious terms by a more modern (since influenced by depth psychology) way of regarding them. Over against those who object to the word Father as applied to God, Baum sees that "God is Father" means that man is a being with a destiny, defined in terms of growth and communion. To believe that God is Father is to become aware of oneself not as a stranger, not as an outsider or an alienated person, but as a son who belongs or a person appointed to a marvelous destiny, one which he shares with the whole community. To believe that God is Father means to be able to say "we" in regard to all men.[83]

Whatever their validity may be, these psychological interpretations of Christian Doctrine reflect a real struggle that is taking place. The Christian lives in a secular world where it becomes almost impossible for him to immerse himself in a special language that requires interpretation if it is not to distort reality. Karl Rahner has remarked:

> Propositions such as: there are three persons in God—God sent his Son into the world—we are saved by the blood of Jesus Christ, are purely and simply incomprehensible for a man of today if they remain, in the former way of theologizing or proclaiming, the starting point and the end point of the Christian message. They give the same impression as the pure mythology in a bygone religion.[84]

81 *Ibid.,* p. 243.
82 *Ibid.,* p. 244.
83 *Ibid.,* pp. 194-195.
84 Karl Rahner, "L'avenir de la théologie," p. 14.

He concludes that theology must develop an aptitude to speak of God in a secular language, and the cult, which as been shaped by the traditional formulae, will also be reshaped at its own pace by any reformulation.[85]

The God of the official EPs is wonderfully close to man, but what should a community do if it experiences God more by his absence than by his presence. It makes no sense to say that such a community must make a leap of faith since it has already undoubtedly done so, nor does it make sense to say that it must conform itself to the larger community for it is just possible that the larger community (say, a given national Church), precisely because it is community in mind and heart, may have the same experience. Nor is there any solution in saying that this is the Greek Orthodox approach. For the experience of God's absence that we are talking about is more akin to the "God is dead" school than the ringing affirmation of the Orthodox Church that God lives. Besides a simple glance at the Eastern anaphoras shows that the theology found therein is so rich that it is precisely here that the Roman EP authors turned for models of their own efforts, so different from some of the Oosterhuis EPs.

One possible solution to reconciling the present lack of serenity in faith is to turn to the Psalms of Israel as models, for Israel's experience is a paradigm for the spiritual adventure of all men. This is the solution adopted by the Oosterhuis EPs. A Psalm like Psalm 4 takes into account an audience that experiences the struggle for faith; Psalm 11 articulates the choice between a panicky flight from the world and the surrender of faith; and Psalm 121 uses the idea of pilgrimage as the image for the life of the believer.[86] Franz Jozef van Beeck, who cooperated with Oosterhuis in translating fifty Psalms into Dutch, says of Psalm 63:

> The experience of emptiness and fulness, distance and closeness, exhaustion and life, near-despair and profound trust go hand in hand if a man, carried on the waves of common worship, discovers his deepest and most fundamental aspirations, expresses them in words at once too big and too vulnerable, and finally comes out with the name for it: "You are my God."[87]

There are two things to note here. The first is the pairing of opposite

[85] *Ibid.*, p. 14 and p. 27.
[86] Franz Jozef van Beeck, Huub Oosterhuis, *et al.*, *Fifty Psalms*, David Smith and Forrest Ingram, trans., Herder and Herder, 1969, *passim*.
[87] *Ibid.*, p. 61.

experiences, what Baum would call the becoming and the self-destructive tendencies in man. The believer cannot deny the existence of both within him. That is why the Oosterhuis "we" finds it so difficult to limit the EP to a hymn of pure thanksgiving or a simple remembrance of what Jesus did. There is a need to present both sides of the "we" as well as affirm that Jesus died and rose. In this way the speaker enters into the dying and rising more closely.

The second thing we would like to point out here is the manner in which van Beeck refers to words. He calls them at once too big and too vulnerable. This is the same kind of snesitivity toward words that Oosterhuis evidenced in his Prayers. It is the poet's delight and fear before the words he puts together to interpret the uninterpretable.

Two other comments of van Beeck are enlightening for an understanding of what Oosterhuis is trying to do. Commenting on Psalm 69, he remarks that the Psalms are not perfect prayers in the sense that they only express the so-called higher, purer, or "more perfect" emotions. Their perfection lies in their being immersed in the human situation with all its fears, doubts, and crudities, while at the same time bringing God's presence to bear on all this:

> Chaos, disintegration, injustice, vulgarity, and abuse are real, and as such they can be the stuff of the experience of faith, and in cases even its mainspring.[88]

The EPs of Oosterhuis proclaim their faith through or in spite of the horrible things that life reveals. The EP becomes the heightened place where the community looks evil full in the face at the very moment it is proclaiming the triumph of "that man Jesus." Is this any different *in kind* from what the Roman EPs are doing when they give a heightened sense of thanksgiving, praise and joy to the privileged moment of the Eucharist?

Finally, Psalm 73 elicits the following comment from van Beeck: "This Psalm fathoms in a passionate and almost rigorous way the power of faith in God by comparing it with unbelief."[89] Something of this idea is operating in Oosterhuis' EP 10, where the speaker is convinced of his faith because it is no longer based on any false ideas. It is pure and simple faith in the face of all of reason's unbelief.

These are powerful thoughts. We find them in the Psalms and in

[88] *Ibid.*, p. 65.
[89] *Ibid.*, p. 73.

the Oosterhuis EPs, but we do not find them in the Roman or American EPs, although there are echoes of them in the Maertens EPs. The question is then: may an EP admit of a dialectical approach in the form of a complaint that ends in thanksgiving and praise? Thus, the complaint Psalm and not the Beraka would be the model for the EP. We suggest the following in answer to this question. So long as we think of public worship as assembling Christians from all walks of life, it is difficult to accept an EP that does not concentrate on the praise and thanksgiving as exemplified in the Roman EPs. If, however, we consider a closely united community struggling with its faith, then there may be less objection to what we have called a dialectical development in the EP. Although, in comparison with the EP of the universal Church, the EP of a parish community may seem a very private one indeed, it would appear that the latter should still exhibit some kind of continuity with the tradition. In the Roman tradition, when the celebrant says "Lift up your hearts!" the assembly moves into a hymn of praise and thanksgiving, of joyful acknowledgment. If this attitude is not to be something merely willed nor something to which one gives only intellectual consent, but something which actually is an outpouring of thankful joy, then it must be preceded by a period of preparation different from that presently provided by the liturgy. Otherwise, to a certain respect, the words "Lift up your hearts!" lose some of their meaningfulness. In a sense, a dialectical EP that leads up to joy, after starting from anguish, becomes a real possibility, at least from the criterion of meaningfulness.

We should like to make one final remark here. Religious imagination has not really been put to work in the official EPs, whereas it has been in the Oosterhuis EPs and to some extent in the Maertens EPs. It has been used with less success in the American EPs. In the traditional EP of the Roman canon, one may find many instances of religious imagination at work, notably in the Sanctus. What Oosterhuis has accomplished is the use of religious imagination in a new way so that its effect tends to be striking. Thus Prayers 7 and 10, which resemble respectively a Greek chorus and a Shakespearean soliloquy, startle by their very form for they are closer to the Book of Job and the complaint Psalms than any other EPs we have studied. The problem is, of course, that even if the Beraka form is abandoned, the EP, as Robert Ledogar has remarked, should not cease to be an acknowledgment of gratitude.[90] Throughout the centuries follow-

---

[90] Robert J. Ledogar, "The Eucharist Prayer and the Gifts Over Which It Is Spoken," *Worship* 41, 1967, p. 586.

ing the Reformation, the Protestant Liturgies, which at their origin expressed a deficient notion of joy at the Lord's Supper, rediscovered how central such a notion was to the Eucharist. This, along with other reasons, led to its reestablishment at the outset of their EPs. However, even though the notion of Memorial gives cause for joy, must joy alone be manifest in the EP? Is it not true that even non-liturgical celebrations of joy contain moments that are not expressions of joy, but are nevertheless expressions of human sentiment? Hence, when J. M. R. Tillard writes, with reference to the different Christian communions, that it is up to each ecclesial tradition to interpret—*according to its own ways and its own sensibility*—that the bread and wine become the Body of the one who by His passage from death to life has been made Lord of creation and history,[91] we may legitimately ask whether or not such latitude may be extended within the Roman Catholic communion to national groups such as the Dutch Church, of which the Oosterhuis EPs are only one manifestation and not acceptable to everyone.

Another area of concern that is very central to an understanding of contemporary EPs is what has come to be called God-talk. To ignore this problem is to risk being totally unconscious of one's pre-suppositions; to take the problem too seriously is to risk being reduced to silence. Since the literature on religious language is enormous, there is no sense in trying to pretend that it does not exist. One thing this literature reveals is that there is no one perfect way of talking about God. There is a variety of ways of talking to and about God which depend on our conceptions of Him, our understanding of our relationship to Him, our notion of what is fitting to say to Him, and our idea of the time and place to speak to Him.

In some of the facile criticism of contemporary unofficial EPs, there seems to be an underlying pre-supposition that there is only one way to talk to God in EPs. This one way may be characterized as "lofty," "serene," and "universal." All three adjectives are characteristic of the classical heritage in literature. We may summarize the attitude as follows: a speaker who does not intrude speaks an elevated language that rarely descends to particulars. Thus, sins against this understanding of how to speak to God would be: the speaker who becomes too obvious or intrusive (the Oosterhuis "we"?), a language that is too common (the Maertens EPs?), and an embarrassing concern with everyday realities (the Maertens and some of the American EPs?).

[91] Tillard, "Catholiques Romains. . . ," p. 642.

The official EPs are those most couched in the language that is traditional. It is a language so tied up with belief that often its practitioners find no need to cast a critical eye on it in the way a philosopher of the logical positivist school may do. In fact, those who are aware of this critical eye and oppose it might say that, since religious language is existential and convictional, one does not need to offer a logical analysis of the Creator of Heaven and Earth, nor discard the doctrine of the Trinity simply because the language in which it is expressed may be logically inconsistent; [92] or that analogies used by believers ultimately establish themselves by the living relation in which they stand to the living Word of God, to the worshipping and obedient community, and to the salvation of God's children.[93]

However, the danger in such answers, as Jerry Gill has pointed out, is that there seems to be an attempt to pretend that religious language does not have criteria. Gill says that the approach which would set religious language off as autonomous proceeds from the worthy motive of safeguarding it from rationalism; but such safety comes at the expense of dis-relating religious language from experience by eliminating any inter-subjective criterion of meaning and truth.[94]

This question is one that cannot be avoided. Is the language of worship totally divorced from the language of theological discourse? Does the theologian who speaks of God as the Limit [95] or of God as Being [96] go home and pray in a more concrete language as found in the Roman EPs or the American EPs? Of course, the solution afforded by speaking about God in terms of biblical references or those based on personal models is a convenient one. It is significant, however, that some biblical terms and some personal models are no longer regarded as relevant. The usual example of this is the word King, a model that had great relevance in the past. We have seen that

[92] William F. Zuurdeeg, "Implications of Analytical Philosophy for Theology," *The Journal of Bible and Religion,* July 1961, p. 209.

[93] John McIntyre, "Analogy," *Scottish Journal of Theology,* March 1959, pp. 1-20.

[94] Jerry H. Gill, "Talk about Religious Talk: Various Approaches to the Nature of Religious Language," *Theology No. 4,* Martin E. Marty and Dean G. Peerman, eds., New York, 1967, pp. 99f.

[95] Gordon D. Kaufmann, "On the meaning of 'God': Transcendence without Mythology," *Theology No. 4,* Martin E. Marty and Dean G. Peerman, eds., New York, 1967, pp. 69-78.

[96] John Macquarrie, "How Can We Think of God?" *Philosophy Today No. 2,* Jerry H. Gill, ed., Toronto, 1969, pp. 142-154.

the favorite model used of God is that of Father, but we know that even the word Father can present difficulties to those persons whose idea of father is almost synonymous with that of tyrant.

There are, then, two problems here. Can we talk about God at all? If yes, how are we to talk about him? The first question is obviously the most radical for if the answer for a believer could possibly be "No," then he would be reduced to silence. However, it is precisely as believer that he cannot admit a negative answer. It is his conception of God that influences the way that he will talk about God, and it is for this reason that the second question is the more important one and, in a sense, the more difficult one. In an age when for many Christians God is more present by his absence than by any feeling of closeness, the question, "What model is to be used to talk about or to God?" is more than just academic. What may have to be recognized is that no single liturgical expression may replace a variety of liturgical expressions rising out of different perceptions of reality and different awareness of experience within the Western Church.[97] In this sense, the contemporary EPs—official and unofficial alike—are more than just interesting experiments in a liturgical literary genre; they also reflect varying approaches to reality.

IV
PRESENT ECUMENICAL CONVERGENCE

At the present moment when different Churches in the Christian tradition are meeting together for ecumenical purposes, the official EPs play a role that is proper to them. It is their vocation to articulate the Eucharistic faith of the Catholic Church in a clear way. Our next and final task is to relate several ecumenical statements to this aspect of the Roman EPs.

Within the framework of the theological dialogues between representatives of the United States Catholic Bishops' Committee for Ecumenical and Inter-religious Affairs and the U.S.A. National Committee of the Lutheran World Federation, representatives of both groups were able to come up with a surprising measure of agreement with regard to "sacrifice" and "real presence." Not all differences were resolved, of course, but the outcome of the dialogues that took place between September, 1966 and October, 1967 was judged to be especially significant.[98]

[97] Rahner, "L'avenir de la theologie," p. 9.
[98] *Lutherans and Catholics in Dialogue III: The Eucharist as Sacrifice*, New York, 1968.

Roman Catholics and Lutherans were able to affirm that both acknowledge that in the Lord's Supper "Christ is present as the crucified who died for our sins and who rose again for our justification, as the once-for-all sacrifice for the sins of the world who gives himself to the faithful." Both agree that the celebration of the Eucharist is the Church's sacrifice of praise and self-offering or oblation. Each tradition can make the following statement its own:

By him, with him and in him who is our great High Priest and Intercessor we offer to the Father, in the power of the Holy Spirit, our praise, thanksgiving and intercession. With contrite hearts we offer ourselves as a living and holy sacrifice, a sacrifice which must be expressed in the whole of our daily lives.[99]

Although the Lutherans acknowledged that Trent taught the unrepeatable character of the sacrifice of the Cross, they admitted that formerly they had reason to doubt that this teaching was upheld by practice. They see now, however, that the Catholic affirmation that the Church "offers Christ" in the Mass has in the course of the last half-century been increasingly explained in terms which answer Lutheran fears that this detracts from the full sufficiency of Christ's sacrifice. The members of the body of Christ are united through Christ with God and with one another in such a way that they become participants in His worship, His self-offering, His sacrifice to the Father. Through this union between Christ and Christians, the Eucharistic assembly "offers Christ" by consenting in the power of the Holy Spirit to be offered by Him in the Father. Apart from Christ, we have no worship, no sacrifice of our own to offer to God. All we can plead is Christ, the sacrificial Lamb and victim whom the Father Himself has given us.[100]

With regard to the presence of Christ in the Lord's Supper, the following points were made: "first, the manifold presence of Christ is affirmed, especially that Jesus Christ, true God and true man, is present wholly and entirely, in his body and blood, under the signs of bread and wine in the sacrament of the Lord's Supper; second, the presence of Christ does not come about through the faith of the believer, or through any human power, but by the power of the Holy Spirit through the word." [101] Rounding off this common understand-

[99] *Ibid.*, pp. 188-189.
[100] *Ibid.*, pp. 189-190.
[101] *Ibid.*, pp. 192-193.

ing were the agreement that as long as Christ is sacramentally present, worship, reverence and adoration are appropriate and the statement that, although Lutherans still had difficulties with the term transubstantiation, none of them affected the presence of Christ in the sacrament.[102]

On an international level, agreement between Anglicans and Roman Catholics was announced December 31, 1971, in a statement of "A Shared Belief." [103] With regard to our study, the pertinent parts of this statement are the following:

> When his people are gathered to commemorate his saving acts for our redemption at the Eucharist, Christ makes effective among us the eternal benefits of his victory and elicits and renews our response of faith, thanksgiving, and self-surrender.[104]

> In the eucharistic prayer the Church continues to make a perpetual memorial of Christ's death; and his members, united with God and one another, give thanks for all his mercies, entreat the benefits of his passion on behalf of the whole Church, participate in these benefits and enter into the movement of his self-offering.[105]

> Through the [consecratory thanksgiving prayer], a word of faith addressed to the Father, the bread and wine become the body and blood of Christ by the action of the Holy Spirit, so that in communion we eat the flesh of Christ and drink his blood.[106]

The first statement emphasizes the idea of the continuation of the effects of Calvary in the Mass and the proper response of the participants, which seems to us to be equivalent to *memores offerimus*. It is in the next paragraph that we see how the thanksgiving and self-surrender of the first paragraph are summarized by the *memores offerimus*. To say memorial is to say thanksgiving because Christ's gift and our thankful response in faith are inseparable as two sides of a sheet of paper. So it is also with his self-offering and our self-offering. The one is inseparable from the other. This statement shows

---

[102] *Ibid.*, pp. 195-196.
[103] "The Windsor Statement on Eucharistic Doctrine," *Worship* 46 (1972), pp. 2-5.
[104] *Ibid.*, p. 2.
[105] *Ibid.*, pp. 3-4.
[106] *Ibid.*, p. 5.

to some extent what is expected of an EP for it says expressly, "In the eucharistic prayer" a perpetual memorial is made, thanks is given, entreaty is made, participation in Christ's benefits takes place, and entry into his self-offering is accomplished. If any of these are omitted in an EP, that EP is an incomplete expression of the Church's *minimal* understanding of the Eucharist. This is why the omission of intercessory prayer from the EP ("to entreat the benefits of his passion on behalf of the whole Church") cannot be undertaken lightly.

The last statement of the "Shared Belief" affirms that the whole EP is consecratory and that it is trinitarian: addressed to the Father it is through the action of the Holy Spirit that the bread and wine become the Body and Blood of Christ in which we participate.

More recently the agreement reached by the *Groupe des Dombes,* composed of Protestants as well as Catholic theologians and pastors, has shown a similar convergence.[107] While full doctrinal agreement was not reached by this group, their common understanding—despite different languages (in the large sense of that word)—is remarkable. The vocabulary used to express this agreement is generally theological and biblical for it is only this vocabulary that enables not only agreement but also conciseness. The group's starting point is the text of the agreement *Foi et Constitution* (1968), which it tries to clarify, adapt and complete in the light of the present French interconfessional situation.[108]

In the matters on which we have centered our interest, the document has this to say: "Accomplishing the memorial . . . of Christ, our high priest and intercessor, the Church presents to the Father the unique and perfect sacrifice of his Son." [109] This statement is the closest expression that the Eucharist is a sacrifice. It is, of course, the word "memorial," in its biblical-theological meaning that allows the statement to be made. The expression "presents the unique and perfect sacrifice of his Son" attempts to hold together, from the Catholic point of view, the once for all sacrifice of Christ and the offering the Church makes. And here, in this expression isolated from its context, it is not a question of the Church's self offering only nor of Christ offering Himself to the Father. It is the Church, the mystical body, presenting to the Father the sacrifice of the Son. Actually the Church does not present the sacrifice of the Son without presenting itself. Nor can the Church present itself separate from Christ pre-

---

[107] Groupe des Dombres, *Vers une même foi eucharistique?* Taizé, 1972.

[108] "Accord oecumenique sur l'eucharistie," *Verbum Caro* No. 87 (1968), pp. 1-10.

[109] Groupes des Dombes, p. 20.

senting Himself at the same moment. There is, however, a hesitation to use the word "offer"; in fact, to move from "present" to "offer" would be not just to use a synonym that is more or less the same, it would be to enter into a sacrificial vocabulary that at this precise point the group is not ready to use. Nevertheless, it does not scruple to use such a vocabulary when it says:

> The Eucharist is the great sacrifice of praise.[110] Thus united to our Lord who offers himself to his Father . . . we offer ourselves in a living and holy sacrifice which should express itself in our daily life.[111]

Insofar as the presence of Christ is concerned, the group has this to say:

> The eucharistic action is the gift of the person of Christ. . . . We confess unanimously the real. iiving and acting presence of Christ in this sacrament.[112]

As in other similar documents, this citation shows that the group does not wish to discuss the how of this presence, but it is content to affirm in a language that is theologically rich some of the relationships taking place in the sacrament. It should be noted, however, that not all Catholics are happy with the statement of the Groupe des Dombes. Cardinal Journet has expressed his regrets very clearly with regard to the statement's position on the sacramental presence of Christ in the Eucharist, which he sees expressed in Calvinist terms and not those of the Council of Trent. With regard to the minister of a valid Eucharist, he asks, "Who can validly pronounce the words of consecration?", thereby raising, without entering into, the debate of the validity of orders among Protestants.[113]

For years now, Lutherans and Anglicans have been concerned with expressing their Eucharistic Faith in their Eucharistic Prayer. Given a certain autonomy of different national groups within these communions, their experimentation has been widespread and gen-

---

110 *Ibid.*, p. 19.
111 *Ibid.*, p. 20.
112 *Ibid.*, p. 21.
113 Charles Journet, "Commentaire de l'accord du 'Groupe des Dombes' sur la doctrine eucharistique," *Documentation Catholique* 69 (1972), pp. 625-628; originally in *Nova et Vetera,* No. 2 (1972), pp. 81ff. For a sympathetic presentation that does not overlook the limitations of the document, see Bishop Daniel Pézeril's commentary in *Documentation Catholique* 69 (1972), pp. 527-531.

erally conducted at an official level.[114] The Episcopal Church has prepared for trial use a First and Second Service as well as four additional EPs that show similarities with the New Roman EPs. It would be fair to say that they are closer to the language and structure of the Roman EPs than are most of the unofficial EPs we have studied.[115] This is true also of the Methodist Alternate Service for Holy Communion prepared by the Commission on Worship for the United Methodist Church.[116] Notable in these Prayers are the Thanksgiving Preface that draws on well-known Scriptural sources, the Acclamation of the people, the Anamnesis, and the Epiclesis on people and gifts. It is especially in their manner of expressing the offering that these Prayers differ from the Roman ones. Insofar as the Calvinists are concerned, the Taizé community and the writings of Max Thurian have had a great influence for good in the present period of ecumenical convergence.

It is in the series *Ecumenical Studies in Worship* that Thurian's *The Eucharistic Memorial* was made known to English readers.[117] In this work, which did so much to recover the meaning of the word "memorial" for Christian worship, Thurian was able to discuss the concept of Eucharistic sacrifice within the context of memorial. Therefore, he can say: "In the eucharistic prayer, the Church does not offer a mere human reality; it is enabled to present to the Father, along with its own poverty-stricken offering, the unique and perfect sacrifice of Christ." [118] Furthermore, Thurian defends the concept of applying sacrifice to the Eucharistic celebration.[119] J. M. R. Tillard is only extrapolating on Thurian when he says, in his exposé to the "Shared Belief" committee, that sacrificial language is used to designate justified man's "yes" to God's radical hold on him. That is why it is fully legitimate to use this terminology at the Lord's Supper.[120] Not only is it proper to use a sacrificial terminology in talking about the Eucharist, but it is equally at home in the Eucharistic Prayer itself.

[114] Cf. Colin Buchanan, editor, *Modern Anglican Liturgies, 1958-1968,* London, 1968, and Luther Reed, *The Lutheran Liturgy: A Study of the Common Liturgy of the Lutheran Church in America,* revised edition, Philadelphia, 1959.

[115] In *Prayer Book Studies 21, The Holy Eucharist,* New York, 1970; see also *Service for Trial Use,* New York, 1971, pp. 37-130.

[116] This text may be found in the *Newsletter* of the Roman Catholic Bishops' Committee on the Liturgy, December, 1972.

[117] Max Thurian, *The Eucharistic Memorial,* J. G. Davies, trans., Richmond, Part One: *The Old Testament,* 1960, Part Two: *The New Testament,* 1961.

[118] *Ibid.,* Part II, p. 76.

[119] *Ibid.*

[120] Tillard, "Catholiques Romains. . . ," p. 611.

The Real Presence is affirmed by Thurian in his theses concerning it. The first of these theses echoes Trent:

> The body and blood of Christ, His whole humanity and deity, are truly, really and substantially present in the Eucharist.[121]

The liturgy of the Taizé community makes abundantly clear the liturgical expression of these doctrinal elements, in which the idea of sacrifice may not be separated from the idea of presence. This is seen especially in the Epiclesis and the Offering. The Epiclesis, before the Institution Narrative, beseeches the Father:

> send thy Holy Spirit upon us and open our Eucharist: consecrate this bread to be the body of Christ and this cup to be the blood of Christ; that the Creator Spirit may fulfill the Word of thy beloved Son.[122]

Then after the Institution Narrative, the Memorial continues:

> We also present unto thee, Lord of glory, as our thanksgiving and intercession, the signs of the eternal sacrifice of Christ, unique and perfect, living and holy, the Bread of life which cometh down from heaven and the Cup of the meal in thy Kingdom.[123]

Christ present in the signs is presented to the Father. It is clear that this kind of statement in the Eucharistic Prayer is closer to the official EPs than some of the contemporary unofficial EPs by Catholics. Indeed, it is especially on the level of ecumenical concern, scholarship, and episcopal authority (that is, those responsible for Eucharistic faith and practice in a special way) that we see a desire for a clear expression of what the Church teaches about the Eucharist. The Preamble to the Missal of Paul VI makes very clear the

---

[121] Thurian, Part II, p. 120.

[122] Max Thurian, editor, *The Eucharistic Liturgy of Taizé,* John Arnold, trans., London, 1963, p. 46. The 1971 French edition contains seven EPs.

[123] *Ibid.,* p. 48. Recently Thurian has acknowledged the theoretical need of small groups for new EPs beyond the present official ones. Nevertheless he cautions that, if one keeps to the structure and themes essential to every EP, their number could hardly exceed ten. This is so because the EP should have a universal quality in its structure, in its doctrine and in its literary genre. Also an EP should be able to be used by all the local Churches of the same rite. See "De novis Precibus Eucharisticis," *Questions liturgiques,* 53 (1972), pp. 252-254.

continuity of the faith from the Council of Trent to Vatican II and after. It expressly reiterates the traditional teaching of the Catholic Church with regard to the sacrifice of the Mass. What is more, it does this by citing Eucharistic Prayers III and IV. The *lex orandi* of the Church expresses its *lex credendi:*

> The doctrine enunciated with precision in the Leonian sacramentary, "Each time we celebrate this sacrifice in remembrance, the work of our redemption is carried out," is developed clearly and carefully in the Eucharistic Prayers: in these prayers when the priest carries out the anamnesis, by addressing God in the name of all the people, he gives thanks and offers him the living and holy sacrifice, that is, the oblation of the Church and the victim by whose immolation God wished to be appeased, and he prays so that the body and blood of Christ may be a sacrifice worthy of the Father and for the salvation of the world.

Furthermore, it is reiterated that the Mass is in its entirety a sacrifice of praise, thanksgiving, propitiation and satisfaction. Not that this is a new sacrifice, but there is an identity between the sacrifice of the Cross and its sacramental renewal at the Mass. Only the manner of offering is different.[125]

As for the real presence, this too is safeguarded, not only by the very words of the consecration but also by the exterior manifestation of respect surrounding the mystery.[126] The role of the Roman EPs is twofold: it is directed outwards in relationship to other Christian communities, and it is directed inwards in relationship to its own communion, where it seeks to preserve tradition across space and time. This, we have suggested, is the official EPs' special vocation. It does not mean that it should eliminate the different role that unofficial EPs are attempting to play.

124 "Prœmium," *Missale Romanum,* editio typica, Typis Polyglottis Vaticanus, 1970, pp. 19-20. My translation.
125 *Ibid.,* p. 20.
126 *Ibid.*

CONCLUSION

The contemporary Eucharistic Prayers that we have studied show similarities and differences between official and unofficial ones. Insofar as the differences are concerned, it is clear that many of them result from initial fundamental options, the most important of which are: the official Prayers are composed for a world-wide community in Latin by an international (though mainly Western European) group relying heavily on tradition; the unofficial Prayers are composed for a small group in the vernacular by single individuals (or members of a national team) who feel less bound to imitate traditional liturgies. The official Prayers represent a necessary stage to avoid anarchy and at the same time show clearly the *lex orandi, lex credendi* of the Church's Eucharistic Prayer. The hundreds of unofficial Eucharistic Prayers, of which we have studied a small but representative group, show a desire to go beyond this consolidating stage.

The significant areas of difference that our study has shown are the following:

1. *Structural Differences.* Unofficial Prayers do not include all the elements found in the official ones. Most often missing are the Sanctus, the *Vere Sanctus,* and Epiclesis on the gifts. Other elements, such as the Thanksgiving Preface, the Institution Narrative, the Epiclesis on the community, and the Doxology are significantly adapted either to highlight a theme or vary the traditional formula.

The frequent omission of the Sanctus and references to the saints, thereby leaving unexpressed the idea of an earthly liturgy joining in a heavenly liturgy, accents the community's desire to assume responsibility for their worship and their work to bring all men into the Kingdom. Those Prayers which omit an Epiclesis on the gifts or vary frequently the Institution Narrative or continue to refer to the bread and wine after the Institution Narrative as bread and wine or by some more general term are all de-emphasizing a vision of the Eucharist that places great stress on the change of the bread and wine into the Body and Blood of Christ. The change the unofficial Prayers are interested in is the community's change of heart so that it might fulfill the command to love God and neighbor. The presence of Christ guarantees the change of heart whereby the community discovers Christ in many places in their everyday lives. Thus, on the level of structure, the unofficial Prayers place less emphasis on the change of the species and more on the change to be effected in the community.

2. *Referential Differences.* The unofficial Prayers express a greater awareness of the community that prays, tend to highlight the humanity of Jesus, are uneasy with the traditional manner of expressing the sacrifice of the Mass, and lack a clear theology of the Holy Spirit at their base. Two things should be noted: first, while often the sacrificial aspect of unofficial Prayers is insufficient, they never present the Eucharistic celebration as a new sacrifice. Second, every Eucharistic Prayer, official or unofficial, is shaped by the community's understanding of itself as Church and by the weight it gives its religious experience. At the same time it cannot separate itself from the principal ideas underpinning the society to which it belongs since these enter in as unconscious assumptions. This we saw in the varying "we's" of the unofficial Prayers which were manifestly different from the official ones.

3. *Language Differences.* There is an obvious attempt in unofficial Prayers to speak in an up-to-date language. Not surprisingly on this level problems of obscurity, sentimentality leading to subjectivity, and even propagandizing of debatable theological or philosophical stances become evident.

Eucharistic Prayers that remain closest to biblical expressions for God or traditional ways of talking to Him have the virtue of continuity with the past and present expression of the faith. This is only one answer to the search for a contemporary way of talking to God about Jesus Christ, ourselves, and the action the Church is accomplishing at the Eucharist. While here and there the unofficial EPs are inadequate in this respect, at the same time they show that Prayers can be fashioned in a contemporary language.

The very catholicity of the official Prayers requires of them an objective type language and a traditional doctrinal expression. However, it is this characteristic that makes difficult their acceptance by particular groups as the *only* EPs for all Eucharistic celebrations. The unofficial Prayers we have studied all try to remedy in their own way the problem of universal/particular, that is, each group tries to adapt the Eucharistic Prayer of its celebration to the service of a definite group. At its simplest this adaptation consists in using a language whose formulation is considered to be one that speaks to today's man.

When at Vatican II the Church chose to up-date itself, it could not avoid confronting the problems facing modern man. Unofficial Eucharistic Prayers by starting precisely there have the great difficulty of avoiding the confusions of the present time. Official Prayers by taking their starting point in tradition risked not being Prayers of contemporary man. To the extent that these latter are complementary expressions of the substance of the Church's Eucharistic faith, they take approaches to express this faith that do not exhaust all other possible approaches. Therefore, we see at the end of our study that the unofficial Prayers are a necessary stage that have their contribution to make in widening the Church's euchology. However, agreement of what constitutes a Eucharistic Prayer and how the faith of the Church is best therein expressed has to be reached if direction is to be given unofficial Prayers. In our day, the present legislation of the Latin Church is that the See of Rome, wherever it has dominion in matters liturgical, determines the fundamental characteristics of the Eucharistic Prayer. This authority determines, from its doctrinal understanding and its idea of a Eucharistic Prayer, which elements should be included, their structuring, and appropriate expression. The hard test, then, for any unofficial Prayer is: does it take a new approach that nevertheless expresses the substance of the faith in the form of a Eucharistic Prayer acceptable to the Church.

Finally, from this viewpoint, if unofficial Prayers were approved, they would have the advantage of placing the burden for creating new Eucharistic Prayers on succeeding generations if the Prayers of our period no longer responded adequately to their experience.

APPENDIX

SACRED CONGREGATION FOR DIVINE WORSHIP

Letter to the Presidents of National Conferences of Bishops, Concerning Eucharistic Prayers

1. The primary objective of liturgical renewal is the participation of the people in the Eucharist knowingly, devoutly and actively.[1] This is especially true of the revision of the Roman Missal, recently put into effect according to the norms of the Second Vatican Council.[2]

It must be acknowledged that the distinguishing characteristic of this Missal, promulgated by authority of Pope Paul VI, is the large number of texts that offer a wide variety in selecting the scriptural readings, songs, prayers and acclamations available to the entire community, as well as in the *presidential* prayers. The eucharistic prayer is no exception, for in addition to the venerable and traditional Roman Canon, three texts have also been introduced into use.[3]

2. The reason why such a variety of texts has been offered, and the end result such new formularies were meant to achieve, are pastoral in nature: namely, to reflect the unity and diversity of liturgical prayer. By using the various texts contained in the Roman Missal, various Christian communities, as they gather to celebrate the Eucharist, are able to sense that they themselves form the one Church praying with the same faith, using the same prayer. They furthermore become one in their ability of proclaiming the same mystery of Christ in different ways—especially when the vernacular is used. Each of the faithful can more easily lift their hearts to God in prayer and thanks,[4] and share in the celebrations with greater spiritual benefits.

3. Although several years have passed since the promulgation of the revised Roman Missal, it has not yet been fully introduced everywhere, since the vast work of providing vernacular editions for so many countries has required a considerable period of time.[5] Furthermore the many ways of increasing the pastoral effectiveness of a celebration are not always known, nor is sufficient attention paid to the spiritual good of the assembly in planning the celebration.[6]

4. In addition many have voiced the desire of adapting the eucharistic celebrations further with the composition of new formularies, including new eucharistic prayers. They maintain that the options among the *presidential* prayers and the four eucharistic prayers of the Order of Mass still do not fully satisfy the many demands of various groups, areas and peoples. This Sacred Congregation has received several requests to approve, or grant the faculty of approving, and to allow the use of new texts for prayers and eucharistic prayers in modern language and thought-patterns.

In the past few years many authors from different countries, representing many language groups, have published eucharistic prayers composed by themselves for such purposes. In spite of the limitations imposed by the Second Vatican Council [7] and the prohibitions of individual bishops, priests have frequently used privately circulated texts for their celebrations.

5. Consequently this Sacred Congregation, at the request of the Holy Father and in consultation with experts from various parts of the world, has carefully studied the question of the composition of new eucharistic prayers or of giving the faculty to episcopal conferences for such approval, together with other questions connected with such prayers and their consequences. The results of this study, made by the members of this Congregation in plenary session, together with the decisions of other Sacred Congregations having competence in such matters, were presented to the Pope. Upon mature consideration of the entire matter, it does not seem advisable at this time to grant episcopal conferences the general faculty of either composing or approving new eucharistic prayers. On the contrary it seems more advisable to recommend that a broader catechesis be undertaken concerning the nature and purpose of a eucharistic prayer.[8] Since it is indeed the center of the celebration, it should also be central to a fuller catechesis. It seems necessary to provide priests with a more

detailed instruction on the possibilities they have to encourage the full participation of the people by using the existing norms found in liturgical legislation and the formularies of the Roman Missal.

6. The four eucharistic prayers presently appearing in the revised Roman Missal remain, and no other eucharistic prayers composed without the express approval or permission of the Holy See may be used. Episcopal conferences and individual bishops are strongly asked to lead their priests in a reasonable way to maintain the one practice of the Roman Church. This will result in the good of the Church as well as preserve the arrangement proper to liturgical celebrations.

The Holy See is motivated by a pastoral love of unity in reserving to itself the right of regulating so important a matter as the order of the eucharistic prayer. In preserving the unity of the Roman rite it will not refuse to consider legitimate requests, and will give willing consideration to such requests received from episcopal conferences for new eucharistic prayers to be composed for particular needs and introduced into the liturgy. It will also set forth those norms to be observed in each individual case.

7. Together with this important decision, it seems useful to suggest several considerations which render its meaning and execution easier to understand. Some of these relate to the nature and importance of the eucharistic prayer in liturgical tradition, especailly the Roman tradition. The rest take into account what can be done to accommodate a celebration to individual groups without changing the text of the eucharistic prayers.

8. By its very nature the eucharistic prayer is the "center of the entire celebration," and "a prayer of thanksgiving and sanctification" whereby "the entire congregation of believers join Christ in acknowledging the works of God and offering the sacrifice." [9] This prayer is proclaimed by the presiding priest. He expresses the voice of God as it is addressed to the people, and the voice of the people as they turn to God. He alone should proclaim this prayer, while those assembled for the sacred celebration observe a reverent silence.

Besides its catechetical nature which attempts to clarify all that is proper to each particular celebration, the prominent feature of this prayer is one of thanksgiving for the universal mystery of salvation, or for some particular aspect of that mystery celebrated within the liturgical action in keeping with the day, feast or season.[10]

To allow those participating to praise God and give him even greater thanks, the revised Roman Missal already contains a "great number of prefaces, derived from the older tradition of the Roman Church or newly composed. In this way the different aspects of the mystery of salvation will be emphasized, and there will be richer themes of thanksgiving." [11]

To this same end, the presiding priest has the faculty of briefly introducing the eucharistic prayer.[12] He can thereby suggest reasons for giving thanks which are there and then meaningful to a particular group of people. The community will then be able to feel that its own life is an intimate part of the history of salvation, and so draw greater benefits from their eucharistic celebration.

9. As for the very purpose of the eucharistic prayer and its inner meaning or structure, there is a secondary aspect of petition or intercession. The revised liturgy provides this notably in the general intercessions, in a form that is much freer and more adaptable to Church and all mankind. The new liturgical books supply many formats for this type of intercession for insertion into the eucharistic prayers, as the structure of each allows. They are to be used in particular celebrations, especially during ritual Masses.[13] In this way the purpose of each celebration becomes more clearly defined, while at the same time signifying that this prayer is offered in union with the whole Church.[14]

10. The variations listed above permit the elements of thanksgiving and intercessions to be more closely related with the celebration as a whole. In order to develop the particular aspect of the mystery of Christ that is celebrated on special solemnities during the liturgical year, the Roman tradition has other special formularies for use (*infra actionem*).[15]

As is evident, the same tradition makes proper provision for the immutability of the text as a whole, while not excluding any appropriate variations. Thus the people can more readily associate themselves with the presiding priest with the frequent proclamation of the same texts. At the same time, the variations within the text, however few in number, are not only useful but welcome, for they foster devotion and attentiveness, and embellish the prayer in a unique way.

In all that pertains to the principles found in Nos. 8-10, there is nothing to prevent episcopal conferences from providing similar variations for their own regions, and to request approval for them from the Holy See. The same holds true for a bishop in regard to the Proper for his diocese, and for the competent authority in regard to the Proper for each religious family.

11. The ecclesial dimension of the eucharistic celebration should be considered paramount. While it is within such a celebration that "the unity of all believers who form one body in Christ is both expressed and brought about," [16] the "celebration of Mass is, in itself, a profession of faith whereby the entire Church recognizes and expresses her own nature." [17] Nowhere is this more apparent than in the eucharistic prayer, for there it is not just an individual person, nor even a local community, but "the one and only Catholic Church, existing in the local churches" [18] that addresses itself to God.

Whenever eucharistic prayers are used without any approval of the Church's authority, unrest and even dissensions arise, not only among priests, but within the communities themselves, even though the Eucharist should be a "sign of unity, and the bond of charity." [19] Many people complain about the overly subjective quality of such texts, and participants have a right to make such a complaint. Otherwise the eucharistic prayer, to which they give their assent in the "Amen" they proclaim, becomes disorderly, or is imbued with the personal feelings of the person who either composes or says it.

Hence it is necessary to demand that only those eucharistic prayers be used which have been approved by the lawful authority of the Church, for they clearly and fully manifest the sentiments of the Church.

12. Due to the very nature of the eucharistic prayer, a more precise adaptation for different groups or circumstances, and a more highly developed catechesis are not always possible nor suitable at that point of the celebration. They should be made, however, in those parts and formularies of the liturgical action which permit and call for variations.

13. For those who both prepare and participate in celebrations, the first variations to be kept in mind are those granted by the General Instruction of the Roman Missal.[20] In certain cases different formularies of the Mass may be chosen, together with additional texts for the various parts of the Mass, such as the readings, prayers and songs "so that they correspond to the needs, spiritual preparation, and attitude of the participants."[21] It is also well to remember that other documents, promulgated since the publication of the Roman Missal, offer further norms and suggestions for preparing celebrations which are alive and planned according to pastoral need.[22]

14. Among the possibilities for further accommodating any individual celebration, it is important to consider the admonitions, the homily and the general intercessions.

First of all are the admonitions. These enable the people to be drawn into a fuller understanding of the sacred action, or any of its parts, and lead them into a true spirit of participation. The General Instruction of the Roman Missal entrusts the more important admonitions to the priest for preparation and use. He may introduce the Mass to the people before the celebration begins, during the liturgy of the word prior to the actual readings, and in the eucharistic prayer before the preface; he may also conclude the entire sacred action before the dismissal.[23] The Order of Mass provides others as well, which are important to certain portions of the rite, such as during the penitential rite, or before the Lord's Prayer. By their very nature these brief admonitions do not require that everyone use them in the form in which they appear in the Missal. Provision can be made in certain cases that they be adapted to some degree to the varying circumstances of the community. In all cases it is well to remember the nature of an admonition, and not make them into a sermon or homily; care should be taken to keep them brief and not too wordy, for otherwise they become tedious.

15. In addition to the admonitions, the homily must be kept in mind, for it is "part of the liturgy itself." [24] It proclaims the Word of God in the liturgical gathering for the community assembled. It explains that Word in view of the total celebration respecting the ability of the people to understand and in terms of their daily life.

16. Importance must also be accorded to the general intercessions as a means of allowing the community to respond to the Word of

God as it has been explained and received. To be effective, the petitions that are made for the needs of all men everywhere should win the assent of the people gathered locally. Insight and a certain freedom should go into the composition of these intercessions, for they are both essential to the very nature of this prayer.

17. In addition to the selection of appropriate texts, a truly living and communal celebration requires the president and all other ministers to carefully examine different forms of verbal communication with the congregation; this refers to the readings, homily, admonitions, introductions, and similar parts.[25]

When the priest says a prayer, especially a eucharistic prayer, he should not only avoid a dry, monotonous style of delivery, but an overly subjective and emotional way of speaking and acting as well. As he presides over the liturgical action, whether by reading, singing, or by use of gestures, he should carefully help the participants achieve a true sense of community as they celebrate and live the memorial of the Lord.

18. A sacred silence must be observed at the proper times,[26] in order that texts may achieve their full effect and enable the greatest possible spiritual benefits to be gained. As an integral part of the liturgical action, the nature of this silence and the time when it is introduced allow individuals to become recollected, or to meditate briefly upon what they have heard, or to pray and praise God in their hearts.[27]

19. Considering all this, it is hoped that pastors would take greater care to instruct their people, rather than introduce novelties into the texts and rites of the sacred action. This will enable them to understand better the nature, structure and elements of celebration, particularly the eucharistic prayer, and to take part in each celebration more fully and with greater awareness. The sacred liturgy does not draw its force and effectiveness from what is new and optional alone, but from sharing more deeply in the mystery of salvation which is truly present and operative within the liturgical action. As people profess one faith and express one prayer to God they will not only be able to work out their own salvation, but will also share it with all their brothers and sisters.

This circular letter was prepared by the Sacred Congregation, and

His Holiness, Pope Paul VI, approved its contents on April 18, 1973, ordering its publication.

From the Sacred Congregation for Divine Worship, April 27, 1973.

Arthur Cardinal Tabera,
Prefect

✠ A. Bugnini,
Titular Bishop of Diocletian,
Secretary

NOTES

[1] See II Vatican Council, const. on the Sacred Liturgy, *Sacrosanctum Concilium,* art. 48: AAS 56 (1964), 113.

[2] See Paul VI, apost. const. *Missale Romanum,* April 3, 1969: AAS 61 (1969), 217-222.

[3] See *ibid.,* p. 219.

[4] See *Institutio generalis Missalis Romani,* no. 54.

[5] As regards the principles governing translations, see Consilium for the Implementation of the Constitution on the Sacred Liturgy, *Instruction sur la traduction des textes liturgiques pour la célébration avec le peuple,* January 25, 1969: *Notitiae* 5, 1969, 3-12.

[6] See *Institutio generalis Missalis Romani,* no. 313.

[7] See II Vatican Council, const. *Sacrosanctum Concilium,* no. 22, para. 3: AAS 56 (1964), 106.

[8] See Benno Cardinal Gut, Letter to Presidents of Episcopal Conferences, June 2, 1968: *Notitiae* 4, 1968, 146-148: *Indications pour faciliter le catechèse des anaphores de la Messe: ibid.,* 148-155.

[9] *Institutio generalis Missalis,* no. 54.

[10] See *ibid.,* no. 55a.

[11] Paul VI, apost. const. *Missale Romanum,* April 3, 1969: AAS 61 (1969), 219.

[12] See *Institutio generalis Missalis Romani,* no. 11.

[13] As regards Eucharistic Prayer I, or the Roman Canon, apart from permission for introducing names into the remembrances of the living and the dead, see the special remembrances for godparents in the Mass of Christian Initiation for Adults and the formulas for the *Hanc igitur* from the Mass of the Easter Vigil up to the Second Sunday of Easter, in Masses for adult converts or adult baptisms, for those being confirmed or ordained, for bride and groom, newly professed religious, and the Consecration of Virgins; as regards Eucharistic Prayers II, III, and IV, see the embolisms for adult converts, newly professed religious, and for the Consecration of Virgins.

[14] See *Institutio generalis Missalis Romani,* no. 55g.

[15] See the proper *Communicantes* for Christmas and its octave for Epiphany, for Masses from the Easter Vigil up to the Second Sunday of Easter, on the Ascension of the Lord, and for Pentecost.

[16] II Vatican Council, const. *Lumen Gentium,* no. 3: AAS 57 (1965), 6.

[17] Secretariat for Promoting Christian Unity, Instruction *In quibus rerum circumstantiis,* June 1, 1972, no. 2b: AAS 64 (1972), 520.

[18] See II Vatican Council, const. *Lumen Gentium,* no. 23: AAS 57 (1965), 27.

[19] Augustine, *In Ioannis Evangelium Tractatus* 26, 13: CCL 36, 266; See II Vatican Council, const. *Sacrosanctum Concilium,* no. 47: AAS 56 (1964), 113.

[20] See *Institutio generalis Missalis Romani,* no. 314-324.

[21] *Ibid.,* no. 313.

[22] See S. Congr. for Divine Worship, Instruction *Actio Pastoralis,* May 15, 1969: AAS 61 (1969), 806-811; Instruction *Memoriale Domini,* May 29, 1969: AAS 61 (1969), 541-547; Instruction *Sacramentali Communione,* June 29, 1970: AAS 62 (1970), 664-667.

[23] See *Institutio generalis Missalis Romani,* no. 11.

[24] II Vatican Council, const. *Sacrosanctum Concilium,* no. 52: AAS 56 (1964), 114.

[25] See *Institutio generalis Missalis Romani,* no. 18.

[26] See II Vatican Council, const. *Sacrosanctum Concilium,* no. 30: AAS 56 (1964), 108; Sacred Congregation of Rites, Instruction *Musicam Sacram,* March 5, 1967, no. 17: AAS 59 (1967), 305.

[27] See *Institutio generalis Missalis Romani,* no. 23.

BIBLIOGRAPHY

The texts studied are found in the following works:

Hoey, Robert F. *The Experimental Liturgy Book.* New York: Herder and Herder, 1969.

Maertens, Jean-Thierry; De Bilde, Marguerite; *et al. Livre de la prière.* Paris: Editions du Centurion, 1969.

Missale Romanum: Editio Typica. Typis Polyglottis Vaticanis, 1970.

Oosterhuis, Huub. *In het Voorbijgaan.* Utrecht: Ambo, 1968. Translated into English in two volumes. *Prayers, Poems & Songs.* Translated by David Smith. New York: Herder and Herder, 1970. *Open Your Hearts.* Translated by David Smith. New York: Herder and Herder, 1971.

*   *   *

Amon, Karl. "Reformwünsche zum innersten Bereich der eucharistischen Feier." *Bibel und Liturgie* 35 (1961/1962), pp. 107-109.

——. "Wünsche an die künftige Messliturgie." *Bibel und Liturgie* 38 (1964/1965), pp. 208-217.

——. "Gratias Agere: zur Reform des Messkanons." *Liturgisches Jahrbuch* 15 (1965), pp. 79-98.

Arranz, Michel. "L'économie du Salut dans la prière du Post-Sanctus des anaphores de type antiochéen." *La Maison-Dieu,* No. 106 (1971), pp. 46-75.

Assemblées du Seigneur, 2ème série. *La Prière Eucharistique,* No. 1 and *Anaphores nouvelles,* No. 2. Paris: Editions du Cerf, 1968.

Audet, J. P. "Literary Forms and Contents of a Normal εὐχαριστία in the First Century." Kurt Aland *et al.,* editors, *Studia Evangelica: Papers Presented to the International Congress on 'The Four Gospels in 1957'.* Oxford, 1957. Berlin: Akademie Verlag, 1959, pp. 643-662 = *Texte und Untersuchungen* 73.

————. "Esquisse historique du genre littéraire de la 'bénédiction' juive et de l'eucharistie chrétienne." *Revue Biblique* 65 (1958), pp. 371-399.

————. "Genre littéraire et formes cultuelles de l'eucharistie." *Ephemerides Liturgicae* 80 (1966), pp. 353-385.

Averbeck, Wilhelm. *Der Opfercharacter des Abendmahls in der neueren evangelischen Theologie.* Paderborn: Bonafacius, 1966.

Bakker, Leo. "Holland, Versuchsfeld der Kirche Gottes?" *Orientierung* 5 (1968), pp. 59-63.

Baum, Gregory. *Man Becoming: God in Secular Meaning.* New York: Herder and Herder, 1970.

Baumstark, Anton. *Liturgie Comparée.* Chevetogne: Editions de Chevetogne, 1939.

Bieritz, Karl-Heinrich. *"Oblatio ecclesiae:* Bemerkungen zu den neuen eucharistischen Hochgebeten der römischen Liturgie." *Theologische Literaturzeitung* 94 (1969), cols. 241-252.

Bishop, Edmund. *Liturgica Historica.* Oxford: Clarendon Press, 1918.

Bobrinskoy, Boris. "Présence réelle et communion eucharistique." *Revue des sciences philosophiques et théologiques* 53 (1969), pp. 402-420.

Botte, Bernard. *La Tradition apostolique de saint Hippolyte,* Sources Chrétiennes II. Paris: Editions du Cerf, 1946.

————. "Liturgie chrétienne et liturgie juive." Cahiers Sioniens 7 (1949), pp. 215-223.

————. "Communication." *QLP* 38 (1957). pp. 122-123.

————. "Où en est la réforme du canon de la messe?" *QLP* 49 (1968), pp. 138-141.

————. "Extendit manus suas cum pateretur." *QLP* 49 (1968). p. 307.

————. "Les anaphores syriennes orientales." Lex Orandi 47. Paris: Editions du Cerf, 1970, pp. 7-24.

————. "Epilogue." *Eucharisties d'Orient et d'Occident, II.* Lex Orandi 47. Paris: Editions du Cerf, 1970, pp. 293-296.

Bousset, W. "Eine judische Gebetssamlung im siebenten Buch der Apostolischen Konstitution." *Nachrichten von der K. Gesellschaft der Wissenschaften zu Göttingen, Philologische-Historische Klasse, 1915,* 1916.

Bouyer, Louis, *Eucharist.* Translated by Charles Underhill Quinn. Indiana: University of Notre Dame Press, 1968.

————. "The New Eucharistic Prayers of the Roman Rite." Patrick

McGoldrick, editor. *Understanding the Eucharist*. Dublin: Gill and Macmillan, 1969, pp. 161-178.

Boyd, Malcolm. *Are You Running With Me, Jesus?* New York: Holt, Rinehart & Winston, 1965.

Brightman, F. E. *Liturgies, Eastern and Western, Volume I, Eastern Liturgies*. Oxford: Oxford University Press, 1896.

Brilioth, Yngve. *Eucharistic Faith and Practice: Evangelical and Catholic*. Revised and shortened. Translated by A. G. Hebert. London: SPCK, 1956.

Brinckhoff, Lukas. "Die liturgische Situation in Holland." Theodor Bogler, editor, *Deutsche Liturgie? Sind wir auf dem weg dahin?* Maria Laach: Ars Liturgica, 1967, pp. 59-63.

Bruylants, Placide. "Les Préfaces du Missel romain." *La Maison-Dieu*, No. 87 (1966), pp. 111-132.

Cazelles, Henri. "L'anaphore et l'ancien testament." *Eucharisties d'Orient et d'Occident I*, Lex Orandi 46. Paris: Editions du Cerf, 1970, pp. 11-20.

Childs, Brevard S. *Memory and Tradition in Israel*. London: SCM Press, 1962.

Chirat, Henri. *L'assemblée chrétienne à l'âge apostolique*, Lex Orandi 10. Paris: Editions du Cerf, 1949.

Congregation for the Doctrine of the Faith. "Regarding the Safeguarding of Faith in the Mysteries of the Incarnation and the Most Blessed Trinity from Some Recent Errors." *L'Osservatore Romano*, weekly English edition. March 30, 1972, p. 6.

Connolly, R. H. *The so-called Egyptian Church Order and Related Documents*. Cambridge: University Press, 1916.

Congar, Yves. "L' 'Ecclesia' ou Communauté chrétienne, sujet intégral de l'action liturgique." *La Liturgie après Vatican II* (Unam Sanctam 66). J.-P. Jossua and Yves Congar, eds. Paris: Editions du Cerf, 1967.

Coppens, Joseph. "Eucharistie." *DB Sup*. Vol. II. Paris: Librairie Letouzey et Ané, 1934, cols. 1146-1215.

Crichton, J. D. "The New Eucharistic Prayers." *Liturgy* 34 (1968), pp. 89-101.

Crystal, David. *Linguistics, Language and Religion*, Faith and Fact Books 131. London: Burns and Oates, 1965.

Cuming, C. G. *A History of Anglican Liturgy*. London: Macmillan. 1969.

Dalmais, Irénée. *Eastern Liturgies*. Translated by Donald Attwater. *The Twentieth Century Encyclopedia of Catholicism, vol. 112*. New York: Hawthorn Books, 1960.

————. "Quelques grands thèmes théologiques des anaphores orientales." *Eucharisties d'Orient et d'Occident,* Lex Orandi 47. Paris: Editions du Cerf, 1970, pp. 179-195.

Danneels, Godfrey. "A la recherche des lois de composition de la prière eucharistique." Godfrey Danneels and Thierry Maertens, editors, *La Prière eucharistique,* Vivante Liturgie 79. Paris: Editions du Centurion, 1967, pp. 65-94.

de Certeau, Michel. *L'étranger ou l'union dans la différence,* Foi Vivante 116. Paris: Desclée de Brouwer, 1969.

————. "How is Christianity Thinkable Today." *Theology Digest* 19 (1971), pp. 334-345.

Decretum SRC *Prece eucharistica. Ephemerides Liturgicae* 82 (1968), pp. 162-180; also in *Notitiae* 4 (1968), pp. 157-179.

de Lubac, Henri. *Les églises particulières dans l'église universelle.* Paris: Aubier, 1971.

————. "Sur les rapports entre Eglise universelle et Eglises particulières." *L'Osservatore Romano* (French edition) January 8, 1971, pp. 9f.

Denzinger-Schönmetzer. *Enchiridion Symbolorum.* 33rd Edition, Freiburg: Herder and Herder, 1965.

Dix, Gregory. *The Treatise on the Apostolic Tradition of St. Hippolytus of Rome.* London: SPCK, 1937.

————. *The Shape of the Liturgy.* London: Dacre Press, 1945.

Doncoeur, Paul. "Comment se pose la problème de la liturgie populaire?" *QLP* 27 (1946), pp. 173-183.

Dumas, Antoine. "Les nouvelles préfaces du Missel romain." *La Maison-Dieu* No. 94 (1968), pp. 159-164.

Eizenhofer, L. "'Te Igitur' und 'Communicantes' im Römischen Messkanon." *Sacris Erudiri* 8 (1956), pp. 14-75.

Elbogen, I. *Der jüdische Gottesdienst in seiner geschichtlichen Entwicklung.* 4th Edition. Hildesheim: G. Olms, 1962.

Fiala, Virgil. "Les prières d'acceptation de l'offrande et le genre littéraire du canon romain." *Eucharisties d'orient et d'occident,* Lex Orandi 46. Paris: Editions du Cerf, 1970, pp. 117-133.

Froger, Jacques. "The Chants of the Mass in the Eighth and Ninth Centuries." *The Gregorian Review,* January-February, 1956, pp. 11-24.

Gallen, John. *Eucharistic Liturgies.* New York: Paulist Press. 1970.

Gavin, F. *The Jewish Antecedents of the Christian Sacraments.* London: SPCK, 1928.

Gill, Jerry H. "Talk about Religious Talk: Various Approaches to the Nature of Religious Language." Martin E. Marty and Dean Peerman, editors, *Theology No. 4.* New York: Macmillan Press, 1967, pp. 99-123.

Goar, Jacques. *Euchologium Graecorum.* Paris: 1647.

Grisbrooke, W. Jardine. "Intercession at the Eucharist II Intercession at the Eucharist Proper." *Studia Liturgica* 5 (1966), pp. 20-44 and 87-103.

Groupe des Dombes. *Vers une même foi eucharistique? Accord entre catholiques et protestants.* Les Presses de Taizé, 1972.

Guardini, Romano. "Letter from Romano Guardini." *Herder Correspondence,* August, 1964, pp. 237-239.

———. *The Church and the Catholic* and *The Spirit of the Liturgy* (in one volume). Translated by Ada Lane. New York: Sheed and Ward, 1935.

Hausherr, Irénée. *Noms du Christ et Voies d'oraison.* Orientalia Christiana Analecta, 157. Rome: Pont. Inst. Orientalium Studiorum, 1960.

Hirtzenberger, Gottfried. *Der Magische Rest: Ein Beitrag zur Entmagisierung des Christentums.* Dusseldorf: Patmos-Verlag, 1969.

Hordern, William. *Speaking of God: the Nature and Purpose of Theological Language.* New York: Macmillan Company, 1964.

"Instruction du 'Consilium' sur la traduction des textes liturgiques pour la célébration avec le peuple." *Notitiae* 44 (1969), pp. 3-12. Reprinted in *La Documentation Catholique* 66 (1969), pp. 367-372.

Jounel, Pierre. "La Composition des Prières Eucharistiques." *La Maison-Dieu,* No. 94 (1968), pp. 38-76.

Journet, Charles. "Commentaire de l'accord du 'Groupe des Dombes' sur la doctrine eucharistique." *Documentation Catholique* 69 (1972), pp. 625-628.

Jungmann, Joseph. *The Place of Christ in Liturgical Prayer.* 2nd Edition, revised. Translated by A. Peeler. New York: Alba House, 1965.

———. *The Mass of the Roman Rite (Missarum Sollemnia).* Translated into two volumes by Francis A. Brunner. New York: Benziger Brothers, 1950.

———. *The Eucharistic Prayer.* Translated by Robert L. Batley. Notre Dame, Indiana: Fides, 1960.

———. "Eucharistiefeier und Frömmigkeit." *Liturgisches Jahrbuch* 5 (1955), pp. 96-104.

————, editor. "Konstitution über die heilige Liturgie." *Das Zweite Vatikanische Konzil: Documente und Kommentare, Teil I, LTK.* Freiburg: Herder, 1966, pp. 10-109.

————. "Ende der Kanonstille." *Liturgisches Jahrbuch* 17 (1967), pp. 220-232.

Kaufmann, Gordon D. "On the Meaning of 'God': Transcendence without Mythology." Martin E. Marty and Dean Peerman, editors, *Theology No. 4.* New York: Macmillan Press, 1967, pp. 69-98.

Kavanagh, Aidan. "Thoughts on the New Eucharistic Prayers." *Worship* 43 (1969), pp. 2-12.

Kilmartin, Edward J. "Sacramental Theology: The Eucharist in Recent Literature." *Theological Studies* 32 (1971), pp. 233-277.

Kleinheyer, Bruno. *Erneuerung des Hochgebetes.* Regensburg: Verlag Friedrich Pustet, 1969.

Knutson, Kent S. "Contemporary Lutheran Theology and the Eucharistic Sacrifice." *Lutherans and Catholics in Dialogue III: The Eucharist as Sacrifice.* New York: Lutheran World Federation, 1968.

Kohler, Kaufmann. "Ueber die Ursprunge und Grundformen der synagogalen Liturgie." *MGWJ* (1893), pp. 441-451, 489-497.

Küng, Hans. "Das Eucharistiegebet: Konzil und Erneuerung der römischen Messliturgie." *Wort und Wahrheit* 18 (1963), pp. 102-107.

La Maison-Dieu No. 94, Les nouvelles prières eucharistiques. Paris: Editions du Cerf, 1968.

Leblanc, P. J. "A Consideration of Intercessory Prayer within the Eucharist." *The Dunwoodie Review* 8 (1968), pp. 115-132.

Ledogar, Robert. "The Eucharistic Prayer and the Gifts Over Which It is Spoken." *Worship* 41 (1967), pp. 578-596.

————. *Acknowledgment: Praise-verbs in the Early Greek Anaphora.* Rome: Herder, 1968.

Lengeling, Emil. "De Precibus Eucharisticis." *Notitiae* 8 (1972), pp. 132-134.

————. "Le Problème des nouvelles prières eucharistiques dans la liturgie romaine." *Questions Liturgiques* 53 (1972), p. 251.

————. "Hippolyt von Rom und die Wendung 'Extendit . . .' " *QLP* 50 (1969), pp. 141-144.

Lewis, Charles A. *The Silent Recitation of the Canon of the Mass.* Excerpt from a dissertation in the Gregorian University theology faculty. Bay Saint Louis: Divine Word Missionaries, 1962.

Lumen Gentium in Walter M. Abbott, S.J., General editor, *The*

Documents of Vatican Two, Joseph Gallagher, translation editor, New York: Herder and Herder, The Association Press, 1966, pp. 14-101.

Luther, Martin. "A Treatise on the New Testament, that is, the Holy Mass (1520)." Translated by Jeremiah J. Schendel. E. Theodore Bachmann, editor. *Luther's Works,* Vol. 35, *Word and Sacrament I.* Philadelphia: Muhlenberg Press, 1960, pp. 75-112.

Lutherans and Catholics in Dialogue III: The Eucharist as Sacrifice. New York: Lutheran World Federation, 1968.

McIntyre, John. "Analogy." *Scottish Journal of Theology* (1959), pp. 1-20.

McNierney, Stephen W., editor. *The Underground Mass Book.* Baltimore: Helicon Press, 1968.

MacQuarrie, John. "How Can We Think of God." *Philosophy Today, No. 2.* Toronto: The Macmillan Company, pp. 142-154.

Maertens, Thierry. *Pour une meilleure intelligence de la prière eucharistique.* Second Edition, revised. Bruges: Biblica, 1963.

Maertens, Thierry and Frisque, Jean. *Guide for the Christian Assembly,* five volumes. Bruges: Biblica, 1965.

Maertens, Thierry. "Les nouvelles prierès eucharistiques au service de l'assemblée." *Liturgie et Vie Chretienne* 65 (1968), pp. 194-202.

Maldonado, Luis. *La Plegaria Eucaristica: Estudio de teologia biblica y liturgica sobre la misa.* Biblioteca de Autores Christianos 273. Madrid: Editorial catolica, 1967.

Manders, Herman. "Who Performs the Liturgy?" *Theology Digest* 16 (1968), pp. 227-231. A condensation of "Wie voltrekt de liturgie?" *Tijdschrift voor Theologie* 3 (1967), pp. 268-287.

————. "Het eucharistisch gebed." *Tijdschrift voor Liturgie* 51 (1967), pp. 27-47.

Mateos, Joseph. "L'action du Saint-Esprit dans la liturgie dite de s. Jean Chrysostom." *Proche-Orient Chrétien* IX (1959), pp. 193-208.

Ménard, Jacques. "La restauration de la bénédiction eucharistique." *Liturgie et Vie chrétienne* 65 (1968), pp. 180-193.

Mohrmann, Christine. *Liturgical Latin, Its Origins and Character.* Washington: Catholic Univ. of America Press, 1957.

————. *Etudes sur le latin des chrétiens.* Rome: Ed. di Storia e Letteratura, Tome I, 1958, Tome II, 1961, Tome III, 1965.

"Newsletter of the Roman Catholic Bishops' Committee on Liturgy." December, 1972.

Oesterley, W. O. E. *The Jewish Background of the Christian Liturgy.* London: Oxford University Press, 1925.

Oosterhuis, Huub. *Your Word Is Near.* Translated by David Smith. Westminster, Md.: Newman Press, 1968.

Pézeril, Daniel. "Vers une même foi eucharistique?" *Documentation Catholique* 69 (1972), pp. 527-531.

Powers, Joseph. *Eucharistic Theology.* New York: Herder and Herder, 1967.

Prayer Book Studies 21, The Holy Eucharist. New York: The Church Hymnal Corporation, 1970.

Raes, Alphonse. Introduction to "Pars Tertia: Anaphorae Orientales." Anton Hänggi and Irmgard Pahl, editors, *Prex Eucharistica.* Fribourg: Editions Universitaires, 1968.

Rahner, Karl and Häussling, Anselm. *The Celebration of the Eucharist.* New York: Herder and Herder, 1968.

Rahner, Karl. "L'avenir de la théologie." *NRT* 93 (1971), pp. 3-28.

Rankin, O. S. "The Extent and the Influence of the Synagogue Service upon Christian Worship." *The Journal of Jewish Studies* 1 (1948), pp. 27-32.

Ratzinger, Joseph. *Introduction to Christianity.* Translated by J. R. Foster. New York: Herder and Herder, 1970.

Refoulé, François. *Au bord du schisme? L'affaire d'Amsterdam et l'Eglise de Hollande.* Paris: Editions du Cerf, 1969.

Renaudot, Eusèbe. *Liturgiarum orientalium Collectio.* Paris: 1716.

Roguet, A-M. "Les prières eucharistiques." *Vie Spirituelle* 118 (1968), pp. 70-87.

Roy, Lucien and Ingram, Forrest, editors. *Step Beyond Impasse: A Chronicle of the Dutch Church.* New York: Newman Press, 1969.

Ryan, Herbert. "Anglican/Roman Catholic Doctrinal Agreement on the Eucharist." *Worship* 46 (1972), pp. 6-14.

Sacrosanctum Concilium in Walter M. Abbott, S.J. General editor, *The Documents of Vatican Two,* Joseph Gallagher, translation editor, New York: American Press, 1966, pp. 137-178.

Schnitzler, Theodore. *Die drei neuen eucharistischen Hochgebete und die neuen Präfationem: in Verkündigung und Betrachtung.* Freiburg: Herder, 1968.

Schroeder, H. J., editor. *Canons and Decrees of the Council of Trent.* St. Louis: Herder, 1950.

Services for Trial Use. New York: The Church Hymnal Corporation, 1970.

Soubigou, Louis. *A Commentary on the Prefaces and the Eucharistic Prayers of the Roman Missal.* Translated by John Ott. Collegeville: Liturgical Press, 1971.

Spanier, A. "Zur Formengeschichte des altjüdischen Gebetes." *MGWJ* (1934), pp. 438-447.

————. "Stilkritisches zum jüdischen Gebet." *MGWJ* (1963), pp. 339-350.

Tappert, T. G., editor. *The Book of Concord.* Philadelphia: Mühlenberg Press, 1959.

"The Windsor Statement on Eucharistic Doctrine." *Worship* 46 (1972), pp. 2-5.

Theisen, Reinold. *Mass Liturgy and the Council of Trent.* Collegeville, Minn.: St. John's Univ. Press, 1965.

Thompson, Bard, editor. *Liturgies of the Western Church.* Cleveland: The World Publishing Company, 1961.

Thurian, Max. *The Eucharistic Memorial.* Ecumenical Studies in Worship 7 and 8. Translated by J. G. Davies. Richmond: John Knox Press, 1960, 1961.

————, editor. *The Eucharistic Liturgy of Taizé.* Translated by John Arnold. London: The Faith Press, 1963.

————. "La théologie des nouvelles prières eucharistiques." *La Maison-Dieu,* No. 94 (1968), pp. 77-102.

———— "De novis Precibus Eucharisticis." *Questions liturgiques* 53 (1972), pp. 252-254.

Tillard, J. M. R. "L'Eucharistie et Saint-Esprit." *NRT* 90 (1968), pp. 363-387.

————. "Catholiques romains et Anglicans." *NRT* 93 (1971), pp. 602-656.

Vagaggini, Cipriano. *The Canon of the Mass and Liturgical Reform.* Translated by Peter Coughlan *et al.* New York: Alba House, 1967.

van Beeck, Franz Jozef *et al. Fifty Psalms.* Translated by David Smith and Forrest Ingram. New York: Herder and Herder, 1969.

Vergote, Antoine. *The Religious Man: A Psychological Study of Religious Attitudes.* Translated by Marie-Bernard Said. Dayton, Ohio: Pflaum Press, 1969.

Verheul, Ambrose. *Introduction to the Liturgy: Towards a Theology of Worship.* Translated by Margaret Clarke. Collegeville, Minnesota: The Liturgical Press, 1968.

von der Goltz, Eduard F. *Tischgebete und Abendmahlgebete in der altchristlichen und in der griechischen Kirche.* Leipzig: J. C.

Hinrichs' sche Buchhandlung, 1905. (Texte und Untersuchungen zur Geschichte der altchristlichen Literatur, Neue Folge, XIV Band, Heft 2b. Oscar v. Gebhardt und Adolf Harnack editors.)

Ware, Timothy. *The Orthodox Church*. Penguin Books. Harmondsworth, 1964.

Wegman, H. "Monde d'aujourd'hui et liturgie d'hier." *Communauté Chrétienne* 44 (1969), pp. 117-130.

Werner, E. *The Sacred Bridge*. London: D. Dobson, 1959.

Willis, G. G. "The New Eucharistic Prayers: Some Comments." *The Heythrop Journal* 12 (1971), pp. 5-28.

Zuurdeeg, William F. "Implications of Analytical Philosophy for Theology." *The Journal of Bible and Religion* 29 (1961), pp. 204-210.